ON PRESERVING:
ESSAYS ON PRESERVATIONISM AND PARACONSISTENT LOGIC

# On Preserving

Essays on Preservationism and Paraconsistent Logic

*Edited by*
*Peter Schotch, Bryson Brown, and Raymond Jennings*

UNIVERSITY OF TORONTO PRESS
Toronto Buffalo London

© University of Toronto Press Incorporated 2009
Toronto Buffalo London
www.utppublishing.com
Printed in Canada

ISBN 978-0-8020-9838-2

Printed on acid-free paper

Toronto Studies in Philosophy
Editors: Donald Ainslie and Amy Mullin

---

**Library and Archives Canada Cataloguing in Publication**

On preserving: essays on preservationism and paraconsistent logic
edited by Peter Schotch, Bryson Brown, and Raymond Jennings.

(Toronto studies in philosophy)
Includes bibliographical references and index.
ISBN 978-0-8020-9838-2

1. Inconsistency (Logic). 2. Logic. I. Schotch, Peter K. II. Brown, Bryson III.
Jennings, R. E. (Raymond Earl) IV. Series.
BC41.O5 2008    160    C2008-905807-0

---

University of Toronto Press acknowledges the financial assistance to its publishing program of the Canada Council for the Arts and the Ontario Arts Council.

University of Toronto Press acknowledges the financial support for its publishing activities of the Government of Canada through the Book Publishing Industry Development Program (BPIDP).

This book has been published with the help of a grant from the Canadian Federation for the Humanities and Social Sciences, through the Aid to Scholarly Publications Program, using funds provided by the Social Sciences and Humanities Research Council of Canada.

# Contents

# Acknowledgments

This book owes a great deal to a great many people. So many indeed that we have probably forgotten some of them; to those we apologize in advance.

First, since the work reported in this volume sprang from some initial work of Ray Jennings and Peter Schotch, the Social Sciences and Humanities Research Council of Canada deserves a particularly hearty vote of thanks. The Council made that collaboration possible under a number of operating grants over those first crucial years. Jennings and Schotch had a chance not only to meet face to face, but also to make their work known to a larger audience by giving talks and attending conferences over much of the learned world. Without that support, it is hard to see any of this having happened.

Second, and nearly tied for first, we must thank our students over the years. They have been many, but we owe them a great debt not only for their enthusiasm and hard work, but also because many of them were responsible for proving things that needed proving. At the head of that list is Bryson Brown, a one-time research assistant who rose to become a famous philosopher. Along the way, he with Peter Apostoli proved the first representation theorem and many graph-theoretic results which do not appear in this volume.[1]

Apart from Bryson Brown, the names Blaine d'Entremont and David Johnston were among the early adopters of our ideas and each has made a signal contribution. The latest generation includes Dorian Nicholson,

---

[1]But which will appear in a projected companion volume focused on applications of the preservationist approach.

Darko Sarenac and Gillman Payette. Two of those have contributed to this volume and all have contributed to the project in ways too valuable to describe in a paragraph.

It also goes without saying that we owe an enormous debt of gratitude to our wives and families, who have had to put up with us while we searched for a proof or even just a way of explaining something that seemed clear to us alone.

ON PRESERVING:
ESSAYS ON PRESERVATIONISM AND PARACONSISTENT LOGIC

# One

# Introduction to the Essays

PETER SCHOTCH

The essays in this volume are intended to serve as an introduction to a research project that started a long time ago, back in the twentieth century. But it didn't start as a project about paraconsistent logic or about what we have come to call preservationism.

## 1.1  The Origins of Preservationism

Instead it started in the summer of 1975, at Dalhousie University, when Ray Jennings[1] and Peter Schotch decided to write a 'primer' of modal logic – a project that never quite made it into the dark of print. So it was modal and decidedly not paraconsistent logic which was uppermost in the minds of Jennings and Schotch. In this connection one should keep in mind that neither had so much as heard the word 'paraconsistent' at the time we are considering.[2]

---

[1] Jennings was then (and now) a member of the philosophy department at Simon Fraser University, but he had accepted a summer-school job at Dalhousie in order to work with Schotch.

[2] In fact the first time they heard that word was at the 1978 meeting of the Society for Exact Philosophy, held in Pittsburgh. And in all truth, they paid little enough attention to the word the first time they did hear it.

What got the ball rolling was the discovery by Jennings, which he communicated to Schotch, that so-called normal modal logic was not suitable for certain philosophical applications of a deontic cast. In particular, there seemed to be distinctions which one might draw intuitively that evaporate in normal modal logic.[3] Now the only restriction on the kind of modal logic involved was that it be normal, so enabling distinctions which cannot be made in that logic was not going to be a simple matter of dropping some modal axioms or, on the semantic side, relaxing a frame condition.

If we are talking about normal modal logic in general, then there are no frame conditions to relax. The fundamental normal modal logic, often called K, is determined by the class of all frames. Period.

But later that afternoon, it started to seem that perhaps the semantics of normal modal logic did impose some restrictions after all. To begin with, there was the restriction that the universe of the frame, its set of 'possible worlds,' must be non-empty. That didn't seem a very promising condition to relax, though there certainly have been those who were prepared to give it up, if only to see what happens to modal logic.[4] No, it would have to be a condition on the frame relation which did the trick. Which condition was it? There could be only one, and that is the condition that the frame relation be binary. And there it was.

Jennings and Schotch then began trying to work out what the truth-condition for necessity would have to be when the frame relation was not binary but say, ternary. Later that evening they had narrowed it down to only one possibility:

---

**Definition 1.** $\Box \alpha$ *is true at a point $x$ in a model $M$ if and only if for every ordered pair $\langle y, z \rangle$ such that $Rxyz$, either $\alpha$ is true at $y$ or $\alpha$ is true at $z$.*

---

[3]The particular example mooted by Jennings had to do with two modal formulas, one of which had a necessity operator outside of a conditional and the other having the necessity distributed over the conditional. Perhaps the easiest version of this kind of distinction, and the one which became absolutely central to the program, is the one between $\Box \alpha \supset \neg \Box \neg \alpha$ and $\neg \Box \bot$. The latter claims that no contradiction can be necessary while the former asserts that if any formula is necessary, its negation is not.

[4]Charles Morgan has constructed this kind of modal logic.

The generalization to $n$-ary frame relations is trivial.

In the hot flush of discovery, Jennings and Schotch imagined that they were treading on *terra incognita*, but as Goethe reminds us,

> All the great thoughts have already been thought. Our job is merely to think them again.

$n$-ary frames had already been introduced by Bjarni Jónsson and Alfred Tarski (Tarski and Jónsson, 1951). In that work $n$-ary frames are a way of representing Boolean algebras with $(n-1)$-ary operators. Modal logic following Kripke had rediscovered (a decade after the original discovery) the special case of this idea for binary frames.

The problem for Jennings and Schotch was how to axiomatize a fragment of the Tarski and Jónsson $n$-ary frames, the *diagonal* fragment. In other words, in the original work the extra operator is $(n-1)$-ary, let's call it $\boxplus$. So for every $(n-1)$-tuple of formulas $\alpha_1, \ldots, \alpha_{n-1}$ the 'modal' formula is $\boxplus(\alpha_1, \ldots, \alpha_{n-1})$. This notion, as interesting and useful as it no doubt is, isn't the modal notion selected by Jennings and Schotch. Theirs, the unary $\Box\alpha$, is represented in Tarski and Jónsson's terms as $\boxplus(\alpha, \ldots, \alpha)$ where the '...' represents $n-3$ iterations of the formula $\alpha$.

This was not a problem which had ever been considered before so Jennings and Schotch were happily refuting Goethe, or at least attempting to do that. However, using the resources of normal modal logic, the problem is extremely difficult.

If we stick to the ternary case for ease of exposition, one quickly finds that the principle of *complete modal aggregation*

$$[\text{K}] \quad \vdash \Box\alpha \wedge \Box\beta \supset \Box(\alpha \wedge \beta)$$

doesn't hold, although the rule of monotonicity (sometimes called regularity) and the rule of (unrestricted) necessitation (also called the rule of normality):

$$[\text{RM}] \quad \vdash \alpha \supset \beta \implies \vdash \Box\alpha \supset \Box\beta$$

$$[\text{RN}] \quad \vdash \alpha \implies \vdash \Box\alpha,$$

both hold in ternary frames (and indeed in $n$-ary frames).

So now comes the problem: How do you axiomatize this semantics? It turns out to be quite a trick without [K]. In fact, it turns out to be impossible without *some* kind of aggregation principle, as Jennings and Schotch realized early on in the project. The correct version of aggregation seemed to be the principle;

[K3] $\vdash (\Box\alpha_1 \wedge \Box\alpha_2 \wedge \Box\alpha_3) \supset \Box((\alpha_1 \wedge \alpha_2) \vee (\alpha_2 \wedge \alpha_3) \vee (\alpha_1 \wedge \alpha_3))$.

But how to prove this conjecture? The situation is entirely different in K, where all the instances of the principle of complete modal aggregation that you might need follow transparently from [K]. In the general case, one needs to show that every aggregation principle which holds in virtue of 'pigeonhole reasoning'[5] (the way [K3] does) follows from [K3]. That is a non-trivial piece of combinatorial work.

While pondering this question and writing a few papers on modal aggregation (none of which solved the problem), Jennings and Schotch chanced to attend the June 1978 meeting of the Society for Exact Philosophy in Pittsburgh. It was there that they first heard of paraconsistent logic via a paper on the subject presented by Robert Wolf. It was also there that they first saw normal modal logic axiomatized by the rule:

$$[N] \; \Gamma \vdash \alpha \implies \Box[\Gamma] \vdash \Box\alpha$$

(where $\Box[\Gamma]$ stands for $\{\Box\gamma | \gamma \in \Gamma\}$), when it was used in a paper presented by Brian Chellas.[6]

In the question period following the presentation by Jennings and Schotch, Barbara Partee happened to remark that it all seemed to her like an attempt to represent a kind of non-trivial reasoning from inconsistent data, since, without complete modal aggregation one cannot construct $\Box\bot$ from $\Box\alpha$ and $\Box\neg\alpha$. So in particular, if one thought of the $\Box$ as some sort of belief operator, then lack of the principle [K] for that operator would allow an individual's set of belief to contain conflicting beliefs without having to contain all beliefs. Jennings and Schotch took

---

[5]By this is meant merely the principle that if there are $k$ objects to distribute over $k - 1$ containers, at least one container must contain at least two objects.

[6]Chellas later attributed the rule to Dana Scott.

note of how the audience perked up at this, and kindly thanked Professor Partee for the observation.

It was on the flight back to Halifax[7] that Jennings urged Schotch to consider the Chellas axiomatization in connection with their $n$-ary modal logic. What Jennings had seen is that the rule [N] characterizes necessity in terms of some notion of inference.[8] For the necessity of normal modal logic in the usual sense, the 'corresponding'[9] inference relation is simply the classical one. But Jennings presumed, since the $n$-ary semantics lacked complete modal aggregation, the inference relation that characterized the new notion of necessity cannot be classical.

This turned out to be an absolutely crucial insight, and one which led ultimately to the program now called preservationism. Schotch began trying to discover an inference relation which bears the same relation to $n$-ary modal logic as the classical relation bears to normal modal logic. There will of course be infinitely many such relations corresponding to the different orders of the frame relations. The project didn't take long since it was possible to – in effect – *read off* the relation from the modal semantics.

## 1.2 How Paraconsistent Inference Fell out of Modal Semantics

The trick is to begin as though you already have the relation in question and then start the 'hard' direction of the fundamental theorem for all, let's say, ternary modal logics. These will be all the extensions of the base logic K3 which logic is axiomatized by the single rule (on top of classical sentence logic):

$$[N3] \ \Gamma \vartriangleright_3 \alpha \implies \Box[\Gamma] \vdash \Box\alpha$$

---

[7]Where Jennings was teaching summer school again.

[8]An algebraist would say that the two concepts inference and necessity, are Galois connected.

[9]Depending upon how precise one wishes to make the notion of correspondence used here, one might be restricted to the necessity operator of the logic K, rather than the necessity operator of any normal modal logic.

In order to discover just what properties $\rhd_3$ has to have, we see what is required to prove:

$$\Box\alpha \notin \Sigma \implies \langle \mathcal{M}_{K3}, \Sigma \rangle \nvDash \Box\alpha,$$

where $\mathcal{M}_{K3}$ is the K3 canonical model and $\Sigma$ is an element of the K3-canonical domain, which is to say a maximal K3-consistent set of formulas. The converse of this is trivial so long as we define the K3-canonical relation, $R_{K3}$ over the elements of K3-canonical domain, in the obvious way as

$$R_{K3}\Gamma\Delta_1\Delta_2 \iff (\forall\alpha)(\Box\alpha \in \Gamma \implies \alpha \in \Delta_1 \text{ or } \alpha \in \Delta_2).$$

So assume $\Box\alpha \notin \Sigma$. We need to find a pair of maximally K3-consistent sets to which $\Sigma$ is related, neither of which contains $\alpha$. The existence of such a pair amounts to the failure of $\Box\alpha$ at the element $\Sigma$ of the K3-canonical model, which is what we are trying to show. To show that a pair of maximally K3-consistent sets exists to which $\Sigma$ stands in the canonical relation, it suffices to show that there is some partition of the set $\Box(\Sigma) = \{\beta|\Box\beta \in \Sigma\}$, both cells of which are K3-consistent. In such a case each cell can be extended to maximal K3-consistency in the usual way. We also require that $\alpha$ not belong to either of the maximally K3-consistent sets thus constructed. The only way to make sure of this is to add $\neg\alpha$ to each cell of the partition. From this point we argue by *reductio*.

Suppose that no such partition can be found, which is to say that for every partition of $\Box(\Sigma)$ into two K3-consistent cells, at least one of the cells is not K3-consistent with $\neg\alpha$. By classical reasoning, this amounts to saying that at least one cell of every partition of $\Box(\Sigma)$ into two K3-consistent sets (classically) proves $\alpha$. If our axiomatization of K3 is going to work, what we just wrote must amount to a statement that $\Box(\Sigma) \rhd_3 \alpha$. This is because if and only if the inference relation is defined in that particular way then, by appeal to the rule [N3], we must have

$$\Box[\Box(\Sigma)] \vdash \Box\alpha.$$

But the set on the left of $\vdash$ is a subset of $\Sigma$ since it collects those formulas in $\Sigma$ which are 'guarded' by $\square$. More precisely, the first (inner) operation forms the set of those formulas in $\Sigma$ which begin with $\square$ and strips off the leading $\square$, while the second (outer) operation prefixes each of those formulas with $\square$. This operation leaves us with exactly those formulas in $\Sigma$ which have an initial $\square$. This subset will usually be proper, since an arbitrary set like $\Sigma$ will normally contain lots of formulas $\alpha$ which do not begin with $\square$, such that $\square\alpha$ does not belong to $\Sigma$.

Now if a subset of $\Sigma$ proves $\square\alpha$ then $\Sigma$ itself must likewise prove that formula by monotonicity of inference.[10] But, by classical reasoning, every maximally K3-consistent set is a theory, which is to say that it contains every formula that it proves. So $\square\alpha \in \Sigma$, which contradicts the hypothesis. Thus K3 is determined by the class of all ternary frames.

In order for $\vartriangleright_3$ to be a paraconsistent inference relation, it must be an inference relation. There is cheerful news on that matter: The relation satisfies all the classical structural rules. So yes, it is inference of some kind, but is it really paraconsistent?

Well, yes and no. It is at least a partially paraconsistent relation, since, if the premise set contains only two contradictory premises without either being self-contradictory, then the closure of the set under the relation $\vartriangleright_3$ will not contain every formula.

On the other hand the premise set might contain a subset like

$$\{\alpha_1, \neg\alpha_1 \wedge \alpha_2, \neg\alpha_1 \wedge \neg\alpha_2\},$$

for which any individual member is consistent by itself but each is inconsistent with the other two. Any set containing a subset like this cannot be partitioned into only two consistent cells. So, contrary to the spirit of paraconsistency perhaps, all such sets prove (in the sense of $\vartriangleright_3$) every formula.

So $\vartriangleright_3$ allows sets to explode inferentially even though they may be representable as the union of sets all of which are consistent. Elsewhere

---

[10]This is, in effect, an appeal to the classical structural rule of dilution.

this condition is vilified by branding it as a kind of inconsistency.[11] Now, of course we can move to a relation defined in terms of partitions containing three cells. In that situation there will be an inference relation, call it $\triangleright_4$, which does what we want, but it will, in turn, fall prey to sets of four formulas each consistent in isolation but explosive in combination with any of the others.[12]

Are we to be driven to infinity here? No, but before we see why not, let us come clean. There are premise sets such that no partition into consistent cells (even allowing infinite partitions) is possible. These are the sets that contain formulas which are, by themselves, inconsistent. Such formulas are often called *absurd*, with $\alpha \wedge \neg\alpha$ serving as the most popular classical example.

*Those* inconsistent sets, the ones containing absurd formulas, cannot be fixed. No matter which version of our new relation we take, the consequences of such a set under that relation will be the set of all formulas. If the goal of paraconsistent logic is prevent even absurd formulas from exploding, then our relations are, none of them, paraconsistent. Fortunately, neither Jennings nor Schotch (nor the angels, we are tempted to say) believes that paraconsistent logic has that goal.

Thus was a great gulf fixed between the preservationist approach, and the 'dialethic' approach championed by several people in the southern hemisphere.[13] It is characteristic of the latter view that both a sentence and its negation might be true, and that there could be a way of making $\alpha \wedge \neg\alpha$ true while at the same time making $\beta$ false. Hence, even absurd formulas might be redeemed.

It is tempting to refer to this program as 'non-negative' on the ground that whatever else may be going on, if you succeed in making both $\alpha$ and $\neg\alpha$ true, then you must be using the symbol $\neg$ to represent something other than negation. This temptation is reinforced by the fact that the dialethists insist on referring to the preservationist program as 'non-adjunctive.'

---

[11] In Schotch and Jennings (1989) inference relations which allow sets to explode without their containing an absurd formula are called *inconsistent\**.

[12] $\triangleright_4$ and the earlier $\triangleright_3$ are examples of what we call *fixed-level* forcing relations.

[13] The name Graham Priest springs to mind.

## 1.3   The Concept of Level

In the previous section it seemed as though there was no limit upon how large we might have to make a partition in order to ensure that every premise set (not containing an absurdity) could be partitioned into that many consistent cells. That is no doubt true but not entirely to the point. What we clearly need to do is to treat every premise set on its own merits, rather than assuming that there is some fixed number $n$ such that the premises can be partitioned into no more than $n$ consistent cells.

Rather, let us say that the *level* of a set, say $\Gamma$ of formulas, modulo some technicalities which will be explained in detail below, is the least number of cells (if there is such a thing) such that $\Gamma$ can be partitioned into that many consistent cells. If there is no such number, which is to say if $\Gamma$ contains an absurd formula, then assign the symbolic value $\infty$ to be the value of the level function applied to that set.

And now we have what we might regard as a wholehearted paraconsistent inference relation. We refer to this relation as the *forcing* relation indicated by $[\Vdash$, and it is defined not in reference to some fixed number of cells, but to partitions into the number of consistent cells equal to the level of the premise set. If, on every such partition, at least one of the cells proves $\alpha$, then $\Gamma[\Vdash \alpha$.

## 1.4   Preservation

At this point the modal-logical motivation has fallen away. In the first place, the version of the generalized form of the rule [N], which has forcing on the left of $\implies$, doesn't correspond to any particular $n$-ary modal semantics, but rather to a semantics in which the frame relation is allowed to vary. This is a bit of an odd duck, modally speaking. In the second place, the problem which started the whole thing off, that of showing that the $n$-ary semantics can be axiomatized using [RN], [RM], and the appropriate $n$-ary form of the aggregation principle [KN], is still unsolved![14]

---

[14] As a matter of historical fact, several years had to pass before that problem was finally solved. See chapter 4 in this volume.

So where does preserving come in? During several presentations that Jennings and Schotch made in the early 1980s more than once the complaint was heard that the notion of inference based on forcing and its near relations seemed at odds with the 'truth-preservation' account.[15] When this complaint was considered outside of heated debate, it seemed to come apart in one's hands.

To say that forcing (or any of its fixed-level modal cousins) does not accord with truth-preservation is to say that some inferences licensed by the latter are not licensed by the former. This is without doubt true, but those inferences are precisely the ones that forcing is designed to block. In other words the complaint seems to come down to the fact that forcing doesn't behave as stupidly as does classical inference in the face of (many) inconsistent premise sets. To which one might well reply 'And ...?'

But since merely preserving truth opens the door to a lot of inferences we'd rather not draw, perhaps forcing & Co. can still be thought of as preserving something worthwhile. And it is relatively easy to see that forcing preserves *level*, which includes preserving truth when the premises taken all together are capable of being true.[16] So level preservation can be thought of as a way of fixing truth-preservation at the precise place where it is broken – when there is no truth to preserve. In that case, forcing finds something else, or rather something in addition, that can still be preserved even while truth is on vacation.

Now the dialethists can and do argue that *they* are the ones who really fix truth-preservation, since their notion of paraconsistent reasoning preserves truth and not something other or over and above, like level. Unfortunately this claim stands or falls with the claim that both a sentence and its negation can be true on the same occasion of evaluation. This is a major sticking point, even a deal breaker, for many of those outside the dialethic school. Not to put too fine a point on the matter, an uncharitable person might remark that dialethism, rather than fixing truth-preservation, breaks it beyond any hope of repair.

---

[15]This paradigm is considered at much greater length in the essay 'Preserving What?' (chapter 6) in this volume.

[16]Which is of course to say that the set of premises is consistent. This is taken up in much more detail in 'Preserving What?' chapter 6 in this volume.

## 1.5 The Essays

In 'Paraconsistency: Who Needs It?' Ray Jennings and Peter Schotch present an informal account of the core motivating examples that lead to a preservationist approach to paraconsistency. They take up the usual examples of belief and obligation and also a not-so-usual one in recasting the motivation of C.I. Lewis for his notion of strict-implication. In effect, they suggest that Lewis was a pioneer of paraconsistency.

In 'Weakly Additive Algebras and a Completeness Problem,' Alasdair Urquhart presents a solution to the problem of showing that the $K_n$ logics are complete with respect to their intended semantics. This is the problem mentioned above that had to wait several years for its solution. At the same time, Urquhart presents his result as an extension of the original algebraic approach of Tarski and Jónsson, which approach in effect 'started the whole thing off.'

In 'A Dualization of Neighbourhood Structures' Dorian Nicholson introduces a dualization of neighbourhood semantics for the purpose of obtaining a simplified proof that weakly aggregative modal logic is complete with respect to $(n + 1)$-ary relational frames. The proof makes no mention of chromatic compactness and thus comes closer to being a 'pure' proof of this result. In this case claims for purity rest on the fact that the algebraic approach is entirely absent. In addition to treating the usual normal $n$-ary logics, Nicholson also discusses non-normal logics.

In 'Polyadic Modal Logics and Their Monadic Fragments,' Kam Sing Leung and Ray Jennings present the long awaited treatment of $n$-ary modal logics, and in a particularly elegant way. The focus of the paper is on $n$-ary modal correspondence theory. That is, the relationship between conditions on the $n$-ary frame relation and modal axioms.

In 'Preserving What?' Gillman Payette and Peter Schotch examine the somewhat shaky status of the truth-preservation paradigm for right reason and suggest alternatives. They treat the concepts of level and forcing with much greater precision and generality than we manage above.

In 'Preserving Logical Structure,' Gillman Payette explores properties of the structure of consequence relations and languages that are preserved in the 'move up' to the forcing relation. A number of crucial things about compactness in the context of level are proved, and these results are used to derive a very important theorem concerning the place of forcing among all other similar inference relations. The work on compactness is based on joint work with Blaine d'Entremont.

In 'Representation of Forcing,' Dorian Nicholson and Bryson Brown show how to represent the forcing relation in terms of a more syntactical presentation of the logic. In a traditional context, what we here call representation would be *axiomatization*. They then extend these results to the more general sequent-logic-like case, in which the relation is reconceived as a relation between sets of formulas (premise sets) and sets of formulas (conclusion sets). This important essay corrects a number of mistakes in the earlier 'On Detonating' (Schotch and Jennings, 1989).

'Forcing and Practical Inference' is the essay in which Peter Schotch takes up the issue of modifying the definition of forcing, in two different ways. In the first modification, the notion of level upon which the forcing relation is based is required to respect certain natural 'clumps' of premises in the sense that no logical cover of a set of premises can break up any of these clumps. The second variation recognizes that logical consistency is a very weak idea and that in ordinary and technical reasoning both, we recognize that the collection of 'bad guys' extends far beyond the logically absurd. This recognition requires an obvious change in the definition of logical cover.

Finally, in 'Ambiguity Games and Preserving Ambiguity Measures' Bryson Brown steers preservationism into previously uncharted waters. By defining ambiguity measures as an alternative to partitions for getting something consistent out of an inconsistent set of sentences, Brown not only produces a property worthy of preservation but also a way of connecting preservationism to what was once thought of as an incompatible way of dealing with inconsistency – dialethism. This is rather startling to say the least.

The essays are, generally speaking,[17] capable of standing alone, although there is considerable overlap. All of them give short shrift to one or another important feature (or features) of the preservationist program,

---

[17]J.S. Minas used always to add the gloss: 'which is to say', in no particular case.'

though none performs such disservice to all the important features. In fine, the essays act together to fix each others' expository flaws, while the flaws themselves make the essays more readable than completeness would allow.

# Two

# Paraconsistency: Who Needs It?

RAY JENNINGS AND PETER SCHOTCH

**Abstract**

In this essay Ray Jennings and Peter Schotch present some of the central motivation for what has come to be called the preservationist approach to paraconsistent logic.

## 2.1  Introduction

The classical account of consistency is inadequate in many situations in which we certainly require a notion *like* it. This is tantamount to saying that there are situations in which classical logic is not adequate. While such an assertion might have enjoyed a certain amount of shock value in the early twentieth century, things have changed since those heady days. Now most people agree that some changes are often necessary in the classical account of inference, though there is nothing approaching widespread agreement on the precise nature of those changes.

One can distinguish two broad strategies for fixing a misbehaving logic. What we count as misbehaviour here is the licensing of inferences which we imagine ought not to be licensed, or the refusal to recognize some inferences as valid which we ordinary reasoners find entirely con-

17

genial and unproblematic. The strategies referred to just now we may term *replacement* and *revision*.

When a logic misbehaves in the second way, we most frequently revise it. We don't need to look far for an example: The logic of 'un-analysed sentences' fails to recognize the correctness of the move from 'All women are mortal' and 'Xanthippe is a woman' to 'Xanthippe is mortal.' Annoyed by this denial of such an obvious example of correct reasoning, we call for the logic of sentences to be extended to include terms and individual quantifiers. We are inclined to take as characteristic of the revision strategy that the revised logic contain the one which had revision visited upon it.

When a logic misbehaves in the first way, things aren't quite so clear. At first blush it seems that all we can do is sue for replacement of the offending logic. This is certainly what C.I. Lewis seemed to be doing in the early twentieth century, when he proposed that so-called material implication be replaced with what he called strict implication. Nor was he alone in pointing to perceived flaws in the classical account of reasoning and suggesting that it be given up at least partially, if not root and branch. The purveyors of many-valued logics and the intuitionists, to name just two, were also early adopters of the replacement strategy.

Now 'replace' is a strong word, and we must temper our understanding of it in this context with the realization that the classical account of inference is as inclusive as it could be, barring triviality. If we were to take any inference from propositional logic which is not classically valid, and add it to classical logic as an extra principle, the logic so constituted would allow any formula to be derived from any premise set – which is to say it would be trivial. The upshot of this fact, first proved by Post, is that any non-trivial logic over the classical language is almost sure to be a sublogic of classical logic. So a logic offered for replacement is not normally going to depart from the classical canon in the sense of being disjoint from it. This is certainly the case with intuitionistic logic and many-valued logics, which are easily shown to be included in classical logic.

This leaves all those logics which, like the Lewis ones, wish to replace the classical $\supset$ with a connective more like what we really mean when we use words like 'implication.' In many, but not all of these cases replacement is the order of the day. But even in these cases, it has sometimes turned out that the proposed replacement is actually a revision, with the new notion of implication representable as some species of modalized classical conditional. This befell the C.I. Lewis program, much to his chagrin, one suspects, but we shall revisit his motivation a bit later in this essay to see if any lessons remain to be learned from it.

There is an important socio-historical point to be made here. Classical logic is not so called because of its antiquity;[1] it is in fact an invention of the late nineteenth and early twentieth century. When the first calls for replacement went forth, philosophers and mathematicians were not being asked to jettison some cherished theory handed down by their respected forefathers. Instead, they were being asked to reconsider their allegiance to a relatively new and untried theory. That situation has changed. By the turn of the twenty-first century classical logic had become entrenched. This means that the scientific community now has a very large investment in the theory. In practical terms it means that replacement theorists are going to have uphill sledding to do, and even revisionists will have to endure a certain lack of goodwill if not downright surliness.

Of all the replacement theories, pride of place must go to intuitionistic logic. There is no single reason for this notable success, but one may discern at least two strands to the story. The first is that intuitionism began early enough not to have to fight an entrenched opponent. Trench warfare being what it is, this is a weighty consideration. The second is that what we might call the structures which match the formalized account of the intuitionist calculus,[2] seem to arise in many different parts of formal science.[3] This is often taken to be an outward and visible sign of the worthiness of the logic displaying it.

---

[1] As one wag has put it, classical logic is so called because of its name.

[2] But what irony that the formalized part of the intuitionistic program carries so much of the weight of promoting the popularity of that program. Intuitionism arose historically as a protest against formalism.

[3] Topology, category theory, and quantum physics are three examples.

## 2.2 The Strange Case of C.I. Lewis

Of all the replacement theories which have been co-opted by classical logic into revision theories, the best known is modal logic. C.I. Lewis lived long enough to see his recommendations concerning strict implication dissolve, by turns, into a proposal to treat the modals as new connectives to be added to the classical store. Of course the proposal even in this new revisionist garb was far from non-controversial. Quine and his students were the most prominent adversaries of this idea and they (and others) were able to cast a pall over modal logic as an area of research. This pall had dispersed by the late 1960's however and the area has been as respectable as any other since then.

To put the early controversy in a nutshell, Lewis thought that the classical account of implication was wrong. By this he meant that some of the classical theorems were wrong when we read the symbol $\supset$ as 'implies.' In defence of this view he would produce what had come to be called 'paradoxes of material implication.' Most prominent among these were:

$$\alpha \supset (\beta \supset \alpha)$$

$$\neg\alpha \supset (\alpha \supset \beta)$$

where these were required to bear the respective interpretations 'A true proposition is implied by any proposition' and 'A false proposition implies any proposition.' According to Lewis, genuine, or what he called strict implication must be interpreted in terms of deduction. In his informal semantics of implication, we would only say that $\alpha$ implies $\beta$ provided there is some way of deducing the latter from the former.

To briefly rehearse some of the more puissant of Quine's criticisms of this position: Implication is a relation rather than a connective. When we read $\supset$ as 'implies,' as Russell often seems to do, this is nothing more substantial than a *façon de parler*. When we read, for instance, $\alpha \supset \beta$ as $\alpha$ implies $\beta$, we intend nothing more mysterious than the assertion that $\alpha$ and $\beta$ (in that order) are connected by $\supset$. As for 'real' or 'genuine' implication, who knows what that is?[4]

---

[4]This is the Quinean sense of not knowing what $X$ is, on which I don't know what $X$ is, and if you think you do, you're mistaken.

Actually, as devastating as the criticism might be, Quine could have done rather better than this. Alas, he was one of those who had been so steeped in the nineteenth century approach to logic that he took the so-called logical truths to be what logic is about. Once we rid ourselves of that unfortunate affliction, we may say to Lewis: 'It's a bit silly to insist that we have a genuine implication (or strict implication, if you must) between the propositions $\alpha$ and $\beta$ only when one can deduce $\beta$ from $\alpha$. This is silly because we already have a representation for that in our logic, namely $\vdash$. So your strict implication is simply another word for provability – and why would we need to rename provability?'

Thus do we sound the death knell for Lewis' complaint about classical logic. It is simply based on a mistake or, to be as charitable as possible, a confusion between which matters belong to the object language and which to the metalanguage.[5] Once we see this, we can dismiss the complaint with its fear-mongering talk of paradox as airily as Quine and his followers. Or can we?

As the old saying has it, there is no smoke without fire. Even if Lewis was partially blinded by the smoke, there might yet be a hot coal or two which remains once the smoke has been contemptuously dispersed. To say this is to say that perhaps all this talk of paradox reverberates into the metalanguage. We shall consider this radical idea more carefully.

Start with 'a false proposition implies an arbitrary proposition,' which is impressive enough to have the Latin name *ex falso quodlibet*. There is an exegesis of this which puts it squarely at the metalinguistic level: 'If all we know about some premise set is that it contains a falsehood, then that is sufficient to allow the inference of any formula at all as a conclusion.' Symbolically,

$$\{\alpha, \neg\alpha\} \vdash \beta$$

This is no longer about implication, it is now an observation and, dare we say it, a complaint, about the classical account of *provability*. When Lewis says, as he does of the 'paradox,' that there is no genuine sense of deduction in which this assertion makes sense, he echoes generations of

---

[5]This is understandable for Lewis, who never really accepted the concept of a metalanguage. At any rate there is no textual evidence that he did.

beginning logic students who think that it is cheating to use *reductio* to derive some formula $\beta$ from a set of assumptions which already contains a contradiction before we assume (for *reductio* as we blithely say) $\neg\beta$. There is no sense in which the assumption of the hypothesis *leads to* an absurdity. To assert the contrary is like saying of a man born with a single arm that the first sight of his mother's face led to his losing an arm.

We must take care here, since Lewis would distinguish the case in which all we know is that a premise is false from the case in which we know that a premise is *necessarily* false. For Lewis, the paradigm of a necessarily false premise is a self-contradictory or, as we often say, an *absurd* one. In this case, says Lewis – bolstered by a famous proof – we really and truly can deduce, using entirely non-controversial rules of proof, anything at all.

The dual paradox that if all we know is that a conclusion is true, then it may be derived from any premises at all, requires an approach to inference in which we allow sets of conclusions on the right-hand side of $\vdash$. These right-handed sets are understood dually to the left-handed ones. In other words, while the comma in $\{\alpha_1, \ldots, \alpha_n\}$ is understood 'conjunctively' if the set is left-handed, it is understood 'disjunctively'[6] if the set is right-handed. So to say that all we know is that a (right-handed) set contains a truth, is to say that the set in question contains something like $\{\alpha, \neg\alpha\}$, and in that case classical logic tells us that

$$\Gamma \vdash \{\alpha, \neg\alpha\}$$

for any set of premises $\Gamma$.

If we follow Lewis once more we must distinguish this case from the one in which the conclusion set contains a dual self-contradiction, namely a tautology.

Now the fact is, as the complaints of our students indicate, classical logic does not permit us to make any distinction of this sort. And if we think about it for a bit, we may be able to find other reasons to criticize classical logic on that ground.

---

[6]The reason for placing these terms in quotes is that we cannot understand a set of formulas disjunctively or conjunctively if the sets in question are infinite. Too, there may be a problem if either of disjunction or conjunction does not occur in the object language.

## 2.3   The Inconsistency of Belief

We begin with an historical example – Hume's Labyrinth:

> I find myself in such a labyrinth, that, I must confess, I nei-
> ther know how to correct my former opinions, nor how to
> render them consistent.

It is no good telling Hume that if his inconsistent opinions were,
all of them, true then every sentence would be true. Even if he could
accept this startling claim, it would have brought him no comfort. The
most which might be wrung out of it is that not all of his opinions could
be true. This, so far from being news to Hume, was precisely what
occasioned much of the anguish which he evidently felt. What we need
in such circumstances is a way to cope.

Nor is it merely in the realm of metaphysics that inconsistent opinions charm us. In the physical sciences as well we seem to have inconsistent consequences thrust upon us by equally well-confirmed hypotheses. And even if, as we reassure ourselves, the inconsistences are not
ineluctable, we must live with them whilst awaiting the crucial experiment, or the new paradigm, or the new metaphor, or merely promotion.
Eventualities may render the inconsistencies resolvable or illusory or
unimportant. In the meantime, however, we must draw inferences from
them which do not depend upon their inconsistency, but which are informed by it.

A more humanistic logic is required. Such a logic would accord
with what we must frequently do, namely the best we can with data
which, although inconsistent, are nevertheless the best data we are able
to command. We would like to be able to reflect but also judge the
reasonings of ordinary doxastic agents. We wish to offer them standards
of correctness which survive conflicts of belief without triviality. This
humane approach need not pander. It would accept classical consistency
as an ideal without the pretence that it is pervasive or even especially
common in actual belief sets.

We say nothing controversial when we claim that often, perhaps usually, a set of sentences to which someone will actually assent would, if

scrutinized, be discovered to be classically inconsistent. The question is: What are we to make of this observation? There appear to be two distinct reactions. The first is to say that some such apparently inconsistent belief sets are real and constitute a genuine difficulty for the received theory of inference. The second takes such inconsistencies to be mere appearance — a fanciful mask over the underlying consistent reality.

Our choice between these is important, for our ordinary understanding of rationality involves drawing inferences from our beliefs. We are not positively *required* to draw these inferences but we *are* required to accept the conclusion once the validity of such an inference has been made known to us. But how is non-trivial reasoning possible in the face of inconsistency? We are like jurors made trusting by cruel penalties. To the extent that we accept the classical account of reasoning, to that extent we resist the view that the set of a person's beliefs can really be inconsistent in a full-blooded sense. We want either to acquit or somehow diminish responsibility.

We have recourse to such strategies as distinguishing between *active* beliefs, which must indeed be consistent, and mothballed beliefs which lie strewn about in their cells unregarded and out of mind. We will be inclined to wink at inconsistencies among this disused bric-a-brac or between them and the brighter ornaments of present thought.

It is tempting to think of this distinction as being congruent with the distinction sometimes made between explicit and implicit contradiction. We are happy to offer forgiveness, if not pardon, for the latter but visit upon the former harshness without mitigation. We must step carefully here for the implicit/explicit distinction can be variously applied, to confusing effect. We may wish to say that there is an explicit contradiction in a person's beliefs when she actively adheres to two or more mutually contradictory opinions. Implicit contradictions, on this score, would be those between two inactive beliefs or between one which is active and another which isn't. This is not Hume's predicament.

His problem lay in his *active* acceptance of contradictory opinions. On the latest account of the distinction, Hume's contradictions were explicit. Yet he did not recognize whatever harsh penalties later logic would have meted out to him. It did not trivialize his inquires. It simply provided him with 'a sufficient reason to entertain a diffidence and modesty in all my decisions.'

There is an alternative account of the distinction according to which Hume's contradictions would count as implicit rather than explicit. On this account, an explicit contradiction is a single sentence which is self-contradictory, whereas for one's set of beliefs to contain an implicit contradiction one must maintain mutually inconsistent opinions, whether actively or inactively. The two ways of drawing the distinction are not always kept separate and the fear of explicit contradictions of the second sort may make us wary of the first sort also.

The prohibition against explicit contradictions of the second sort may be expressed as the requirement that every member of a set of beliefs must be logically capable of being true. This stricture seems plausible enough but it does not preclude sets of beliefs which contain implicit contradictions of the second sort. Moreover, it seems likely that implicitly inconsistent belief sets of the second sort are quite common.[7]

On the other hand, the notion of someone believing an explicit contradiction of the second kind seems devoid of content. One might argue that it is part of the root meaning of 'belief' that the sentence expressing it must, at a minimum, be capable of being true. If the classical penalties of triviality are to be imposed anywhere, let them fall upon a transgression which no one is capable of committing. We feel no qualms at the prospect of requiring anybody who believes an explicit contradiction to believe everything.

The stronger restriction upon belief sets corresponds to the requirement that such sets be satisfiable, which is to say that all the members be capable of simultaneous truth. It is this condition that flies so directly in the face of our ordinary experience of belief. We have now arrived at a crux.

If we let ordinary experience (not to say common sense) be our guide, allowing our belief sets to contain implicit contradiction (of the second kind) but not explicit contradictions, we must of necessity abandon classical logic as an account of how one belief (or set of beliefs) can justify another. For by means of the classical picture of inference we

---

[7]Some have argued that to be rational one must have such a belief set. See Campbell (1980).

may always derive an explicit contradiction from a set of beliefs which is implicitly inconsistent. Thus classical modes of reasoning trample what is manifestly a useful distinction – the one we earlier attributed to Lewis.

How far ought this felt need for a non-classical logic be indulged? Appeals to experience can easily lead us astray. After all, almost anybody who proposes some species of non-classical logic is tempted to argue that since the world is non-classical so should our logic be. To travel too far along this road is to invite some form of the genetic fallacy.

If our arithmetic or our syllogisms are not in accord with the classical canons, the fault might well lie in our inability to calculate or to construct Venn diagrams. The observation that the reasonings of actual people are sometimes non-classical, in order to bite, must be coupled with evidence that such reasoning is correct, or at the very least not evidently mistaken. If invention is to be mothered let it be through necessity and not through the failure to take suitable precautions.

Nevertheless some of the evidence is compelling. Even when our stock of beliefs is inconsistent we routinely draw a distinction between what follows from it and what does not, and regard certain inferences from our beliefs as improper, in spite of the circumstances. If our procedures were genuinely classical we would not, indeed could not, make such a distinction. There is no classical issue to be taken with any inference from an inconsistent set.

Failure to take this sort of evidence into account seems as misguided as any of the worst excesses of those who would base logical theory democratically upon the actual inferential practice of the proletariat. It is no doubt true that if the rule A then B; B; therefore A (sometimes known as Modus Morons) were from time to time invoked in country districts or local government, we should nevertheless resist viewing it as a ratiocinative dialect or alternative inferential lifestyle. But if humanity universally manages to distinguish, at least in some cases, valid arguments from inconsistent premises on the one hand from invalid arguments from those same premises, this is another and weightier matter.

The view that everyone commits a logical error in making such a distinction is an adaptation for logic of the doctrine of original sin.

We have already considered one non-classical view of the matter, namely, the view that when we argue from our beliefs we disregard some, reasoning only from the active portion of our belief set. That this is non-classical is evident from the fact that it is non-monotonic. Whatever sense of inferable we adopt, it is clear that we do not think of our conclusions as inferable in that significant way from an inconsistent set. The reason for such a non-monotonic stance is precisely that the whole of one's belief set might be seen to be inconsistent if examined, that an inference drawn from the set taken as a whole might be trivial. To escape this consequence we must take the further step of claiming that the only real beliefs are the active ones.

This protestant view, which is really an attempt to deny that beliefs can be inconsistent, suffers from two flaws. The first is that on this doctrine it is nearly impossible to identify a belief set. Suppose someone's apparent belief set is inconsistent. Which subset of the set of apparent beliefs constitutes the *real* belief set? (Assuming that the real beliefs are also apparent; otherwise the problem becomes even worse.) Even if we insist that the real beliefs form a maximal consistent subset of the apparent beliefs we do not thereby guarantee uniqueness. We must elaborate more sophisticated side conditions to ensure this, perhaps invoking the probability calculus to assist. In this case we must have handy some interpretation of probability other than one of its belief interpretations. The project seems a mare's nest. But these difficulties would not deter us from the task were it not for the second flaw.

The second flaw is that the basic premise is false. Try any thinking beyond the wallpaper or musak variety of daily life, and inconsistent pairs of beliefs *do* turn up, the one belief as active as the other.

## 2.4 Inconsistency and Ethics

It seems to be part of our ordinary moral experience that we can find ourselves in a dilemma, which is to say a situation in which the demands of morality cannot (all) be heeded. Let us suppose that such situations

might extend beyond the world of everyday all the way into philosophy.[8]
Let us next ask the question of whether or not obligations[9] are 'closed
under logical consequence.' This is an example of a question which is
of interest to ethical theory and also to logic. Some philosophers, even
some ethicists, might object that the question is one that only a logician
could love, and that they, as ethicists, have not the slightest interest in
it. Such a position betrays a lack of thought.

The issue is really quite deep. If you deny that the logical consequences of obligations are also obligations, then you are saying that
moral argument, at least moral argument of a certain standard kind, is
impossible. When you and I enter into a moral dispute, a dispute over
whether or not you ought to bring it about that, say $P$, then what often, perhaps usually, happens is that I try to demonstrate that $P$ follows
from something, some general moral principle, to which you subscribe.
In stage one we obtain the subscription:

> Don't you think that we ought to help those who cannot help
> themselves?
> Not in every case, suppose somebody is both helpless and
> not in need of help?
> Very well, we ought to help those in need who cannot help
> themselves?
> Wonderfully high minded, but impossible I'm afraid.
> Why impossible?
> We are overwhelmed by the numbers, don't you see?
> The numbers of what? Those in need?
> Precisely! We would spend all our resources helping the
> needy only to join their ranks before long.
> Ah, well how about this modification then: We ought to help
> those in need who cannot help themselves, but not to the
> point of harming ourselves or even seriously inconvenienc-

---

[8]Such a supposition is by no means beyond the bounds of controversy. There are moral
philosophers who argue that such conflicts of obligation are merely apparent.

[9]We are sacrificing rigour in the cause of clarity in this example. Strictly speaking we are not
talking about 'obligations' at all, since those are typically *actions*. We should be talking rather
about 'sentences which ought to be true.' This is a much more awkward form of words, however,
and it would interfere with the flow without adding very much to what we are saying.

ing ourselves?
Yes, it doesn't sound so high-minded, but now it's something
I can support.

Now we close in for the kill:

Would you say that Jones is in need of help?
Yes, not much doubt about that, poor bloke.
We should pass the hat, don't you think? Everybody could
put in what they can easily spare.
I don't see the point in that.
Do you imagine then that Jones can pull himself up by the
bootstraps, that all he needs is sufficient willpower?
No, I wouldn't say that, not in his present state at least.
Then, we ought to help him, wouldn't you say?
Well somebody needs to help him if he's going to be helped,
but I don't see how that got to be my problem.

What has been shown is that 'We help Jones' is a logical consequence of 'We help those in need who cannot help themselves and
whose help is not a significant burden to us.' This much is uncontro-
versial, once we have agreed upon 'We ought to help those in need ...'
But the remaining step, the step from the foregoing to 'We ought to
help Jones,' will follow only if the logical consequences of obligations
are themselves obligations. It is just crazy to say that the issue is of no
interest to ethicists, unless the ethicists in question have no interest in
arguments like our sample.

Nor can the relevance of logic to ethics be exhausted by this one
example. Suppose that, in exasperation, our stubborn ethicist agrees
that the issue is of interest after all. But the interest is over once we
see that we must answer 'yes' to the question of whether or not the
consequences of obligations are themselves obligations, isn't it? Not at
all. Recall how this got started.

We were wondering about moral dilemma, about *conflict of obligations*. In view of what we just said about obligations and logical consequences, we now have a problem. Suppose I am in a moral dilemma,

that there are two sentences $P$ and $Q$ which I believe should both be true (I believe that each, individually, *ought* to be true). But the two cannot be true together – hence the dilemma.

This is bad enough, but it gets worse. One of the consequences of the set of sentences which we say ought to be the case, the set of obligations, is the sentence $P \wedge Q$. But since the two sentences cannot both be true at the same time, this consequence is equivalent to $P \wedge \neg P$. Since the consequences are also obligations, $P \wedge \neg P$ is an obligation. But *everything* follows from $P \wedge \neg P$, so in the case of a moral dilemma one is obliged to do *everything*. This seems a bit burdensome.

## 2.5  Summing Up

The unhappy fact of the matter is that sometimes, through no fault of our own, we are simply stuck with bad data. This can happen in any of the variety of circumstances in which we gather information from several sources. Should the sources contradict each other, we may have a way of measuring their relative reliability in some reasonable way. Equally often, however, either the means at our disposal will not settle the matter conclusively (as in the case of beliefs) or we simply have no means for the adjudication of conflict between our sources.

The classical theory of inconsistency must retire in such a situation, since non-trivial classical reasoning is impossible in the face of inconsistent premise sets. All that the classical logician can advise in these circumstances is to start over again with a consistent set of premises. Sometimes this is wise counsel, but more often it is of a piece with what the doctor said when told by a patient, 'It hurts when I do this.'

To get back to our earlier example, both belief and obligation seem to call for the Lewis distinction (at least the one that remains after we 'fix' the original claim). We need to be able to distinguish premise sets which contain full-blooded self-inconsistencies from those which contain pairs of premises which are inconsistent although the individual premises are not.

This is the path which we shall follow – the one we shall eventually call *preservationist*. But we should point out that there is another path which is quite distinct from ours but which claims for itself all the merits of our approach and perhaps others besides.

This other account is distinguished from ours by being a whole-hearted replacement theory, where ours is a revision theory. According to dialethism, as its defenders have come to call it, there can be premise sets in which both a sentence A and its negation not-A appear without any ill effect. Without, that is, the premises having as the set of consequences the set of all sentences. What is more, such a set will also contain the single conjunction 'A and not-A.' Subscribers to this account suppose that the true meaning of 'not' is such as to make 'A and not-A' capable of being true. This move allows the satisfiability condition to reappear since many more sets (perhaps even every set) will be satisfiable.

As a replacement theory this has all the drawbacks of such theories when the target of replacement is classical logic. But quite apart from the resistance of vested interests, the dialethists must also endure the scorn of the naive and uncommitted. The very idea of 'true contradiction' seems to be about as counterintuitive as one could imagine, unless one is addicted to continental philosophy of the more literary sort.

In mincing negation, this scheme avoids the classical consequences of contradiction by changing the meaning of 'contradiction.' Let us say at once that the dialethists have many virtues. The boldness of their approach is admirable, and they have been far from lazy. Both the theory underlying the move and its inferential consequences have been energetically worked out and widely published. But where one ought to feel release and fill one's lungs, one feels a kind of dull unease. For even if classical negation is not primordial in human language but merely a contrivance of latter days, it is nonetheless with us and, even if not all, at least some of our contradictions seem to be on that scale.

# Three

# Weakly Additive Algebras and a Completeness Problem

ALASDAIR URQUHART

## Abstract

In this essay an extension of existing approaches to the algebra of modal logic is studied. Where the originating work by Jónnson and Tarski concerned the representation of Boolean algebras with additive operators, the present effort considers the representation of bounded distributive lattices with *weakly* additive operators. Where Jónnson and Tarski rely upon Stone's representation theory for Boolean algebras, this essay relies upon Priestley's representation theory (usually called Priestly duality) for bounded distributive lattices.

## 3.1 Introduction and Brief History

In a series of papers,[1] Ray Jennings and Peter Schotch have developed a generalized relational frame theory that goes beyond the standard approach in modal logic Schotch and Jennings (1980a,b); Jennings and Schotch (1981, 1984). The key idea is to generalize the usual truth condition for the necessity operator by using multi-place relations rather

---

[1] For further details concerning the origin of these papers see the the introductory chapter of this volume.

33

than the usual binary relation. Thus, if $R$ is an $(n + 1)$-place relation defined on a set $W$, then Jennings and Schotch state the truth condition for the generalized necessity operator as follows. If $x \in W$, then

$$x \models \Box\alpha \iff \forall y_1, \ldots, y_n [Rxy_1, \ldots, y_n \Rightarrow \exists i (y_i \models \alpha)].$$

This definition validates the scheme $K_n$ of $n$-ary aggregation,

$$\Box\alpha_0 \wedge \cdots \wedge \Box\alpha_n \supset \Box[ \bigvee_{0 \leq i < j \leq n} \alpha_i \wedge \alpha_j ].$$

In Jennings and Schotch (1984), the authors claim without proof that the class of formulas valid in all frames based on an $(n+1)$-place relation is axiomatized by the scheme $K_n$, together with rules of necessitation and monotonicity. This claim is proved by Apostoli and Brown in Apostoli and Brown (1995). An earlier completeness proof was given by Schotch and Jennings (1980a), which exploited the idea that necessity operators and inference relations are related in a certain way which is reminiscent of a Galois connection.

As clever (and fecund) as this approach is, it is not in the mainstream of modal logic. It isn't, in other words, *pure*, since it brings in ideas that are not part of what we might call *classical* modal logic. This is because it makes essential use of a non-classical inference relation (called $n$-forcing). The same holds for the proof by Apostoli and Brown, since it depends on an intermediate lemma stating chromatic compactness for hypergraphs. Though the Apostoli Brown proof was substantially simplified by Nicholson, Jennings, and Sarenac (2000), the notion of chromatic compactness was still used. There is now a proof due to Dorian Nicholson, detailed in chapter 4, which is probably the best one can do in the way of a pure proof.

A proof of completeness for the logic $K_n$ is presented in section 3.4 of this essay, where it is derived as a corollary to the main representation theorem for weakly additive algebras. Is this proof also pure? It certainly brings in something that seems external to classical modal logic, but how much is in that seeming? One might well argue that the representation theory of certain sorts of algebras is the basis of classical modal semantics, whether or not modal logicians acknowledge the fact. Agree to that, and you agree that the proof below is pure.

In the early 1950s Bjarni Jónsson and his thesis advisor[2] Alfred Tarski began work on the representation of Boolean algebras with extra operators (Jónsson and Tarski, 1951, 1952). One is tempted to conjecture that Tarski was the one who suggested this topic, which was a kind of melding of his friend Marshall Stone's ground-breaking work on the representation of Boolean algebras[3] and his own work with J.C.C. McKinsey on the algebra of closure operators (McKinsey and Tarski, 1948).

The representations in question work like this: We can easily see that every finite Boolean algebra is 'the same' as an algebra of sets, namely the set of all subsets of some finite set, called the underlying set, with the Boolean operations of meet, join, complement, 1, and 0 represented by set intersection, set union, relative set complement, the underlying set, and the empty set. We can spell out the sameness in several different (and equivalent) ways. One of them is this: There is a translation $T$ which maps the atoms of the Boolean algebra (all finite Boolean algebras are atomic) to the unit subsets of the underlying set of the set algebra and the equation $x \wedge y = 1$ holds in a given Boolean algebra, with underlying set $\Sigma$ if and only if $T(x) \cap T(y) = \Sigma$.

The algebraic point to make here is that such a translation $T$ can be reversed by the obvious inverse translation $T^{-1}$, which takes unit sets to atoms, intersections to meets, etc. Moreover, the existence of these two translations amounts to an isomorphism between the Boolean algebra and the set algebra.

This is pretty much old news by the 1930s. But it raises a question: Can this result extend to arbitrary Boolean algebras? In other words, is it the case that every Boolean algebra whatever is isomorphic to an algebra of sets? There is a lot of content in the 'whatever,' since there are infinite Boolean algebras and, also, non-atomic ones. Stone proved that this question has a positive answer though the set algebra in question isn't what the novice might expect.[4] The sets, in general, are drawn

---

[2] In fact, Jónsson appears to have been the very first graduate student to work with Tarski after the latter's move to the United States.

[3] Which work is reported in Stone (1936).

[4] And, it should be noted, the notion of isomorphism has to be enlarged too. In fact some assert that this enlargement pointed the way to the theory of categories, well before that theory

from a topological space and have certain curious properties. They are both open and closed. The set operations are more complicated too. We can continue to translate meet by intersection, but joins are not in general simple unions. Instead they are the closures of such unions.

Jónnson and Tarski consider the problem of what changes must occur to preserve this isomorphism when we introduce extra operations. They consider the case of a single $n$-ary operation, which we shall call $\Diamond_n$ (with the subscript suppressed when no confusion will result) which is a generalization of the closure operation. What they show is that such expanded Boolean operations can be represented by the original set algebras provided that we introduce an $(n+1)$-ary *relation* to deal with the added operator. The translation which makes everything work is that the generalized closure $\Diamond_n(x_1, \ldots, x_n)$ goes to the set of sets $\{b_1, \ldots, b_n\}$ such that $a$ is an element of $T(x_i)$ and $Rab_1 \ldots b_n$.

**Example 1.** The ordinary closure is a unary operation. In that case the closure $\Diamond(x)$ is represented by the set of elements $b$ such that $a \in T(x)$ and $Rab$. It is easy to see the connection between this condition and the usual 'Kripke' truth condition for possibility.[5]

Of course not any old generalized closure operator will be representable in this way. In fact, Jónnson and Tarski restrict their operators to those they call *additive*. The additivity condition can be expressed by the Boolean inequality,

$$\Diamond_n(x_1, \ldots, x_i \vee y_i, x_{i+1}, \ldots, x_n) \leq$$

$$\Diamond_n(x_1, \ldots, x_i, x_{i+1}, \ldots, x_n) \vee \Diamond_n(x_1, \ldots, x_{i-1}, y_i, x_{i+1}, \ldots, x_n)$$

so long as the generalized closure operator is *normal*, which is to say that $\Diamond(x_1, \ldots, x_i, 0, x_{i+1}, \ldots, x_n) = 0$.

Another popular condition is *(upward) monotonicity*, which is to say that $\Diamond_n(x_1, \ldots, x_n) \leq \Diamond_n(y_1, \ldots, y_n)$ whenever $x_i \leq y_i$ for $1 \leq i \leq$

---

had been framed.

    [5]Kripke (1963) refers (in a footnote) to the work of Jónnson and Tarski more than a decade before his publication as 'a surprising anticipation,' though it isn't clear to the casual reader who should be (most) surprised.

$n$. This condition applies in particular to the algebras which correspond to the Jennings and Schotch $K_n$ logics.

The present essay sets the modal-logical results in a broader framework, by presenting the theory of Jennings and Schotch as a generalization of the work of Jónsson and Tarski. To be consistent with this earlier work, the theory is couched in terms of the possibility operator rather than the dual necessity operator used in the work of Jennings and Schotch (and in modal logic generally speaking). The emphasis on possibility does not reflect some preference for this modality over necessity, but rather a desire to focus on the notion of *closure*, which is more likely to be familiar to mathematicians. The topological equivalent of a necessity operator is an *interior* operator which, while not unfamiliar, is not as popular – topologically speaking.

As a corollary to our main representation theorems, we show that the operators on a given distributive lattice $L$ satisfying a generalized form of the dual of the axiom scheme $K_n$ are exactly the closure under composition of the additive operators on $L$.

## 3.2 Weakly Additive Operators

Let $L$ be a bounded distributive lattice. Such an object is a generalization of the (perhaps) more familiar Boolean algebra in the sense that every Boolean algebra is a bounded distributive lattice, but the converse is not true. To take a single (but prominent) example, a Heyting algebra is a bounded distributive lattice which is not a Boolean algebra.

We shall use vector notation $\vec{a}, \vec{b}, \ldots$ to refer to sequences of elements from $L$, including the zero vector $\Lambda$. Operations and relations on such vectors are to be understood in terms of the product lattices $L^k$. In other words, a binary operation, let's call it $\wedge$, on two vectors $\vec{a}$ and $\vec{b}$ is to be understood as resulting in a unique vector $\vec{a} \wedge \vec{b}$ in which the elements of this sequence are defined as the $\wedge$ of the corresponding elements of $\vec{a}$ and $\vec{b}$.[6] Of course this assumes that the two vectors have the same length.

---

[6]This is often described as defining the $\wedge$ of two vectors *componentwise*.

We use $|\vec{a}|$ for the length of the vector $\vec{a}$; the vector of length $k$ in which all of the entries are the element $a$ is written $a^k$ (when $k = 0$, this is the empty vector $\Lambda$). If $\vec{k}$ is a sequence of integers, then we write $\sum \vec{k}$ for the sum of the elements in the sequence.

In the succeeding section on duality theory, we need notations and definitions for sequences of elements from an arbitrary set. We write $x \in \vec{y}$ if $x$ is a member of the sequence $\vec{y}$. If $\vec{x}$ is a sequence of elements from a set $S$ and $A \subseteq S$, then we write $\vec{x} \subseteq A$ if every element in the sequence $\vec{x}$ is in $A$. If $\vec{x}$ is a sequence of subsets of a fixed set $S$, then we use the notation $\bigcap \vec{x}$ for the intersection of all the sets in the sequence $\vec{x}$; in the case of the empty sequence $\Lambda$ of sets, $\bigcap \Lambda = S$.

---

**Definition 1.** *If $\vec{x}$ and $\vec{y}$ are sequences of elements from a set $S$ with an ordering relation $\leq$ defined on it, and $|\vec{x}| \leq |\vec{y}|$, then we write $\vec{x} \leq \vec{y}$ if $x_i \leq y_i$ for all $i$, where $1 \leq i \leq |\vec{x}|$.*

---

Let $\diamond$ be an $n$-place operation defined on $L$.

---

**Definition 2.** *For $k > 0$, we say that $\diamond$ is $k$-additive in the $i$-th place if it is normal and satisfies the conditions*

$$\diamond[\vec{a}, \bigwedge_{0 \leq h < j \leq k} (b_h \vee b_j), \vec{c}] \leq \bigvee_{0 \leq j \leq k} \diamond[\vec{a}, b_j, \vec{c}]$$

*for $\vec{a} \in L^{i-1}, \vec{c} \in L^{n-i}$ and $b_0, \ldots, b_k \in L$.*

---

**Example 2.** Suppose $\diamond$ is binary. Then $\diamond$ is 1-additive in the second place if and only if

$$\diamond(x, (b_0 \vee b_1)) \leq [(\diamond(x, b_0) \vee \diamond(x, b_1)]$$

While $\diamond$ is 2-additive in the first place if and only if

$$\diamond((b_0 \vee b_1) \wedge (b_0 \vee b_2) \wedge (b_1 \vee b_2), y) \leq [\diamond(b_0, y) \vee \diamond(b_1, y) \vee \diamond(b_2, y)]$$

In the following definition we define something a bit more general than our earlier notion of monotonicity, which applies only where the relation $\leq$ assumes that the related vectors are of equal length.

---

**Definition 3.** $\Diamond$ *is said to be monotone if it satisfies the condition* $\Diamond\vec{a} \leq \Diamond\vec{b}$ *whenever* $\vec{a} \leq \vec{b}$.

---

**Definition 4.** *An operator on a bounded distributive lattice is defined to be* weakly additive *if it is monotone and in all of its argument places it is $k$-additive for some $k > 0$.*

---

**Definition 5.** *An additive operator in the sense of Jónsson and Tarski (1951; 1952) is a monotone operator that is 1-additive in all of its argument places.*

---

**Definition 6.** *We say that an $n$-place weakly additive operator $\Diamond$ is of type $\vec{k}$ if $\vec{k}$ is a vector of positive integers of length $n$ so that $\Diamond$ is $k_i$-additive in its $i$-th place.*

---

For example:

**Example 3.** If $\Diamond(a, b, c)$ is 1-additive in its first place, 3-additive in its second place, and 2-additive in its third, then it is of type $\langle 1, 3, 2 \rangle$.

---

**Definition 7.** *We define a* weakly additive algebra of type $\vec{k}$ *to be a bounded distributive lattice $L$ together with a weakly additive operator of type $\vec{k}$ defined on $L$.*

---

If we translate the $K_n$ modal logics considered by Jennings and Schotch into algebraic form, the result is a special case of the general framework outlined above. Consider a propositional logic satisfying the scheme $K_n$ of $n$-ary aggregation, as well as the rules of necessitation and monotonicity. We can define a possibility operator in the usual way as the dual of the necessity operator; that is to say, $\Diamond\alpha \leftrightarrow \neg\Box\neg\alpha$. Then the scheme $K_n$ is provably equivalent to the dual scheme,

$$\Diamond[ \bigwedge_{0\leq i < j \leq n} \alpha_i \vee \alpha_j] \supset \Diamond\alpha_0 \vee \ldots \vee \Diamond\alpha_n.$$

Hence, the algebraic version of the Jennings/Schotch system with the axiom scheme $K_n$ is the theory of Boolean algebras with a one-place monotone normal operator $\Diamond$ satisfying

$$\Diamond[ \bigwedge_{0\leq i < j \leq n} (b_i \vee b_j)] \leq \bigvee_{0\leq i \leq n} \Diamond b_i$$

that is to say, Boolean algebras with a one-place weakly additive operator of type $\langle n\rangle$. In what follows, we shall call these *Jennings/Schotch algebras*; we shall denote the variety of weakly additive algebras satisfying the above inequality by the notation $V_n$.

The Jennings/Schotch truth condition for $\Box$, when translated into its dual form, is as follows:

$$x \models \Diamond\alpha \iff \exists y_1,\ldots,y_n[Rxy_1,\ldots,y_n \wedge \forall i(y_i \models \alpha)].$$

## 3.3  A Further Generalization

Weakly additive operators can be defined from multi-place relations, in a way that generalizes both the Jennings/Schotch truth condition for possibility, and a construction of Jónsson and Tarski (Jónsson and Tarski, 1951, Definition 3.2). Let $\vec{k}$ be a length $n$ sequence of non-negative integers, $X$ a non-empty set and $R$ a $(\sum \vec{k} + 1)$-place relation on $X$. We define an $n$-place operation $\Diamond_R$ on $\mathcal{P}(X)$ as follows:

---

**Definition 8.**     $x \in \Diamond_R(A_1,\ldots,A_n) \iff$

$$\exists \vec{y}_1,\ldots,\vec{y}_n[Rx\vec{y}_1,\ldots,\vec{y}_n \wedge \forall i\,[1 \leq i \leq n \Rightarrow \vec{y}_i \subseteq A_i]]$$

---

where for each $i$, $1 \le i \le n$, $\vec{y}_i$ is a vector of length $k_i$.

**Theorem 1.** *For $\vec{k}$ a sequence of non-negative integers of length $n$, and $R$ a $(\sum \vec{k} + 1)$-place relation on a non-empty set $X$, $\diamond_R$ is a weakly additive operator of type $\vec{k}$ on $\mathcal{P}(X)$.*

Proof. Let $L$ be $\mathcal{P}(X)$. We need to prove for $k = k_i > 0$ the inclusion

$$\diamond_R[\vec{A}, \bigcap_{0 \le h < j \le k} (B_h \cup B_j), \vec{C}] \subseteq \bigcup_{0 \le j \le k} \diamond_R[\vec{A}, B_j, \vec{C}],$$

where $\vec{A} \in L^{i-1}, \vec{C} \in L^{n-i}$ and $B_0, \dots, B_k \in L$. Assume

$$x \in \diamond_R[\vec{A}, \bigcap_{0 \le h < j \le k} (B_h \cup B_j), \vec{C}],$$

so that there exist $\vec{y}_1, \dots, \vec{y}_n$ satisfying the conditions,

$$Rx\vec{y}_1, \dots, \vec{y}_n \wedge \forall j \, (1 \le j < i \Rightarrow \vec{y}_j \subseteq A_j),$$

$$\forall j \, (i < j \le n \Rightarrow \vec{y}_j \subseteq C_j),$$

$$\vec{y}_i \subseteq \bigcap_{0 \le h < j \le k} (B_h \cup B_j).$$

Let us suppose that for all $j$, $0 \le j \le k$, $\vec{y}_i \not\subseteq B_j$. Then for any such $j$, there is a $z \in \vec{y}_i$ so that $z \notin B_j$. Since $|\vec{y}_i| = k$, it follows (by the pigeonhole principle) that there are distinct $h, j$ so that for some $z \in y_i$, $z \notin B_h \cup B_j$, contrary to assumption. Hence for some $j$, $\vec{y}_i \subseteq B_j$, proving the inclusion. The remaining conditions defining a weakly additive operator of type $\vec{k}$ are easily verified. $\square$

## 3.4 Duality Theory for Weakly Additive Operators

The duality for weakly additive operators described in this section is piggy-backed on Priestley's duality for bounded distributive lattices. We begin by giving the main results of this duality theory without proofs. For detailed discussion of the theory, the reader is referred to articles by

Priestley (1970, 1984), Davey and Duffus (1982) and to the textbook by Davey and Priestley (1990).

An *ordered topological space* is a topological space with a partial order relation defined on it. A subset $E$ of a partially ordered set is *increasing* if $x \in E$, $x \leq y$ imply $y \in E$. A map $f$ between partially ordered sets is *increasing* if $x \leq y$ implies $f(x) \leq f(y)$, and *decreasing* if $x \leq y$ implies $f(y) \leq f(x)$. A map between two ordered spaces is said to be an *order-homeomorphism* if it is both a homeomorphism and an isomorphism with respect to the orderings on the spaces. A *Priestley space* is an ordered topological space $\mathcal{S}$ that is compact and totally order-disconnected; that is, for points $x, y$ of $\mathcal{S}$, if $x \not\leq y$ then there is a clopen increasing set $U$ such that $x \in U$, $y \notin U$.

If $L$ is a bounded distributive lattice, then the *dual space* of $L$, $\mathcal{S}(L)$, is the ordered topological space in which the set of points $S$ is the family of all prime filters of $L$, ordered by containment, and the topology is defined by taking as a sub-base the family of all sets $\{\nabla \in S : a \in \nabla\}$ and $\{\nabla \in S : a \notin \nabla\}$ for $a \in L$. Conversely, if $\mathcal{S}$ is a Priestley space then the dual lattice of $\mathcal{S}$, $L(\mathcal{S})$, is the set of all clopen increasing sets of $\mathcal{S}$, with the lattice operations of set intersection and union.

**Theorem 2.**    *1. If $L$ is a bounded distributive lattice, then $\mathcal{S}(L)$ is a Priestley space, and $L$ is isomorphic to $L(\mathcal{S}(L))$ under the mapping*

$$\eta(a) = \{x \in \mathcal{S}(L) : a \in x\}.$$

*2. If $\mathcal{S}$ is a Priestley space, and $L(\mathcal{S})$ its dual lattice, $\mathcal{S}$ is order-homeomorphic to $\mathcal{S}(L(\mathcal{S}))$ under the mapping*

$$\theta(x) = \{B \in L(\mathcal{S}) : x \in B\}.$$

We obtain the duality theory for weakly additive operators by building on Priestley's duality theory. Let $\vec{k}$ be a sequence of non-negative integers, and $\sum \vec{k} = n$ the sum of the entries in $\vec{k}$. We define a *relational space of type* $\vec{k}$ to be a structure $\langle \mathcal{S}, R \rangle$, where $\mathcal{S}$ is a Priestley space, and $R$ is a $(\sum \vec{k} + 1)$-place relation on $S$, satisfying the following conditions:

1. If $A_1, \ldots, A_n \in L(\mathcal{S})$, then $\Diamond_R(A_1, \ldots, A_n)$ is clopen.

2. If $Rx\vec{y}$ and $x \leq z$ then $Rz\vec{y}$.

3. If for all $i$, $1 \leq i \leq n$, $|y_i| = k_i$ and $\neg Rx\vec{y}_1, \ldots, \vec{y}_n$, then $(\exists A_1, \ldots, A_n \in L(\mathcal{S}))$ such that

$$[\forall i \, (1 \leq i \leq n \Rightarrow \vec{y}_i \subseteq A_i) \wedge x \notin \Diamond_R(A_1, \ldots, A_n)].$$

If $\mathcal{R} = \langle \mathcal{S}, R \rangle$ is a relational space of type $\vec{k}$, then the *dual algebra* of $\mathcal{R}$ is the algebra $A(\mathcal{R})$ defined on the lattice $L(\mathcal{S})$ by adding the operation $\Diamond_R$. If $\langle L, \Diamond \rangle$ is a weakly additive algebra, where $\Diamond$ is an $n$-place operator, and each $\vec{y}_1, \ldots, \vec{y}_n$ is a sequence of filters in $L$, then the relation $R_\Diamond$ is defined by

$$R_\Diamond x \vec{y}_1, \ldots, \vec{y}_n \Leftrightarrow \forall \vec{a} \in L^n [\forall i (a_i \in \bigcap \vec{y}_i) \Rightarrow \Diamond(a_1, \ldots, a_n) \in x].$$

If $A = \langle L, \Diamond \rangle$ is a weakly additive algebra of type $\vec{k}$, then the dual space of $A$, $\mathcal{R}(A)$, is defined by adding to the Priestley space of $L$ the relation $R$ defined by

$$Rx\vec{y}_1, \ldots, \vec{y}_n \Leftrightarrow R_\Diamond x \vec{y}_1, \ldots, \vec{y}_n \wedge \forall i \, [1 \leq i \leq n \Rightarrow |\vec{y}_i| = k_i],$$

where $n = |\vec{k}|$.

If $L$ is a distributive lattice, then we employ the following terminology for vectors $\vec{u}$, where each $u_i$ is a subset of $L$. For such vectors $\vec{u}$ and $\vec{v}$, where $|\vec{u}| \leq |\vec{v}|$, we write $\vec{u} \subseteq \vec{v}$ if for all $i$ where $1 \leq i \leq |\vec{u}|$, $u_i \subseteq v_i$ (this terminology is consistent with the corresponding terminology introduced above for vectors of points in ordered sets). If $\mathcal{F}$ is a family of such vectors, and the maximum length of a vector in $\mathcal{F}$ is $k$, then we define $\bigcup \mathcal{F}$ to be the vector $\vec{v}$ of length $k$ where $v_i = \bigcup \{u_i | \vec{u} \in \mathcal{F}\}$.

For a lattice $L$, $x$ a filter in $L$, and $a$ an element of $L$, we denote by $x[a]$ the smallest filter containing $x$ and $a$. The principal filter containing $a$ is denoted by $[a]$.

**Lemma 1.** *Let* $\langle L, \Diamond \rangle$ *be a weakly additive algebra of type* $\vec{k}$, *where* $|\vec{k}| = n$. *Then for* $a \in L$, $x \in \mathcal{S}(L)$, *if* $\Diamond \vec{a} \in x$, *then*

$$\exists \vec{w}_1, \ldots, \vec{w}_n [\, Rx\vec{w}_1, \ldots, \vec{w}_n \,\wedge\, \forall i [\, 1 \le i \le n \Rightarrow a_i \in \bigcap \vec{w}_i ]\,].$$

Proof. Let $\Diamond \vec{a} \in x$, where $x \in \mathcal{S}(L)$. Define $\mathcal{F}$ to be the family of all sequences $\vec{u}_1, \ldots, \vec{u}_n$, where each $\vec{u}_i$ is a sequence of filters in $L$, so that: (1) $a_i \in \bigcap \vec{u}_i$; (2) for every $i$, $1 \le i \le n$, there are $b_1, \ldots, b_{i-1}, b_{i+1}, \ldots, b_n$ so that for all $y \in \vec{u}_i$, there is an element $a_y \in L$ such that

$$\forall z \in \vec{u}_i (z \ne y \Rightarrow a_y \in z) \,\wedge\, \Diamond (b_1, \ldots, b_{i-1}, a_y, b_{i+1}, \ldots, b_n) \notin x;$$

(3) $R_\Diamond x\vec{u}_1, \ldots, \vec{u}_n$; (4) $|\vec{u}_i| \le k_i$. We define an ordering on $\mathcal{F}$ as follows. For $\vec{u}_1, \ldots, \vec{u}_n \in \mathcal{F}$ and $\vec{v}_1, \ldots, \vec{v}_n \in \mathcal{F}$, $\vec{u}_1, \ldots, \vec{u}_n \le \vec{v}_1, \ldots, \vec{v}_n$ if and only if for all $i$, $\vec{u}_i \subseteq \vec{v}_i$.

First, we show that $\mathcal{F} \ne \emptyset$. For $k_i > 0$, set $\vec{u}_i = \langle [a_i] \rangle$. Then $\vec{u}_1, \ldots, \vec{u}_n \in \mathcal{F}$, since for $y \in \vec{u}_i$, we can set $b_j = 1$ for $j \ne i$, and $a_y = 0$, since $\Diamond (1, \ldots, 1, 0, 1, \ldots, 1) = 0 \notin x$. Second, we show that every chain in $\mathcal{F}$ has an upper bound in $\mathcal{F}$. Let $\mathcal{C} \subseteq \mathcal{F}$ be a chain; for $1 \le i \le n$ define $\vec{u}_i = \bigcup \{ \vec{v}_i \,|\, \vec{v}_1, \ldots, \vec{v}_n \in \mathcal{C} \}$. Then it is straightforward to check that $\vec{u}_1, \ldots, \vec{u}_n$ is in $\mathcal{F}$, and is an upper bound for $\mathcal{C}$.

By Zorn's Lemma, $\mathcal{F}$ contains a maximal element $\vec{w}_1, \ldots, \vec{w}_n$. To complete the proof of the lemma, we need to show that all the filters in $\vec{w}_1, \ldots, \vec{w}_n$ are prime. Suppose that this is not so, so that for some $\vec{w}_i = y_1, \ldots, y_j, \ldots, y_l$, $y_j$ is not prime; thus there are $d, e \in L$ where $d \vee e \in y_j$, but $d, e \notin y_j$. Let $\vec{u}, \vec{v}$ be the vectors that result from $\vec{u}_i$ by replacing $y_j$ by $y_j [d]$ and $y_j [e]$ respectively. Since $\vec{w}_1, \ldots, \vec{w}_n$ is maximal in $\mathcal{F}$, it follows that $\neg R_\Diamond x\vec{w}_1, \ldots, \vec{w}_{i-1}, \vec{u}, \vec{w}_{i+1}, \ldots, \vec{w}_n$ and $\neg R_\Diamond x\vec{w}_1, \ldots, \vec{w}_{i-1}, \vec{v}, \vec{w}_{i+1}, \ldots, \vec{w}_n$. Thus there are $f_1, \ldots, f_n \in L$ so that $f_1 \in \bigcap \vec{w}_1, \ldots, f_i \in \bigcap \vec{u}, \ldots, f_n \in \bigcap \vec{w}_n$, $\Diamond (f_1, \ldots, f_n) \notin x$ and $g_1, \ldots, g_n \in L$ so that $g_1 \in \bigcap \vec{w}_1, \ldots, g_i \in \bigcap \vec{v}, \ldots, g_n \in \bigcap \vec{w}_n$, and $\Diamond (g_1, \ldots, g_n) \notin x$. Let $\vec{z}$ be the vector $\langle \vec{u}, y_j [e] \rangle$. We claim that $R_\Diamond x\vec{w}_1, \ldots, \vec{z}, \ldots, \vec{w}_n$. For if not, there are elements $p_1, \ldots, p_n \in L$ so that $p_1 \in \bigcap \vec{w}_1, \ldots, p_i \in \bigcap \vec{z}, \ldots, p_n \in \bigcap \vec{w}_n$ and

$\Diamond(p_1, \ldots, p_n) \notin x$. But since $p_i \in y_j[d]$ and $p_i \in y_j[e]$, it follows that $p_i \in y_j$, contradicting $R_\Diamond x \vec{w}_1, \ldots, \vec{w}_n$.

We now show that the sequence $\vec{w}_1, \ldots, \vec{z}, \ldots, \vec{w}_n$ also satisfies the second of the three conditions defining the elements of $\mathcal{F}$. Let $b_1, \ldots, b_{i-1}, b_{i+1}, \ldots, b_n$ be the sequence of elements associated with $\vec{w}_i$ by condition (2). For $j \neq i$, let $h_j = b_j \wedge f_j \wedge g_j$. We claim that the sequence $h_1, \ldots, h_{i-1}, h_{i+1}, \ldots, h_n$ satisfies condition (2). For elements $y$ in $\vec{z}$ other than the filters $y_j[d]$ or $y_j[e]$, we can set $a_y$ to be the element $a_y$ associated with $\vec{w}_1, \ldots, \vec{w}_n$ by condition (2). For $y = y_j[d]$, set $a_y = g_i$, and for $y = y_j[e]$, set $a_y = f_i$. Then it follows from our assumptions that $h_1, \ldots, h_{i-1}, h_{i+1}, \ldots, h_n$ and the elements $a_y$ satisfy condition (2).

Since $\vec{w}_1, \ldots, \vec{w}_n \leq \vec{w}_1, \ldots, \vec{z}, \ldots, \vec{w}_n$, and $\vec{w}_1, \ldots, \vec{w}_n$ is a maximal element in $\mathcal{F}$, $\vec{w}_1, \ldots, \vec{z}, \ldots, \vec{w}_n \notin \mathcal{F}$. Because $\vec{w}_1, \ldots, \vec{z}, \ldots, \vec{w}_n$ satisfies conditions (1) to (3) in the definition of $\mathcal{F}$, it follows that $l = |\vec{w}_i| = k_i$. Let $a_0, \ldots, a_l$ be the sequence of elements $a_y$ for $y \in \vec{z}$.

$$\text{Then} \quad \bigwedge_{0 \leq i < j \leq l} a_i \vee a_j \in \bigcap \vec{z},$$

$$\text{so that} \quad \Diamond \, (h_1, \ldots, h_{i-1}, \bigwedge_{0 \leq i < j \leq l} a_i \vee a_j, h_{i+1}, \ldots, h_n) \in x.$$

$$\text{It follows that} \quad \bigvee_{0 \leq i \leq l} \Diamond(h_1, \ldots, a_i, \ldots, h_n) \in x.$$

But then, since $x$ is a prime filter, it follows that for some $i$, $0 \leq i \leq l$, $\Diamond(h_1, \ldots, a_i, \ldots, h_n) \in x$, contrary to the definition of $a_i$.

In the definition of $\mathcal{F}$, we have only required that $|\vec{u}_i| \leq k_i$, for $1 \leq i \leq n$, while the definition of $R$ above requires the condition $|\vec{u}_i| = k_i$. However, if $R_\Diamond x \vec{u}_1, \ldots, \vec{u}_i, \ldots, \vec{u}_n$, then $R_\Diamond x \vec{u}_1, \ldots, \langle \vec{u}_i, z \rangle, \ldots, \vec{u}_n$, where $z$ is any element in $\vec{u}_i$. Consequently, we can conclude that

$$\exists \vec{w}_1, \ldots, \vec{w}_n [ \, Rx\vec{w}_1, \ldots, \vec{w}_n \wedge \forall i [ 1 \leq i \leq n \Rightarrow a_i \in \bigcap \vec{w}_i ] \, ].$$

This completes the proof of the lemma. $\qquad\qquad\qquad \square$

**Theorem 3.**   *1. If $A$ is a weakly additive algebra of type $\vec{k}$, then $\mathcal{R}(A)$ is a relational space of type $\vec{k}$ and $A$ is isomorphic to $A(\mathcal{R}(A))$ under the mapping*

$$\eta(a) = \{x \in \mathcal{R}(A) : a \in x\}.$$

*2. If $\mathcal{R}$ is a relational space of type $\vec{k}$, and $A(\mathcal{R})$ its dual algebra, $\mathcal{R}$ is order-homeomorphic to $\mathcal{R}(A(\mathcal{R}))$ under the mapping*

$$\theta(x) = \{B \in A(\mathcal{R}) : x \in B\}.$$

Proof. (1) The main condition to be verified is that $\Diamond \vec{a} \in x \Rightarrow$

$$\exists \vec{w}_1, \ldots, \vec{w}_n [\, R_\Diamond x \vec{w}_1, \ldots, \vec{w}_n \land \forall i [\, 1 \leq i \leq n \Rightarrow a_i \in \bigcap \vec{w}_i \,] \,],$$

for $x \in \mathcal{S}(L)$. This follows immediately from the definition of $R_\Diamond$ and lemma 1. The conditions defining a relational space of type $\vec{k}$ are then easily verified from the definitions, using this equivalence.

Priestley's representation theorem (theorem 2) implies that $\eta$ is a lattice-isomorphism, so it suffices to show that $\eta$ is an isomorphism with respect to $\Diamond$. That $\eta$ is also an isomorphism with respect to $\Diamond$ is exactly the content of the above condition.

(2) By theorem 2, the map $\theta$ is an order-homeomorphism from $\mathcal{R}$ onto the second dual of $\mathcal{R}$, so it suffices to prove that $\theta$ is an isomorphism with respect to the relation $R$. This follows from the definition of $\Diamond_R$ and the third condition defining a relational space of type $\vec{k}$.   $\square$

The representation theorem we have just proved is an algebraic version of the completeness theorem described in the introductory section. In fact, that completeness theorem can be derived from the representation theorem (theorem 3).

**Theorem 4.** *The logic $K_n$ is complete with respect to the family of all $(n + 1)$-ary relational frames, given the Jennings/Schotch truth condition for the $\square$ operator.*

Proof. We can construct a Boolean algebra with operator $\Diamond$ by the familiar Lindenbaum construction; that is to say, we can construct an algebra in which the elements are classes of provably equivalent formulas.

If we begin from the logic $K_n$, then the result is an algebra $A$ in the variety $V_n$. By theorem 3, this algebra is isomorphic to $A(\mathcal{R}(A))$ under the mapping $\eta(a) = \{x \in \mathcal{R}(A) : a \in x\}$.

Consider the $(n + 1)$-ary relational frame defined on the family of all prime filters in $A$, with the accessibility relation $R$ defined in the dual space $\mathcal{R}(A)$. For a propositional variable $P$, the set of points at which it is true is defined to be $\eta([P])$, where $[P]$ is the set of formulas equivalent to $P$ in $K_n$. It is a straightforward exercise to check that a formula is true at all points in this model if and only if it is a theorem of $K_n$. $\qquad\qquad\square$

# Four

# A Dualization of Neighbourhood Structures

DORIAN NICHOLSON

### Abstract

A dualization of neighbourhood semantics is introduced for the purpose of obtaining a simplified proof that weakly aggregative modal logic is complete with respect to $(n+1)$-ary relational frames. This new class of quasi-semantic structures exploits the theory of transverse hypergamous. Unlike the other proofs in the literature, the one included here does not cite chromatic, or colouring, compactness. Along the way we prove completeness for a denumerable class of non-normal modal logics, which have deontic, as well as philosophical logical motivations.

## 4.1 Introduction

The search for a completeness proof for Jennings and Schotch's weakly aggregative modal logic lasted for nearly twenty years (Johnston, 1978; Schotch and Jennings, 1980a; Jennings and Schotch, 1981; Schotch and Jennings, 1980b) before the goal was attained in 1995 by Apostoli and Brown (1995), and also independently, algebraically, by Urquhart (1995). Apostoli and Brown's proof was subsequently simplified by Nicholson, Jennings, and Sarenac (2000). But both proofs exploit the compactness of colouring for hypergraphs whose edges are finitely long. *Chromatic compactness*, also called *colouring compactness*, is the claim that $\forall H$, if $H$ is a hypergraph then $H$ is $k$-colourable $(k \geq 1)$ iff every finite $G \subseteq H$ is $k$-colourable.[1] A *hypergraph* is a family of sets, called *edges*. A hypergraph $H$ is *k-colourable* iff there is a partition of its union, called its *vertex set*, into $k$ pairwise disjoint, mutually exhaustive sets, or cells, such that no edge of $H$ is a subset of any cell. The simplifying thrust of Nicholson et al. (2000) raises the question whether there is an even simpler completeness proof, one which avoids citing chromatic compactness. In this paper an affirmative answer to this question is demonstrated, by invoking the theory of what are dubbed *hyperframes*. The theory of hyperframes implements the theory of transverse hypergraphs and consists essentially of a dualization of the neighbourhood semantics for modal logic explored by Segerberg (1971), and referred to as 'minimal models' by Chellas (1980).

## 4.2  Hyperframes

A *hyperframe* $\mathfrak{F}$ is pair $(\mathcal{U}, \mathcal{H})$ where $\mathcal{U}$ is a non-empty set (the *universe* of the frame) and $\mathcal{H}$ is a *hypergraph function* from $\mathcal{U}$ to $\mathcal{P}\mathcal{P}(\mathcal{U})$. Accordingly, for each $x \in \mathcal{U}$, $\mathcal{H}(x)$ is a *hypergraph* on $\mathcal{U}$: a family of subsets of $\mathcal{U}$, where the subsets are called the *edges* of the hypergraph, and the elements of the edges are called the *vertices* of the hypergraph. For each $x$ in $\mathcal{U}$, $\mathcal{H}(x)$ is called the *hypergraph on $x$* (relative to $\mathfrak{F}$). A hyperframe is thus, in essence, a neighbourhood frame, as the latter is defined in Segerberg (1971), for example. But a model on a hyperframe is distinct from a model on a neighbourhood frame when it comes to interpreting $\Box$.

   If $\mathfrak{F} = (\mathcal{U}, \mathcal{H})$ is a hyperframe and $\mathcal{V} : Nat \rightarrow \mathcal{P}(\mathcal{U})$ is a valuation function, then $(\mathcal{U}, \mathcal{H}, \mathcal{V})$ is a *(hyper)model* $\mathfrak{M}$ on $\mathfrak{F}$. Truth at a point $x$ in a model $\mathfrak{M} = (\mathcal{U}, \mathcal{H}, \mathcal{V})$, with respect to the language of a standard propositional logic, is defined in the standard way for Boolean connectives. To interpret the unary necessity operator $\Box$, we use the notion of the *transversal* of a hypergraph.

---

[1] Colouring compactness is provable from the compactness of propositional logic.

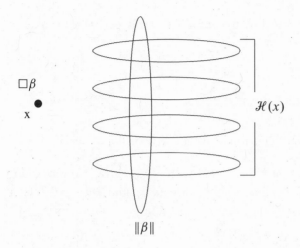

Figure 4.1: The truth condition for □ on hyperframes.

**Definition 1.** *If $\mathcal{H}$ is a hypergraph on a non-empty set $\mathcal{U}$, and $S$ is a subset of $\mathcal{U}$, $S$ is a* transversal *for $\mathcal{H}$ iff $\forall \mathcal{E} \in \mathcal{H}, S \cap \mathcal{E} \neq \emptyset$.*

It follows from this definition that $\emptyset \in \mathcal{H}$ iff $\mathcal{H}$ has no transversals, and $\mathcal{H} = \emptyset$ iff, vacuously, every subset of $\mathcal{U}$ is a transversal for $\mathcal{H}$.

The truth condition for □ is

$$\models^{\mathfrak{M}}_{x} \Box\beta \text{ iff } \|\beta\|^{\mathfrak{M}} \text{ is a transversal for } \mathcal{H}(x).$$

(See figure 4.1.) Introducing $\Diamond\beta$ as an abbreviation for $\neg\Box\neg\beta$, we therefore have

$$\models^{\mathfrak{M}}_{x} \Diamond\beta \text{ iff } \exists \mathcal{E} \in \mathcal{H}(x) : \|\beta\|^{\mathfrak{M}} \supseteq \mathcal{E}$$

If $\mathfrak{M} = (\mathcal{U}, \mathcal{H}, \mathcal{V})$ is a model and $\forall x \in \mathcal{U}, \models^{\mathfrak{M}}_{x} \alpha$, then $\alpha$ is *valid on $\mathfrak{M}$*, written '$\models^{\mathfrak{M}} \alpha$'; if for every valuation function $\mathcal{V}$, $\alpha$ is valid on $(\mathcal{U}, \mathcal{H}, \mathcal{V})$ then $\alpha$ is *valid on $\mathfrak{F} = (\mathcal{U}, \mathcal{H})$*, indicated by '$\mathfrak{F} \models \alpha$'. If

$\alpha$ is valid on every member of a class $\mathfrak{C}$ of frames, then $\alpha$ is *valid with respect to* $\mathfrak{C}$, '$\mathfrak{C} \models \alpha$'.

The logic determined by the class $\mathfrak{C}$ of all hyperframes is axiomatized by $\mathbf{N_q}$,[2] the system defined by

$$[RR] : \vdash \alpha \supset \beta \;\Rightarrow\; \vdash \Box\alpha \supset \Box\beta$$

$$[PL] : \vdash_{PL} \alpha \;\Rightarrow\; \vdash \alpha$$

$$[MP] : \vdash \alpha \supset \beta \;\&\; \vdash \alpha \;\Rightarrow\; \vdash \beta$$

$$[US] : \vdash \alpha \;\&\; \beta \text{ is a substitution instance of } \alpha \;\Rightarrow\; \vdash \beta$$

It is easy to check that $\mathbf{N_q}$ is sound with respect to $\mathfrak{C}$; to prove completeness we use a Henkin construction which capitalizes on the theory of transverse hypergraphs.

---

**Definition 2.** *Let $\mathcal{H}$ be a hypergraph on a set $\mathcal{U}$. A set $\mathcal{E} \subseteq \mathcal{U}$ is a minimal transversal for $\mathcal{H}$ if $\mathcal{E}$ is a transversal for $\mathcal{H}$ and $\forall \mathcal{E}' \subset \mathcal{E}, \mathcal{E}'$ is not a transversal for $\mathcal{H}$. The transverse hypergraph for $\mathcal{H}$, $T(\mathcal{H})$, or just $T\mathcal{H}$ for convenience, is the set of all minimal transversals for $\mathcal{H}$.*

---

**Proposition 1.** *For any hypergraph $\mathcal{H}$ on a set $\mathcal{U}$, $\mathcal{H} = \emptyset$ iff $T\mathcal{H} = \{\emptyset\}$, and $\emptyset \in \mathcal{H}$ iff $T\mathcal{H} = \emptyset$.*

*Proof.* [$\Rightarrow$] Assume that $\mathcal{H} = \emptyset$. Then every subset of $\mathcal{U}$ is a transversal for $\mathcal{H}$; but then if $\mathcal{E} \neq \emptyset$, $\exists \mathcal{E}' \subset \mathcal{E}$ such that $\mathcal{E}'$ is a transversal for $\mathcal{H}$. So every minimal transversal for $\mathcal{H}$ is empty. And, $\emptyset \in T\mathcal{H}$ because $\emptyset$ has no proper subsets. Thus $T\mathcal{H} = \{\emptyset\}$. [$\Leftarrow$] Assume now that $T\mathcal{H} = \{\emptyset\}$. Then $\forall \mathcal{E} \in \mathcal{H}, \emptyset \cap \mathcal{E} \neq \emptyset$. Therefore $\mathcal{H} = \emptyset$.

[$\Rightarrow$] Suppose that $\emptyset \in \mathcal{H}$. Then $\forall \mathcal{E} \in T\mathcal{H}, \mathcal{E} \cap \emptyset \neq \emptyset$. Whence $T\mathcal{H} = \emptyset$. [$\Leftarrow$] Lastly, suppose that $T\mathcal{H} = \emptyset$. If $\mathcal{H} = \emptyset$ then by the above reasoning $\emptyset \in T\mathcal{H}$. So $\mathcal{H} \neq \emptyset$. If, then, $\emptyset \notin \mathcal{H}$, $\exists \mathcal{E}_{\neq \emptyset}$ such that $\mathcal{E} \in T\mathcal{H}$, which is absurd. Therefore $\emptyset \in \mathcal{H}$. $\qquad \Box$

---

[2]The name of this system has been drawn from Jennings and Schotch (1981).

---

**Definition 3.** *A hypergraph $\mathcal{H}$ is simple if $\forall \mathcal{E}, \mathcal{E}' \in \mathcal{H}, \mathcal{E} \not\subseteq \mathcal{E}'$.*

---

**Proposition 2.** *For any hypergraph $\mathcal{H}$ on a set $\mathcal{U}$, $TT\mathcal{H} \subseteq \mathcal{H}$. If $\mathcal{H}$ is simple then $\mathcal{H} = TT\mathcal{H}$.*

*Proof.* Let $\mathcal{H}$ be a hypergraph on $\mathcal{U}$, and let $\mathcal{E} \in TT\mathcal{H}$. Suppose that $\mathcal{E} \not\in \mathcal{H}$. Note that $\forall \mathcal{E}' \in \mathcal{H}, \mathcal{E}'$ is a transversal for $T\mathcal{H}$. Therefore $\forall \mathcal{E}' \in \mathcal{H}, \exists x \in \mathcal{E}'$ such that $x \not\in \mathcal{E}$, in which case $\exists \mathcal{E}' \in T\mathcal{H}$ such that $\mathcal{E} \cap \mathcal{E}' = \emptyset$, contrary to the assumption that $\mathcal{E} \in TT\mathcal{H}$. Therefore $TT\mathcal{H} \subseteq \mathcal{H}$.

Now let $\mathcal{E} \in \mathcal{H}$, and assume that $\mathcal{H}$ is simple. Since $\mathcal{E}$ is a transversal for $T\mathcal{H}$, $\exists \mathcal{E}' \subseteq \mathcal{E}$ such that $\mathcal{E}' \in TT\mathcal{H}$. But the above reasoning shows that $TT\mathcal{H} \subseteq \mathcal{H}$. Therefore, since $\mathcal{H}$ is simple, $\mathcal{E}' = \mathcal{E}$, i.e., $\mathcal{E} \in TT\mathcal{H}$, whence $\mathcal{H} \subseteq TT\mathcal{H}$. □

If **L** is a modal logic and $\alpha$ is a sentence, the *proof set* for $\alpha$ in **L**, $|\alpha|_\mathbf{L}$, is the set of all maximal **L**-consistent sets of which $\alpha$ is a member. The *canonical frame* for **L** is the structure $\mathfrak{F}_\mathbf{L} = (\mathcal{U}_\mathbf{L}, \mathcal{H}_\mathbf{L})$ where $\mathcal{U}_\mathbf{L}$ is the class of all maximal **L**-consistent sets of formulae, and $\forall x \in \mathcal{U}_\mathbf{L}$,

$$\mathcal{H}_\mathbf{L}(x) = T(\{|\gamma|_\mathbf{L} : \Box\gamma \in x\}).$$

The *canonical model* for **L**, $\mathfrak{M}_\mathbf{L}$, is the triple $(\mathcal{U}_\mathbf{L}, \mathcal{H}_\mathbf{L}, \mathcal{V}_\mathbf{L})$ where $\mathcal{V}_\mathbf{L}$ is defined by

$$\forall n \in Nat, x \in \mathcal{V}_\mathbf{L}(n) \text{ iff } p_n \in x.$$

**Theorem 1.** *Let **L** be any logic closed under $[RR], [PL], [MP]$ and $[US]$. Then*

$$\forall \alpha, x \in \mathcal{U}_\mathbf{L}, \|\alpha\|^{\mathfrak{M}_\mathbf{L}} = |\alpha|_\mathbf{L}.$$

*Proof.* We show that $\forall x \in \mathcal{U}_\mathbf{L}, \alpha$ is true at $x$ iff $\alpha \in x$. The proof is by induction on the complexity of $\alpha$. We omit all but the case for $\alpha = \Box\beta$.

Suppose that $x \in \|\Box\beta\|$. Then $\|\beta\|$ is a transversal for $\mathcal{H}_\mathbf{L}(x)$, in which case, by the hypothesis of induction, so is $|\beta|$. Therefore $\exists \mathcal{E} \subseteq |\beta|$ such that $\mathcal{E} \in T(\mathcal{H}_\mathbf{L}(x))$. Whence $\mathcal{E} \in \{|\gamma| : \Box\gamma \in x\}$ (Proposition

2). So let $\mathcal{E} = |\gamma|$. Then $|\gamma| \subseteq |\beta|$ and $\Box\gamma \in x$. But then $\vdash \gamma \supset \beta$, and thus $\vdash \Box\gamma \supset \Box\beta$ (by $[RR]$). Therefore $\Box\beta \in x$.

Suppose now that $\Box\beta \in x$. Then $\forall\mathcal{E} \in \mathcal{H}_{\mathbf{L}}(x), \mathcal{E} \cap |\beta| \neq \emptyset$. I.e., $|\beta|$ is a transversal for $\mathcal{H}_{\mathbf{L}}(x)$. By the induction hypothesis, $|\beta| = \|\beta\|$. Whence $x \in \|\Box\beta\|$.                                                  □

**Corollary 1.** *The system $\mathbf{N_q}$ is determined by the class of all hyper-frames.*

## 4.3    Normal Hyperframes

The logic $\mathbf{N_q}$ is not normal because there is at least one theorem of $\mathbf{N_q}$ whose $\Box$ formula is not a theorem. E.g., $\vdash_{\mathbf{N_q}} \top$ while $\nvdash_{\mathbf{N_q}} \Box\top$. Since there is a hypermodel $\mathfrak{M}$ containing a point $x$ such that $\emptyset \in \mathcal{H}(x)$, it follows that $\mathfrak{C} \nvDash \Box\top$, and hence $\nvdash_{\mathbf{N_q}} \Box\top$ (Corollary 1). By similar, dual reasoning there is a model $\mathfrak{M}$ containing a point $x$ such that $\forall\alpha, \vDash_{\frac{\mathfrak{M}}{x}}$ $\Diamond\alpha$, and thus $\vDash_{\frac{\mathfrak{M}}{x}} \Diamond\bot$. Hyperframes therefore provide an opportunity for the systematic investigation of non-normal logics, that is, logics that are not closed under the rule $[RN]: \vdash \alpha \Rightarrow \vdash \Box\alpha$.

---

**Definition 4.** *If $\mathfrak{F} = (\mathcal{U}, \mathcal{H})$ is a hyperframe then $\mathfrak{F}$ is normal if $\forall x \in \mathcal{U}, \emptyset \notin \mathcal{H}(x)$. A model is normal if it is based on a normal hyperframe.*

---

This is significant from a philosophical perspective for two reasons: First, non-normal logics have deontic motivations insofar as we would like to not have an infinite number of obligations. A logic is normal when $\Box\alpha$ is a theorem whenever $\alpha$ is a theorem. Thus, if $\Box$ represents 'it is obligatory that,' then in any deontic logic with an infinite number of theorems there is an infinite number of obligations.[3] Second, if we read $\Box$ as a necessity operator, then the existence of determined

---

[3]It is important to note, however, that the absence of normality does not guarantee the absence of an infinite number of obligations. Although the absence of normality is necessary, it is not sufficient for this end. What we really need is the rule: $\vdash \alpha \Rightarrow \vdash \neg\Box\alpha$. Jennings has suggested that what we really want is a variety of connexivist implication, which is a restriction of classical logic to contingencies.

non-normal modal logics marks a conceptual divergence between logical validity and its classical, Aristotelian account. According to the classical account, an argument is valid when it is necessary that if the premises are true then the conclusion is true. But there are non-normal logics in which there are logically valid conditionals whose $\Box$ formulae are not theorems. This raises the philosophical question of how theoremhood in such systems should be understood, or alternatively, the question of what the $\Box$ operator represents.

**Theorem 2.** *Let* **L** *be a logic which is closed under* $[RR], [RN], [US],$ $[PL],$ *and* $[MP]$. *Then the canonical hyperframe for* **L** *is normal.*

*Proof.* Let $x \in \mathcal{U}_{\mathbf{L}}$, and suppose that $\emptyset \in \mathcal{H}_{\mathbf{L}}(x)$. Then by proposition 1, $T\mathcal{H}_{\mathbf{L}}(x) = \emptyset$. But $\mathcal{H}_{\mathbf{L}}(x) = T(\{|\gamma| : \Box\gamma \in x\})$; therefore $T\mathcal{H}_{\mathbf{L}}(x) = \{|\gamma| : \Box\gamma \in x\} = \emptyset$ (proposition 2). That is, $\forall\gamma, \Box\gamma \notin x$. But $\vdash \top$, and so by $[RN]$, $\vdash \Box\top$, in which case $\Box\top \in x$, an absurdity. $\Box$

## $(n + 1)$-ary Relational Frames and $n$-Bounded Hyperframes

An $(n + 1)$-*ary relational frame* $(n \geq 1)$ is a pair $(\mathcal{U}, \mathcal{R})$ where $\mathcal{U}$ is a non-empty set and $\mathcal{R} \subseteq \mathcal{U}^{n+1}$. If $\mathcal{V}$ is a function from *Nat* to $\mathcal{P}(\mathcal{U})$ then the triple $(\mathcal{U}, \mathcal{R}, \mathcal{V})$ is an $(n + 1)$-*ary relational model* based on the frame $(\mathcal{U}, \mathcal{R})$. Truth and validity relative to $(n + 1)$-ary relational frames and models are as defined for hyperframes and models, with the exception that truth at a point $x$ for $\Box$ formulae is defined

$$\models_{x}^{\mathfrak{M}} \Box\alpha \text{ iff } \forall\langle y_1, ..., y_n\rangle \in \mathcal{R}(x), \exists i \in [n] :\models_{y_i}^{\mathfrak{M}} \alpha,$$

where for any positive integer $n$, $[n]$ denotes $\{1, 2, ..., n\}$, and if $\mathcal{R} \subseteq \mathcal{U}^{n+1}$, then $\mathcal{R}(x) = \{\langle y_1, ..., y_n\rangle : \langle x, y_1, ..., y_n\rangle \in \mathcal{R}\}$. (See figure 2.)

---

**Definition 5.** *A hyperframe* $\mathfrak{F} = (\mathcal{U}, \mathcal{H})$ *is* $n$-bounded, *for* $n \geq 1$, *if* $\forall x \in \mathcal{U}, \forall \mathcal{E} \in \mathcal{H}(x), |\mathcal{E}| \leq n$. *A model is* $n$-bounded *if it is based on an* $n$-bounded hyperframe.

---

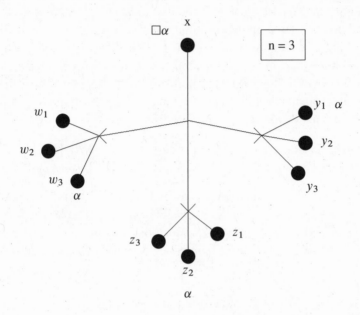

Figure 4.2: The truth condition for $\square$ on $(n + 1)$-ary relational frames.

**Definition 6.** *Let* $\mathfrak{F} = (\mathcal{U}, \mathcal{H})$ *be an n-bounded normal hyperframe, and let the relation* $\mathcal{R} \subseteq \mathcal{U}^{n+1}$ *be defined pointwise:*

$$\mathcal{R}(x) := \{\langle y_1, ..., y_m, \underbrace{y_i, ..., y_i}_{n-m \ times} \rangle :$$
$$\{y_1, ..., y_m\} \in \mathcal{H}(x) \ \& \ i \in [m]\}.$$

*Then the* $(n + 1)$-*ary relational transformation of* $\mathfrak{F}$ *is the* $(n + 1)$-*ary relational frame* $\mathfrak{F}^* = (\mathcal{U}, \mathcal{R})$.

It is easy to see that for any model $\mathfrak{M}$ on an $n$-bounded normal hyperframe there is an equivalent $(n + 1)$-ary relational model. That is:

**Theorem 3.** *For every normal n-bounded hyperframe* $\mathfrak{F} = (\mathcal{U}, \mathcal{H})$, *every model* $\mathfrak{M}^* = (\mathcal{U}, \mathcal{R}, \mathcal{V})$ *on the* $(n + 1)$*-ary relational transformation* $\mathfrak{F}^* = (\mathcal{U}, \mathcal{R})$ *of* $\mathfrak{F}$ *is pointwise equivalent to the hypermodel* $\mathfrak{M} = (\mathcal{U}, \mathcal{H}, \mathcal{V})$, *that is,*

$$\forall x \in \mathcal{U}, \forall \alpha, \ \underset{x}{\overset{\mathfrak{M}}{\vDash}} \alpha \Leftrightarrow \underset{x}{\overset{\mathfrak{M}^*}{\vDash}} \alpha$$

*Proof.* The (omitted) proof is by induction on the complexity of $\alpha$.  $\square$

## 4.4  Weakly Aggregative Modal Logic

A consequence of the theory of $n$-bounded normal hyperframes is a simple proof of the completeness of the system $\mathbf{K_n}$ with respect to the class of all $(n + 1)$-ary relational frames. The system $\mathbf{K_n}$  $(n \geq 1)$ is defined as follows:

$[RR]: \ \vdash \alpha \supset \beta \ \Rightarrow \vdash \Box \alpha \supset \Box \beta$

$[RN]: \ \vdash \alpha \ \Rightarrow \vdash \Box \alpha$

$[PL]: \ \vdash_{PL} \alpha \ \Rightarrow \vdash \alpha$

$[MP]: \vdash \alpha \supset \beta \ \& \ \vdash \alpha \ \Rightarrow \vdash \beta$

$[US]: \vdash \alpha \ \& \ \beta$ is a substitution instance of $\alpha \ \Rightarrow \vdash \beta$

$[K_n]: \ \vdash \Box \alpha_1 \wedge ... \wedge \Box \alpha_{n+1} \supset \Box \bigvee_{1 \leq i < j \leq n+1} \alpha_i \wedge \alpha_j.$

$\mathbf{K_1}$ is just the Kripke system $\mathbf{K}$. For each $n > 1$, $\mathbf{K_n}$ is *weakly aggregative* because it replaces the strong aggregation principle $[K](= [K_1])$ with the weaker $[K_n]$.

It would appear that the completeness proof herein is a simplification of the other proofs in the literature (Apostoli and Brown, 1995; Nicholson et al., 2000), as both of these rely heavily on the colouring theory of hypergraphs, reference to which is omitted in the present proof. In particular, the previous proofs exploit colouring compactness, the claim that if $H$ is a hypergraph each of whose edges is finitely long, then $H$ is $k$-colourable iff every finite subgraph of $H$ is $k$-colourable. In contrast, the crucial lemma used here, in addition to theorem 2, is that the canonical hyperframe for any logic that includes $[K_n]$ ($n \geq 1$) is $n$-bounded.

For convenience, we introduce the convention that if $t_1, t_2, ..., t_{n+1}$ are sets ($n \geq 1$), then $\frac{2}{n+1}(t_i)_{i \in [n+1]}$ denotes $\bigcup_{1 \leq i < j \leq n+1} t_i \cap t_j$, and if $\alpha_1, \alpha_2, ..., \alpha_{n+1}$ are sentences then $\frac{2}{n+1}(\alpha_i)_{i \in [n+1]}$ represents $\bigvee_{1 \leq i < j \leq n+1} \alpha_i \wedge \alpha_j$.

**Lemma 1.** $\forall n \geq 1$, if $\mathcal{H}$ is a hypergraph such that $\forall \mathcal{E} \in \mathcal{H}, |\mathcal{E}| \leq n$, then whenever $t_1, t_2, ..., t_{n+1}$ are transversals for $\mathcal{H}$, so is $\frac{2}{n+1}(t_i)_{i \in [n+1]}$.

*Proof.* Suppose that $\forall \mathcal{E} \in \mathcal{H}$, $|\mathcal{E}| \leq n$ and that $\forall i \in [n+1]$, $t_i$ is a transversal for $\mathcal{H}$. Suppose further that $\frac{2}{n+1}(t_i)_{i \in [n+1]} \cap \mathcal{E} = \emptyset$, for some $\mathcal{E} \in \mathcal{H}$. By a pigeonhole argument, $\exists i, j \in [n+1](i \neq j)$ such that $t_i \cap t_j \cap \mathcal{E} \neq \emptyset$, which is absurd since $t_i \cap t_j \subseteq \frac{2}{n+1}(t_i)_{i \in [n+1]}$. $\square$

**Lemma 2.** Let $\mathcal{H}$ be a simple hypergraph such that $\exists n \geq 1, \exists \mathcal{E} \in \mathcal{H}, |\mathcal{E}| > n$. Then there are $n+1$ transversals for $\mathcal{H}$, $t_1, t_2, ..., t_{n+1}$, such that $\frac{2}{n+1}(t_i)_{i \in [n+1]}$ is not a transversal for $\mathcal{H}$.

*Proof.* Let $\mathcal{H}$ be a simple hypergraph and let $n \geq 1$ be an arbitrary integer such that for some $\mathcal{E} \in \mathcal{H}, |\mathcal{E}| > n$. Suppose that $\mathcal{E} = \{x_1, x_2, ..., x_i, ..., x_{n+1}, ...\}$. Then it is possible to construct $n+1$ transversals for $\mathcal{H}$, $t_1, t_2, ..., t_{n+1}$ such that $\forall i \in [n+1], t_i \cap \mathcal{E} = \{x_i\}$; otherwise $\exists \mathcal{E}' \in \mathcal{H}$ such that $\mathcal{E}' \subset \mathcal{E}$, contrary to the assumption that $\mathcal{H}$ is simple. But then $\frac{2}{n+1}(t_i)_{i \in [n+1]} \cap \mathcal{E} = \emptyset$. $\square$

**Theorem 4.** $\forall n \geq 1$, if **L** is a modal logic which is closed under $[RR]$, $[PL]$, $[US]$, and modus ponens, then if $[K_n] \in$ **L**, it follows that the canonical frame for **L** is $n$-bounded.

*Proof.* Assume that **L** is a modal logic which satisfies the antecedent conditions, including that $[K_n] \in$ **L** for some $n \geq 1$. We show that $\forall x \in \mathcal{U}_\mathbf{L}, \forall \mathcal{E} \in \mathcal{H}_\mathbf{L}(x), |\mathcal{E}| \leq n$. Suppose not. Let $x \in \mathcal{U}_\mathbf{L}$ be such that $\mathcal{E} \in \mathcal{H}_\mathbf{L}(x)$ and $|\mathcal{E}| > n$. From lemma 2 it follows that there are $n+1$ transversals for $\mathcal{H}_\mathbf{L}(x)$, $t_1, t_2, ..., t_{n+1}$, such that $\frac{2}{n+1}(t_i)_{i \in [n+1]}$ is not a transversal for $\mathcal{H}_\mathbf{L}(x)$. But since $t_i$ is a transversal for $\mathcal{H}_\mathbf{L}(x)$ ($i \in [n+1]$), $\exists \mathcal{E}_i \subseteq t_i$ such that $\mathcal{E}_i \in T(\mathcal{H}_\mathbf{L}(x))$, that is, from proposition 2, $\mathcal{E}_i \in \{|\gamma| : \Box\gamma \in x\}$. So let $\mathcal{E}_i = |\gamma_i|$ ($i \in [n+1]$), where $\Box\gamma_i \in x$. Since $[K_n] \in \mathbf{L}$, and $\mathbf{L}$ is closed under uniform substitution, $\Box\gamma_1 \wedge \ldots \wedge \Box\gamma_{n+1} \supset \Box\frac{2}{n+1}(\gamma_i)_{i\in[n+1]} \in x$. Therefore $\Box\frac{2}{n+1}(\gamma_i)_{i\in[n+1]} \in x$, and thus $\underset{x}{\overset{\mathfrak{M}_L}{\models}} \Box\frac{2}{n+1}(\gamma_i)_{i\in[n+1]}$ (theorem 1), in which case $\|\frac{2}{n+1}(\gamma_i)_{i\in[n+1]}\|^{\mathfrak{M}_L}$ is a transversal for $\mathcal{H}_L(x)$. But

$$\left\|\frac{2}{n+1}(\gamma_i)_{i\in[n+1]}\right\|^{\mathfrak{M}_L} = \frac{2}{n+1}(\|\gamma_i\|^{\mathfrak{M}_L})_{i\in[n+1]}$$

$$= \frac{2}{n+1}(|\gamma_i|)_{i\in[n+1]}$$

$$= \frac{2}{n+1}(\mathcal{E}_i)_{i\in[n+1]},$$

and $\frac{2}{n+1}(\mathcal{E}_i)_{i\in[n+1]} \subseteq \frac{2}{n+1}(t_i)_{i\in[n+1]}$. Therefore $\frac{2}{n+1}(\mathcal{E}_i)_{i\in[n+1]}$ is not a transversal for $\mathcal{H}_L(x)$, which is absurd. $\square$

Since $\forall n \geq 1$, $\mathbf{K_n}$ is sound with respect to the class of all normal $n$-bounded hyperframes (see lemma 1), given theorems 2 and 4 we have:

**Corollary 2.** $\forall n \geq 1$, *the modal system* $\mathbf{K_n}$ *is determined by the class of all normal n-bounded hyperframes.*

In closing we have:

**Theorem 5.** $\forall n \geq 1$, *the system* $\mathbf{K_n}$ *is complete with respect to the class of all* $(n+1)$-*ary relational frames.*

*Proof.* Assume that $\alpha$ is valid with respect to the class of all $(n+1)$-ary relational frames. Then $\alpha$ is valid on the $(n+1)$-ary relational transformation of the canonical hyperframe $\mathfrak{F}_{K_n}$ for $\mathbf{K_n}$ (theorems 2, 4). Therefore, by theorem 3, $\alpha$ is valid on the canonical model $\mathfrak{M}_{K_n}$ for $\mathbf{K_n}$, whence $\vdash_{K_n} \alpha$. $\square$

# Five

---

# Polyadic Modal Logics and Their Monadic Fragments

KAM SING LEUNG AND R.E. JENNINGS

---

### Abstract

It is well known that the smallest normal modal logic, called K, is determined by the class of binary relational frames. The collection of normal modal logics can be expanded by considering polyadic modal languages, each possessed of an $n$-ary modal connective and interpreted in $(n + 1)$-ary relational frames. We survey a number of such logics and their classes of frames, and give metatheorems of soundness, completeness, and definability. Finally, a series of monadic logics is obtained by diagonalizing the $n$-ary modal connectives. These monadic fragments support aggregation principles which are weaker than that of K, thus making them more suitable than K for such applications as deontic reasoning.

## 5.1   Introduction

The originating pulse of virtually all of the work presented in this volume lay in the inexpressibility, within the received Kripkean modal systems, of one or two deontically fundamental distinctions. The first was the distinction between deontic conflict, the common-enough moral pickle in which, through incompetence, inattention, or circumstance, we find ourselves forced to neglect one moral duty to fulfil another. The topic has confronted moral systematizers for at least two hundred years. John Stuart Mill evidently supposed that if obligations are objectively grounded, any apparent such conflict can be no more than the starting point of a moral calculation that would ultimately dissolve it. Any like-minded philosopher might find little to complain of in the deontic reading of the modal □ of some of the weaker Kripkean systems as *It ought to be the case that*, where a claim of deontic conflict $\Box\alpha \wedge \Box\neg\alpha$ (a conjunction of contradictory obligations) is equivalent to a claim of a single obligatory contradiction $\Box\bot$. Most philosophers are convinced of the principle embodied in the Kantian slogan 'Ought implies can,' representable in the weak form [Con] $\neg\Box\bot$ and some are no doubt happy to learn that as a matter of logic, that fundamental principle, of itself, rules out moral conflict, being equivalent to [D] $\Box p \rightarrow \neg\Box\neg p$. If it is already a matter of logic, then it would seem that the question whether obligations are objectively grounded need not be answered. For some, no doubt, that resolution is a vindication of the Kripkean analysis of deontic necessity. For such people, it is an early discovery of deontic logic that the principle (call it 'Kant') that ought implies can is equivalent to the principle that there are no moral conflicts, and allows the latter to be elevated to the status of 'The Deontic Law.'

But for deontic logicians there can be no such repose; nor for moral philosophers who accept the Kantian proscription of unfulfillable single obligations, but who recognize the presence of pairs or triples or larger families of obligations that force us to a kind of moral triage. For such theorists even the question as to what principles of deontic reasoning can be relied upon to constrain deontic conclusions remains itself a deontic matter. Logic does not relieve us of the responsibility to sort out such messes; the existence of such messes forces us to choose among logics. For such theorists, the distinctness of the two cases is itself a matter of logic. Accordingly, no system that does not preserve it is adequate.

For the healthy sceptic, *every* principle of logic can be interrogated as to its suitableness for a particular application. For the deontic case, this applies to all of the principles that the Kripke systems force upon us. The principle [K] $\Box p \wedge \Box q \rightarrow \Box(p \wedge q)$ is certainly suspect, but so are the principles of normality and monotonicity. The former is embodied in the rule of necessitation [RN] $\vdash \alpha \implies \vdash \Box\alpha$, which makes every theorem an obligation. There would seem to be a desire in the moral tradition that no obligation be unshirkable. Indeed, when we reflect that language is an evolved biological characteristic of humans, and moral language in particular is likely the product of selective social pressures, the exclusion of logically warranted sentences has some point. It is precisely the *contingency* of social arrangements that presses us to preserve the language by which we promote some and discourage others.

Again, the principle [RM] $\vdash \alpha \to \beta \implies \vdash \Box\alpha \to \Box\beta$ (the rule of monotonicity), which takes all logically provable consequences of obligatory acts as themselves obligations, can be ruled out on the related grounds that theorems are among the logically provable consequences of every obligatory act. Thus the adoption of a rule excluding theorems from obligation would seem to force some restriction on [RM], or the adoption, as the underlying propositional system, of one weaker than the classical PL.

Now all of logic is, within varying limits, negotiable. Systems of logic are artefact, and can be variously fashioned to serve varying goals, however local. Nevertheless, there remains such a thing as pure research, and all of current deontic logical research must yet come under that rubric. So there is some point to exploring systems and classes of systems that have no other desirable feature than that they admit or deny particular distinctions, whatever other, independent distinctions they neglect. We might explore such a system for no purpose other than to satisfy our curiosity or to expand our understanding. In doing so, we might do well to proceed gradually from the familiar to the less familiar, retaining, for the sake of illumination, principles which we expect ultimately to reject. We gain another benefit from this Fabian approach, for we learn about relationships and dependencies among principles that are masked in the more particular setting, but become evident in the more general.

The simple expedient of generalizing the semantic analysis of the $\Box$ to $n$-ary relational frames, substituting the binary truth condition

$$\mathfrak{M}, x \models \Box\alpha \iff (\forall y, Rxy \implies \mathfrak{M}, y \models \Box\alpha)$$

with the general

$$\mathfrak{M}, x \models \Box\alpha \iff$$

$$(\forall y_1, \ldots, y_n, Rxy_1 \cdots y_n \implies \exists i \, (1 \le i \le n), \mathfrak{M}, y_i \models \alpha),$$

preserves both [RM] and [RN] as rules, but fails to validate [K]. Instead, it validates the considerably weaker

$$[\mathrm{K}_n] \quad \Box p_1 \wedge \cdots \wedge \Box p_{n+1} \to \Box \bigvee_{i=1}^{n+1} \bigvee_{j=i+1}^{n+1} (p_i \wedge p_j).$$

In consequence, it distinguishes [D], which corresponds to no first-order restriction on $n$-ary R, and [Con], which corresponds to $n$-ary seriality:

$$\forall x, \exists y_1, \ldots, y_n : Rxy_1 \cdots y_n.$$

As we demonstrate below, the matter is not so simple as that. In the first place, although we do not discuss the matter here, a generalization to a *set* of $n$ binary relations would serve to make at least some of the distinctions that a single binary relation conceals. And $n$-ary relational structures introduce their own conflations. Nor is the language of unary $\Box$ the most natural or most expressive modal language for a study of $n$-ary relational structures. So we begin with a discussion of the correspondences between the language of an $(n-1)$-ary modal connective and the language of a single $n$-ary relation. Again, once we have seen the greater generality, it becomes evident that such a language generates more than one monadic fragment. In this introductory essay, however, we consider only the diagonal fragments of $n$-ary systems.

## 5.2   Polyadic Modal Languages and Multi-ary Relational Frames

In this section, we introduce a series of modal languages, each of which extends the language of propositional logic with an $n$-ary modal operator. The frames and models for interpreting these languages are then described.

**Definition 1.** *The n-adic modal language, denoted $\mathcal{L}_n$, has the following symbols: denumerably many propositional variables $(p_1, p_2, p_3, \ldots)$, connectives ($\bot$, $\neg$, $\vee$, and $\square_n$), and punctuations (the left and right parentheses ( and ), and the comma ,). The set of $\mathcal{L}_n$-formulas is specified by the following rule in BNF:*

$$\alpha ::= p \mid \bot \mid \neg\alpha \mid (\alpha_1 \vee \alpha_2) \mid \square_n(\alpha_1, \ldots, \alpha_n),$$

*where p is any propositional variable.*

Note that $\bot$ is a nullary connective while $\neg$, $\vee$, and $\square_n$ are unary, binary, and $n$-ary connectives, respectively. Other connectives such as $\top$, $\wedge$, $\rightarrow$, $\leftrightarrow$, and $\Diamond_n$ (the dual of $\square_n$) are introduced as shorthand:

$\top$ abbreviates $\neg\bot$.

$(\alpha \wedge \beta)$ abbreviates $\neg(\neg\alpha \vee \neg\beta)$.

$(\alpha \rightarrow \beta)$ abbreviates $(\neg\alpha \vee \beta)$.

$(\alpha \leftrightarrow \beta)$ abbreviates $((\alpha \rightarrow \beta) \wedge (\beta \rightarrow \alpha))$.

$\Diamond_n(\alpha_1, \ldots, \alpha_n)$ abbreviates $\neg\square_n(\neg\alpha_1, \ldots, \neg\alpha_n)$.

We mention here some of the meta-logical conventions adopted in this paper. Outermost parentheses are omitted when writing formulas. $\vee$ and $\wedge$ bind more strongly than $\rightarrow$ and $\leftrightarrow$. Throughout this paper, we use lower case letters from the Greek alphabet $\alpha$, $\beta$, $\gamma$, $\ldots$ to denote formulas, and upper case letters $\Gamma$, $\Delta$, $\Sigma$, $\ldots$, to denote sets of formulas. We write $\forall$, $\exists$, $\neg$, $\&$, $\implies$, and $\iff$ (or iff) for 'for every,' 'there exists,' 'it is not the case that,' 'and,' '(if ...) then,' and 'if and only if,' respectively. Other meta-logical symbols will be introduced when needed.

**Definition 2.** *An n-ary relational frame $\mathfrak{F}$ is a duple $\langle U, R \rangle$, where U, the universe of the frame, is a non-empty set of points,*

*and $R$ an $n$-ary relation on $U$. Given an $n$-ary relational frame*
*$\mathfrak{F} = \langle U, R \rangle$, an $n$-ary relational model $\mathfrak{M}$ is a duple $\langle \mathfrak{F}, V \rangle$ (or a*
*triple $\langle U, R, V \rangle$) where $V$ is a valuation, that is, a function*
*assigning each propositional variable a set of points in $U$.*

**Definition 3.** *An $\mathcal{L}_n$-formula $\alpha$ is said to be true at a point $x$ in an*
*$(n+1)$-ary relational model $\mathfrak{M} = \langle U, R, V \rangle$ (notation:*
*$\mathfrak{M}, x \models \alpha$) according to the following set of inductive conditions*
*(where $\mathfrak{M}, x \not\models \alpha$ means that $\alpha$ is false at $x$ in $\mathfrak{M}$):*

> *For every propositional variable $p_i$, $\mathfrak{M}, x \models p_i$ iff*
> *$x \in V(p_i)$.*
>
> *$\mathfrak{M}, x \not\models \bot$;*
>
> *$\mathfrak{M}, x \models \neg\alpha$ iff $\mathfrak{M}, x \not\models \alpha$;*
>
> *$\mathfrak{M}, x \models \alpha \vee \beta$ iff $\mathfrak{M}, x \models \alpha$ or $\mathfrak{M}, x \models \beta$;*
>
> *$\mathfrak{M}, x \models \Box_n(\alpha_1, \ldots, \alpha_n)$ iff $\forall y_1, \ldots, y_n, Rxy_1 \cdots y_n \implies$*
> *$\exists y_i (1 \leq i \leq n) : \mathfrak{M}, y_i \models \alpha_i$.*

Given the above definition of $\Diamond_n$, we have the following condition:

> $\mathfrak{M}, x \models \Diamond_n(\alpha_1, \ldots, \alpha_n)$ iff $\exists y_1, \ldots, y_n : Rxy_1 \cdots y_n$ & $\forall y_i (1 \leq i \leq n), \mathfrak{M}, y_i \models \alpha_i$.

Truth conditions for the other defined connectives are straightforward
and are omitted here.

**Definition 4.** *An $\mathcal{L}_n$-formula $\alpha$ is said to hold in a model $\mathfrak{M}$*
*(notation: $\mathfrak{M} \models \alpha$) if for every $x$ in $\mathfrak{M}$, we have $\mathfrak{M}, x \models \alpha$.*
*Moreover $\alpha$ is said to be valid on a frame $\mathfrak{F}$ (notation: $\mathfrak{F} \models \alpha$) if*
*it holds in every model on $\mathfrak{F}$. If it is valid on every frame in a class*

> $\mathbb{C}$ *of frames, we say that it is valid on $\mathbb{C}$ (notation: $\mathbb{C} \models \alpha$). If $\alpha$ is valid on the class of all frames, we simply say that $\alpha$ is valid (notation: $\models \alpha$).*

The presentation of formulas of an $n$-adic modal language and properties of an $n$-ary relational frame will be made simpler by adopting the following shorthand.

**Notation 1.**　1. We often drop the subscripts of $\Box_n$ and $\Diamond_n$ since their arities are obvious from the number of propositions that are within their scope.

2. $\vec{p}$ is an $n$-termed sequence $p_1, p_2, \ldots, p_n$, and $\vec{p}_i$ is an $n$-termed sequence $p_{i,1}, p_{i,2}, \ldots, p_{i,n}$. Similarly for $\vec{x}$ and $\vec{x}_1$ etc.

3. $\bot^k$ is a k-termed sequence of $\bot$'s, and similarly for $\top^k$.

## 5.3 Normal Polyadic Modal Logics

A formal system S (in an object language) is essentially a proof-theoretic entity: it consists of a decidable set of formulas (called its axioms) and a finite set of inferential rules, each of which specifies what formula (conclusion) can be derived from other formulas (hypotheses). A formula $\alpha$ is said to be provable from a set $\Sigma$ of formulas (called assumptions) in S if there is a finite sequence of formulas, with the last member being $\alpha$, and each member of the sequence being an axiom, or an assumption, or the conclusion of a rule of inference applied to some previous formulas in the sequence. We call such a sequence a proof of $\alpha$ from $\Sigma$ in S, and record its existence by writing $\Sigma \vdash_S \alpha$ or simply $\Sigma \vdash \alpha$ if the system is clear in the context. If $\alpha$ is provable from the empty set of formulas, we call it a theorem of S and write $\vdash_S \alpha$ or simply $\vdash \alpha$ if the system is obvious. S is said to be inconsistent if the false is a theorem of it ($\vdash_S \bot$), consistent if not ($\nvdash_S \bot$).

A logic, in comparison with a system, is usually characterized as a set of formulas (in an object language) that is closed under certain rules of inference. Given our definition of formal systems above, the set of theorems of a formal system constitutes a logic, but the converse is not generally true: there are logics which cannot be axiomatized as formal systems. Since we deal with axiomatizable logics only in this paper, we will no longer make the distinction between a system and a logic, and use the terms interchangeably from now on.

---

**Definition 5.** *An n-adic modal logic (in the modal language $\mathcal{L}_n$) is a consistent system that has the set of all the tautologies of propositional logic (or a suitable subset of it) included in its set of axioms, and the following rules in its set of inferential rules:*

$$[\text{MP}] \ \frac{\alpha, \alpha \to \beta}{\alpha}$$

$$[\text{US}] \ \frac{\vdash \alpha}{\vdash \alpha[p_i / \beta]}$$

*where $\alpha[p_i / \beta]$ is the formula that results from substituting $\beta$ for every occurrence of $p_i$ in $\alpha$.*

---

Note that an *n*-adic modal logic (or simply an *n*-adic logic) is an extension of propositional logic in the sense that its set of theorems includes all the tautologies of propositional logic and is closed under the rules of modus ponens and uniform substitution. We express the same thing by saying that an *n*-adic logic includes PL. (Here PL refers to the set of tautologies together with the rules [MP] and [US].)

Since the 'early' days of modern modal logic, logicians have worked on monadic systems characterized as 'normal.' Normality in this context means that the systems or logics have the following rules and axioms in addition to PL:

$$[\text{RM}] \ \frac{\vdash \alpha \to \beta}{\vdash \Box \alpha \to \Box \beta}$$

$$[\text{RN}] \ \frac{\vdash \alpha}{\vdash \Box \alpha}$$

[K] $\Box p \wedge \Box q \rightarrow \Box (p \wedge q)$

The smallest normal (monadic) system is called K (after Kripke). Various logics are obtained by adding axioms to K:

KCon [Con] $\neg \Box \bot$

KD [D] $\Box p \rightarrow \Diamond p$

KT [T] $\Box p \rightarrow p$

KB [B] $p \rightarrow \Box \Diamond p$

K4 [4] $\Box p \rightarrow \Box \Box p$

K5 [5] $\Diamond p \rightarrow \Box \Diamond p$.

In what follows, we generalize normal monadic logics to normal $n$-adic logics where $n$ is a positive integer.

---

**Definition 6.** *An n-adic logic is called normal if it has in addition to* PL *the following schemas of rules of inference and axioms (where $1 \leq i \leq n$, and $\beta$, $q$, and $p_i \wedge q$ occur in the i-th argument place of $\Box$ as $\alpha_i$ and $p_i$ do):*

$$[\text{RM}_n^i] \quad \frac{\vdash \alpha_i \rightarrow \beta}{\vdash \Box(\alpha_1, \ldots, \alpha_i, \ldots, \alpha_n) \rightarrow \Box(\alpha_1, \ldots, \beta, \ldots, \alpha_n)}$$

$$[\text{RN}_n^i] \quad \frac{\vdash \alpha_i}{\vdash \Box(\alpha_1, \ldots, \alpha_i, \ldots, \alpha_n)}$$

$$[\text{G}_n^i] \quad \Box(p_1, \ldots, p_i, \ldots, p_n) \wedge \Box(p_1, \ldots, q, \ldots, p_n) \rightarrow$$
$$\Box(p_1, \ldots, p_i \wedge q, \ldots, p_n)$$

---

We mention here an alternative way to characterize normal logics which makes use of PL, [$\text{RN}_n^i$], and the following schema of axioms [$\text{G!}_n^i$]:

$$[\text{G!}_n^i] \quad \Box(p_1, \ldots, p_i \rightarrow q, \ldots, p_n) \rightarrow (\Box(p_1, \ldots, p_i, \ldots, p_n) \rightarrow$$
$$\Box(p_1, \ldots, q, \ldots, p_n)).$$

Note that there are n instances of each of $[RM_n^i]$, $[RN_n^i]$, $[G_n^i]$, and $[G!_n^i]$. We shall refer to any one of them, or all of them, simply as $[RM_n]$, $[RN_n]$, $[G_n]$, and $[G!_n]$, respectively.

We call the smallest normal $n$-adic logic $G_n$. Note that $G_1$ is just K. The name '$G_n$' comes from D.K. Johnston who named the system after Goldblatt because the latter introduced what amounts to $G_2$ in an unpublished paper 'Temporal Betweenness' (1976). Other names have also been used in the literature: $E^{[n]}$ ($E$ for entailment) in Gabbay (1976), $K_\tau$ where $\tau$ is a modal similarity type (Blackburn et al., 2001).

Various normal $n$-adic logics can be obtained by adding to $G_n$ axioms, which are generalizations of their monadic counterparts.

---

**Definition 7.** *The following normal n-adic systems extend* $G_n$ *with the indicated axioms. In what follows,*

$$G_nCon_n \, [Con_n] \, \neg\Box\bot^n$$

$$G_nD_n \, [D_n] \, \Box\vec{p} \to \bigvee_{i=1}^{n} \Diamond (\top^{i-1}, p_i, \top^{n-i})$$

$$G_nT_n \, [T_n] \, \Box\vec{p} \to \bigvee_{i=1}^{n} p_i$$

$$G_nB_n \, [B_n] \, \bigwedge_{i=1}^{n} p_i \to \bigwedge_{i=1}^{n} \Box(\bot^{i-1}, \Diamond\vec{p}, \bot^{n-i})$$

$$G_n4_n \, [4_n] \, \Box\vec{p} \to \bigwedge_{i=1}^{n} \Box(\bot^{i-1}, \Box\vec{p}, \bot^{n-i})$$

$$G_n5_n \, [5_n] \, \Diamond\vec{p} \to \bigwedge_{i=1}^{n} \Box(\bot^{i-1}, \Diamond\vec{p}, \bot^{n-i}).$$

---

Each of the axioms and rules of inference mentioned previously has a dual form, which is logically equivalent to it (in any logic which provides propositional logic). We list the dual forms here for future reference:

$[\text{RM}\Diamond_n^i]$
$$\frac{\vdash \alpha_i \to \beta}{\vdash \Diamond(\alpha_1, \ldots, \alpha_i, \ldots, \alpha_n) \to \Diamond(\alpha_1, \ldots, \beta, \ldots, \alpha_n)}$$

$[\text{RN}\Diamond_n^i]$
$$\frac{\vdash \alpha_i}{\vdash \neg \Diamond(\alpha_1, \ldots, \neg\alpha_i, \ldots, \alpha_n)}$$

$[\text{G}\Diamond_n^i]$ $\Diamond(p_1, \ldots, p_i \vee q, \ldots, p_n) \to$
$$\Diamond(p_1, \ldots, p_i, \ldots, p_n) \vee \Diamond(p_1, \ldots, q, \ldots, p_n)$$

$[\text{G}\Diamond_n^i]$ $\neg \Diamond(p_1, \ldots, p_i, \ldots, p_n) \to (\Diamond(p_1, \ldots, q, \ldots, p_n) \to$
$$\Diamond(p_1, \ldots, \neg p_i \wedge q, \ldots, p_n))$$

$[\text{Con}\Diamond_n]$ $\Diamond\top^n$

$[\text{D}\Diamond_n]$ $\displaystyle\bigwedge_{i=1}^{n} \Box(\bot^{i-1}, p_i, \bot^{n-i}) \to \Diamond\vec{p}$

$[\text{T}\Diamond_n]$ $\displaystyle\bigwedge_{i=1}^{n} p_i \to \Diamond\vec{p}$

$[\text{B}\Diamond_n]$ $\displaystyle\bigvee_{i=1}^{n} \Diamond(\top^{i-1}, \Box\vec{p}, \top^{n-i}) \to \bigvee_{i=1}^{n} p_i$

$[4\Diamond_n]$ $\displaystyle\bigvee_{i=1}^{n} \Diamond(\top^{i-1}, \Diamond\vec{p}, \top^{n-i}) \to \Diamond\vec{p}$

$[5\Diamond_n]$ $\displaystyle\bigvee_{i=1}^{n} \Diamond(\top^{i-1}, \Box\vec{p}, \top^{n-i}) \to \Box\vec{p}$

To conclude this section, we list some of the theorems of normal $n$-adic logics below. (To highlight the axioms and rules used, we assume the base logic is just an $n$-adic logic.)

**Proposition 1.** *The following are provable in any n-adic logic (that is, logic in $\mathcal{L}_n$ that provides* PL*), given the specified rules and axioms:*

1. *In the presence of* $[\mathrm{RM}_n]$ *and* $[\mathrm{RN}_n]$,

$$[\mathrm{B}_n] \leftrightarrow \left( \bigvee_{i=1}^{n} \bigwedge_{j=1}^{n} p_{i,j} \rightarrow \Box(\Diamond \vec{p}_1, \ldots, \Diamond \vec{p}_n) \right).$$

2. *In the presence of* $[\mathrm{RM}_n]$,

$$[\mathrm{B}_n] \rightarrow [\mathrm{G}_n].$$

3. *In the presence of* $[\mathrm{T}_n]$ *and* $[4_n]$,

$$\Box \vec{p} \leftrightarrow \Box(\bot^{i-1}, \Box \vec{p}, \bot^{n-i}),$$

*where* $1 \le i \le n$.

4. *In the presence of* $[\mathrm{T}_n]$ *and* $[5_n]$,

$$\Box \vec{p} \leftrightarrow \Box(\bot^{i-1}, \Diamond \vec{p}, \bot^{n-i}), \text{ where } 1 \le i \le n.$$

5. *In the presence of* $[\mathrm{RM}_n]$ *and* $[\mathrm{G}_n]$,

$$[\mathrm{Con}_n] \rightarrow [\mathrm{D}_n].$$

6. *In the presence of* $[\mathrm{RN}_n]$,

$$[\mathrm{D}_n] \rightarrow [\mathrm{Con}_n].$$

We leave the proof of the above proposition to the reader. Its import is as follows: (1) provides an alternative formulation of our $[\mathrm{B}_n]$ in systems that have $[\mathrm{RM}_n]$ and $[\mathrm{RN}_n]$; (2) is a generalization to the $n$-ary $\Box$ of the result reported in Jennings (1981) for the unary $\Box$; (3) and (4) show that $[4_n]$ and $[5_n]$ are in some sense reduction axioms (in systems that have $[\mathrm{T}_n]$); (5) and (6) show that $[\mathrm{Con}_n]$ and $[\mathrm{D}_n]$ are indeed equivalent in normal $n$-adic systems. Observe that what has been called $[\mathrm{D}_n]$ here is weaker than the following formula:

$$[\mathrm{D!}_n] \quad \Box \vec{p} \rightarrow \Diamond \vec{p}.$$

We remark here that both $[D_1]$ and $[D!_1]$ are the same formula, namely $[D]$ $\Box p \to \Diamond p$. So $[D_n]$ and $[D!_n]$ represent two different ways to generalize $[D]$. In normal monadic logics, $[D]$ and $[Con]$ are inter-derivable. Bearing this in mind, our $[D_n]$ appears to be a better way to generalize $[D]$ than $[D!_n]$ does. (This is also reflected in the correspondence result in the next section: while $[D_n]$ and $[Con_n]$ correspond to seriality, $[D!_n]$ is not even first-order definable.)

## 5.4 Frame Definability

**Proposition 2.** *The following modal formulas correspond to the indicated first-order conditions:*

| | | | |
|---|---|---|---|
| $[Con_n]$ | : | $(\forall x)(\exists \vec{y})Rx\vec{y}$ | (Seriality) |
| $[D_n]$ | : | $(\forall x)(\exists \vec{y})Rx\vec{y}$ | (Seriality) |
| $[T_n]$ | : | $(\forall x)Rxx\cdots x$ | (Reflexivity) |
| $[B_n]$ | : | $(\forall x)(\forall \vec{y})(Rx\vec{y} \to (\forall y_i \in \vec{y})Ry_ix\cdots x)$ | (Symmetry) |
| $[4_n]$ | : | $(\forall x)(\forall \vec{y})(Rx\vec{y} \to (\forall y_i \in \vec{y})(\forall \vec{z})(Ry_i\vec{z} \to Rx\vec{z}))$ | |
| | | | (Transitivity) |
| $[5_n]$ | : | $(\forall x)(\forall \vec{y})(Rx\vec{y} \to (\forall y_i \in \vec{y})(\forall \vec{z})(Rx\vec{z} \to Ry_i\vec{z}))$ | |
| | | | (Euclideanness) |

*Proof.* For correspondence between any one of the modal formulas listed above (say $\alpha$) and the respective first-order condition (say $\phi$), we prove that a frame $\mathfrak{F}$ validates $\alpha$ *if and only if* it validates $\phi$. The *if* direction is trivial and is omitted here. For the *only if* direction, we show that if $\mathfrak{F}$ does not validate $\phi$, then there is a model on $\mathfrak{F}$ in which $\alpha$ fails at some point in the model.

For $[Con_n]$, assume that $\mathfrak{F} = \langle U, R \rangle$ is not serial. Then there exists an $x$ in $U$ which is not related to any $n$-tuple of points in $U$. Consider an arbitrary model $\mathfrak{M}$ on $\mathfrak{F}$. By the truth condition for $\Box$, any $\Box$-formula is true at $x$ in $\mathfrak{M}$. So $\mathfrak{M}, x \not\models \neg\Box\perp^n$.

For $[D_n]$, assume, as in the case of $[Con_n]$, that $\mathfrak{F} = \langle U, R \rangle$ is not serial, and so some $x$ in $U$ is not related to any $n$-tuple of points in $U$. Consider an arbitrary $\mathfrak{M} = \langle \mathfrak{F}, V \rangle$. Trivially $\mathfrak{M}, x \models \Box\vec{p}$, but

$\mathfrak{M}, x \not\models \Diamond(\top^{i-1}, p_i, \top^{n-i})$ for any $i$ such that $1 \leq i \leq n$. So $\mathfrak{M}$ is a counter-model of $[D_n]$.

For $[T_n]$, assume that $\mathfrak{F} = \langle U, R \rangle$ is not reflexive, that is, there is an $x$ in $U$ such that $Rxx \cdots x$ does not hold. Consider a model $\mathfrak{M} = \langle \mathfrak{F}, V \rangle$ with $V(p_i) = U - \{x\}$ for every $i$ between 1 and $n$. It is clear that $\mathfrak{M}, x \models \Box \vec{p}$, since for any $\vec{z}$ such that $Rx\vec{z}$, at least one of $\vec{z}$, say $z_j$, is not $x$, and so $\mathfrak{M}, z_j \models p_j$. On the other hand, $\mathfrak{M}, x \not\models p_1$ and similarly for $p_2, \ldots, p_n$. So $\mathfrak{M}, x \not\models [T_n]$.

For $[B_n]$, assume $\mathfrak{F} = \langle U, R \rangle$ is not symmetric, that is, there exist an $x \in U$ and a $\vec{y} \in U^n$ such that $Rx\vec{y}$ and for some $y_i \in \vec{y}$, it is false that $Ry_i x \cdots x$. Consider a model $\mathfrak{M} = \langle \mathfrak{F}, V \rangle$ with $V(p_1) = \{x\}, \ldots,$ and $V(p_n) = \{x\}$. Clearly, $\mathfrak{M}, x \models p_1 \wedge \cdots \wedge p_n$. But $\mathfrak{M}, y_i \not\models \Diamond \vec{p}$, for if $\mathfrak{M}, y_i \models \Diamond \vec{p}$ then there exists $\vec{z}$ such that $Ry_i \vec{z}$ and $\mathfrak{M}, z_j \models p_j$ for all $j$ from 1 to $n$, which implies that $z_j = x$ and so $Ry_i x \cdots x$, contrary to assumption. So $\mathfrak{M}, x \not\models \Box(\bot^{i-1}, \Diamond \vec{p}, \bot^{n-i})$. It thus follows that $\mathfrak{M}, x \not\models [B_n]$.

For $[4_n]$, assume $\mathfrak{F} = \langle U, R \rangle$ is not transitive, that is, there exist $x \in U$, $\vec{y} \in U^n$, and $\vec{z} \in U^n$ such that $Rx\vec{y}$, $Ry_i \vec{z}$ (for some $y_i \in \vec{y}$), and $\neg Rx\vec{z}$. Consider a model $\mathfrak{M} = \langle \mathfrak{F}, V \rangle$ with $V(p_1) = U - \{z_1\}$, $\ldots,$ and $V(p_n) = U - \{z_n\}$. We argue that $\mathfrak{M}, x \models \Box \vec{p}$ as follows: for an arbitrary $\vec{w} \in U^n$ such that $Rx\vec{w}$ and for some $w_j \in \vec{w}$, we have $w_j \neq z_j$ and so $\mathfrak{M}, w_j \models p_j$. However, $\mathfrak{M}, x \not\models \Box(\bot^{i-1}, \Box \vec{p}, \bot^{n-i})$ since $\mathfrak{M}, y_i \not\models \Box \vec{p}$ (the reason being that $Ry_i \vec{z}$, $\mathfrak{M}, z_1 \not\models p_1, \ldots,$ and $\mathfrak{M}, z_n \not\models p_n$). In other words, $\mathfrak{M}, x \not\models [4_n]$.

For $[5_n]$, assume $\mathfrak{F} = \langle U, R \rangle$ is not euclidean, that is, there exist $x \in U$, $\vec{y} \in U^n$, and $\vec{z} \in U^n$ such that $Rx\vec{y}$, $Rx\vec{z}$, and $\neg Ry_i \vec{z}$, for some $y_i \in \vec{y}$. Consider a model $\mathfrak{M} = \langle \mathfrak{F}, V \rangle$ with $V(p_1) = \{z_1\}$, $\ldots,$ and $V(p_n) = \{z_n\}$. Clearly $\mathfrak{M}, x \models \Diamond \vec{p}$. However $\mathfrak{M}, x \not\models \Box(\bot^{i-1}, \Diamond \vec{p}, \bot^{n-i})$ or equivalently $\mathfrak{M}, x \models \Diamond(\top^{i-1}, \Box \neg \vec{p}, \bot^{n-i})$, since $\mathfrak{M}, y_i \models \Box \neg \vec{p}$, for which we argue as follows: assume arbitrary $\vec{w} \in U^n$ such that $Ry_i \vec{w}$, then $w_j \neq z_j$ (for some $w_j \in \vec{w}$) and so $\mathfrak{M}, w_j \not\models p_j$, i.e. $\mathfrak{M}, w_j \models \neg p_j$. In other words, $\mathfrak{M}, x \not\models [5_n]$.    □

**Theorem 1.** *The classes of $(n+1)$-ary relational frames for the following normal $n$-adic logics are as indicated:*

$G_n Con_n$ *Serial frames*

$G_n D_n$ *Serial frames*

$G_n T_n$ *Reflexive frames*

$G_n B_n$ *Symmetric frames*

$G_n 4_n$ *Transitive frames*

$G_n 5_n$ *Euclidean frames*

*Proof.* The theorem follows directly from proposition 2. ☐

## 5.5 Soundness and Completeness

A consequence of theorem 1 is the soundness of those logics with respect to their classes of frames. In this section, we demonstrate that they are also complete.

Our strategy of proving the completeness of a normal $n$-adic logic L with respect to a class $\mathbb{C}$ of $(n + 1)$-ary relational frames is to show that every set of $\mathcal{L}_n$-formulas consistent in L has a model on a frame in $\mathbb{C}$. In fact, for any normal modal logic, there exists a model that satisfies any consistent set of formulas. (We call this model the canonical model of the logic, and the corresponding frame its canonical frame.) Given this result, all that remains to show the completeness of L with respect to the class $\mathbb{C}$ of frames is to show that the canonical frame of L belongs to $\mathbb{C}$.

In the following, we first define the canonical model of a normal $n$-adic logic. Before showing that the canonical model is indeed a model for any consistent set of formulas, we prove an existence lemma and a truth lemma pertaining to such a logic and its canonical model. (The proof for what we call the existence lemma here is based on Gabbay (1976). Johnston (1976) has another proof. For a more recent version, readers can check Blackburn et al. 2001.)

**Definition 8.** *[Canonical frames and models] Let* L *be a normal n-adic logic (in modal language $\mathcal{L}_n$). The* L*-canonical model, denoted* $\mathfrak{M}_L$, *is a triple* $\langle U_L, R_L, V_L \rangle$ *where*

$U_L$ *is the set of all* L*-maximal consistent set of $\mathcal{L}_n$-formulas.*

*For every* $x$, $y_1, \ldots,$ *and* $y_n$, $R_L x y_i \cdots y_n$ *iff the following condition holds:*

$$\Box(\alpha_1, \ldots, \alpha_n) \in x \implies \exists \alpha_i (1 \leq i \leq n) : \alpha_i \in y_i.$$

*For every* $x$, $x \in V_L(p_i)$ *iff* $p_i \in x$.

*We call the duple* $\langle U_L, R_L \rangle$ *the canonical frame of* L.

**Lemma 1.** (Existence Lemma for normal *n*-adic logics). *Let* $\mathfrak{M}_L = \langle U_L, R_L, V_L \rangle$ *be the canonical model of a normal n-adic logic* L. *For any point* $x \in U_L$ *and $\mathcal{L}_n$-formulas $\alpha_1, \ldots, \alpha_n$, if $\neg\Box(\alpha_1, \ldots, \alpha_n) \in x$, then there exist* $y_1, \ldots, y_n \in U_L$ *such that* $\neg\alpha_1 \in y_1, \ldots,$ *and* $\neg\alpha_n \in y_n$, *and* $R_L x y_1 \cdots y_n$.

*Proof.* Assume $\neg\Box(\alpha_1, \ldots, \alpha_n) \in x$. We show, by induction, that there exist $y_1, \ldots, y_n \in U_L$ such that each $y_i$ $(1 \leq i \leq n)$ satisfies both of the following requirements:

(E1)  $\neg\alpha_i \in y_i$.

(E2)  For any formulas $\gamma_1, \ldots, \gamma_{i-1}, \beta$, if $\neg\gamma_1 \in y_1, \ldots, \neg\gamma_{i-1} \in y_{i-1}$, and $\Box(\gamma_1, \ldots, \gamma_{i-1}, \beta, \alpha_{i+1}, \ldots, \alpha_n) \in x$, then $\beta \in y_i$.

For the existence of $y_1$, we first show that $y_1^0$ defined by letting

$$y_1^0 = \{\neg\alpha_1\} \cup \{\beta | \Box(\beta, \alpha_2, \ldots, \alpha_n) \in x\}$$

is L-consistent. Assume, for reductio, $y_1^0$ is not L-consistent. Then, for some $\beta_1, \ldots, \beta_m \in \{\beta | \Box(\beta, \alpha_2, \ldots, \alpha_n) \in x\}$, the following hold:

$$\{\beta_1, \ldots, \beta_m, \neg\alpha_1\} \vdash_L \bot$$
$$\vdash_L \beta_1 \wedge \cdots \wedge \beta_m \rightarrow \alpha_1$$
$$\vdash_L \Box(\beta_1 \wedge \cdots \wedge \beta_m \rightarrow \alpha_1, \alpha_2, \ldots, \alpha_n) \qquad ([RN_n])$$
$$\vdash_L \Box(\beta_1 \wedge \cdots \wedge \beta_m, \alpha_2, \ldots, \alpha_n) \rightarrow \Box(\alpha_1, \alpha_2, \ldots, \alpha_n) \quad ([G_n])$$
$$\vdash_L \bigwedge_{j=1}^m \Box(\beta_j, \alpha_2, \ldots, \alpha_n) \rightarrow \Box(\alpha_1, \alpha_2, \ldots, \alpha_n) \qquad ([G_n])$$

Since $\Box(\beta_j, \alpha_2, \ldots, \alpha_n) \in x$ for every $j$, and $x$ is maximal L-consistent, we have $\Box(\alpha_1, \alpha_2, \ldots, \alpha_n) \in x$. But this is impossible, for by assumption $\neg\Box(\alpha_1, \alpha_2, \ldots, \alpha_n) \in x$. Thus, by reductio, $y_1^0$ is L-consistent and so has a maximal L-consistent extension $y_1$ (by Lindenbaum's Lemma). It is straightforward to see that $y_1$ satisfies both requirements, (E1) and (E2) (for $i = 1$).

To demonstrate the existence of the other members of the series, namely, $y_2, \ldots, y_n$, assume that we already have $y_1, \ldots, y_k \in U_L$, which satisfy (E1) and (E2) in place (where $k < n$). As in the case of $y_1$, we define an initial set $y_{k+1}^0$ that can be shown to have a maximal L-consistent extension $y_{k+1}$ satisfying both (E1) and (E2). So let

$$y_{k+1}^0 = \{\neg\alpha_{k+1}\} \cup \{\beta | \exists\gamma_1, \ldots, \gamma_k : \neg\gamma_1 \in y_1, \ldots, \neg\gamma_k \in y_k \ \&$$
$$\Box(\gamma_1, \ldots, \gamma_k, \beta, \alpha_{k+2}, \ldots, \alpha_n) \in x\}.$$

To show that $y_{k+1}^0$ is L-consistent, we assume otherwise. Then, for some $\beta_1, \ldots, \beta_m \in y_{k+1}^0 - \{\neg\alpha_{k+1}\}$, the following holds:

$$\{\beta_1, \ldots, \beta_m, \neg\alpha_{k+1}\} \vdash_L \bot$$
$$\vdash_L \beta_1 \wedge \cdots \wedge \beta_m \rightarrow \alpha_{k+1}$$

For each $\beta_j$ $(1 \le j \le m)$, there exist $\neg\gamma_{j.1} \in y_1, \ldots, \neg\gamma_{j.k} \in y_k$ such that

$$\Box(\gamma_{j.1}, \ldots, \gamma_{j.k}, \beta_j, \alpha_{k+2}, \ldots, \alpha_n) \in x.$$

Then, by $[RM_n]$ and $[G_n]$ we get

$$\Box(\bigvee_{j=1}^m \gamma_{j.1}, \ldots, \bigvee_{j=1}^m \gamma_{j.k}, \bigwedge_{j=1}^m \beta_j, \alpha_{k+2}, \ldots, \alpha_n) \in x$$

Since $\beta_1 \wedge \cdots \wedge \beta_m \to \alpha_{k+1} \in x$, we also have the following by [RN$_n$]:

$$\Box(\bigvee_{j=1}^{m} \gamma_{j.1}, \ldots, \bigvee_{j=1}^{m} \gamma_{j.k}, \bigwedge_{j=1}^{m} \beta_j \to \alpha_{k+1}, \alpha_{k+2}, \ldots, \alpha_n) \in x.$$

Thus, by [G$_n$] we have

$$\Box(\bigvee_{j=1}^{m} \gamma_{j.1}, \ldots, \bigvee_{j=1}^{m} \gamma_{j.k}, \alpha_{k+1}, \alpha_{k+2}, \ldots, \alpha_n) \in x.$$

Note that $\neg \bigvee_{j=1}^{m} \gamma_{j.1} \in y_1$, since $\neg \gamma_{j.1} \in y_1$ for all $j$ $(1 \le j \le m)$, and $y_1$ is maximal L-consistent. Similarly, $\neg \bigvee_{j=2}^{m} \gamma_{j.2} \in y_2, \ldots$, and $\neg \bigvee_{j=1}^{m} \gamma_{j.k} \in y_k$. But $\bigvee_{j=1}^{m} \gamma_{j.k} \in y_k$, since $y_k$ complies with our requirement (E2). Hence we derive a contradiction. By reductio $y_{k+1}^0$ is L-consistent, and so has a maximal L-consistent extension $y_{k+1}$. It is straightforward to check that $y_{k+1}$ satisfies requirements (E1) and (E2) (for $i = k + 1$).

We have now demonstrated the existence of $y_1, \ldots, y_n \in U_L$, all of which satisfy requirements (E1) and (E2). It remains to show that $R_L x y_1 \cdots y_n$. Assume that for any $\beta_1, \ldots, \beta_n$, $\Box(\beta_1, \ldots, \beta_n) \in x$, $\beta_1 \notin y_1, \ldots, \beta_{n-1} \notin y_{n-1}$. Then $\neg \beta_1 \in y_1, \ldots, \neg \beta_{n-1} \in y_{n-1}$. Since $y_n$ satisfies (E2), we have $\beta_n \in y_n$. Thus $R_L x y_1 \cdots y_n$ according to the definition of $R_L$. This completes our proof of the Existence Lemma.                                                                                      $\Box$

**Lemma 2.** (Truth lemma for $n$-adic logics). *Let* L *be a normal $n$-adic logic. For any* $\mathcal{L}_n$*-formula*

$$\mathfrak{M}_L, x \models \alpha \iff \alpha \in x.$$

*Proof.* The proof is by induction on $\alpha$. In the following we show the modal case only. Let $\alpha$ be $\Box(\alpha_1, \ldots, \alpha_n)$, and show that for an arbitrary $x \in U_L$,

$$\mathfrak{M}_L, x \models \Box(\alpha_1, \ldots, \alpha_n) \iff \Box(\alpha_1, \ldots, \alpha_n) \in x$$

by assuming the inductive hypothesis that the theorem holds for $\alpha_1, \ldots,$ and $\alpha_n$.

For the direction $\Longrightarrow$, assume that $\Box(\alpha_1, \ldots, \alpha_n) \notin x$, that is, $\neg\Box(\alpha_1, \ldots, \alpha_n) \in x$. Then, by the existence lemma, there exist $y_1, \ldots, y_n \in U_L$ such that $\neg\alpha_1 \in y_1, \ldots,$ and $\neg\alpha_n \in y_n$, and $R_L x y_1 \cdots y_n$. Then for each $i$ such that $1 \leq i \leq n$, $\alpha_i \notin y_i$ and by the inductive hypothesis $\mathfrak{M}_L, y_i \not\models \alpha_i$. Thus $\mathfrak{M}_L, x \not\models \Box(\alpha_1, \ldots, \alpha_n)$, as desired.

For the direction $\Longleftarrow$, assume that $\Box(\alpha_1, \ldots, \alpha_n) \in x$. To show that $\mathfrak{M}_L, x \models \Box(\alpha_1, \ldots, \alpha_n)$, we consider arbitrary $y_1, \ldots, y_n \in U$ such that $R_L x y_1 \cdots y_n$. Then by the definition of $R_L$, $\alpha_i \in y_i$ for some $i$ where $1 \leq i \leq n$. It follows from the inductive hypothesis that $\mathfrak{M}, y_i \models \alpha_i$, whence we conclude that $\mathfrak{M}_L, x \models \Box(\alpha_1, \ldots, \alpha_n)$. $\quad\Box$

**Corollary 1.** *Let* L *be a normal n-adic logic. Then any* L-*consistent set of formulas is satisfiable in the canonical model of* L.

*Proof.* Let $\Sigma$ be an L-consistent set of formulas. By the Lindenbaum Lemma, $\Sigma$ can be extended to a maximal L-consistent set $x$ of formulas. But every formula in $\Sigma$ is true at $x$ in $\mathfrak{M}_L$, the canonical model of L, according to the truth lemma. In other words, $\Sigma$ is satisfiable in $\mathfrak{M}_L$. $\quad\Box$

**Theorem 2.** *The following normal n-adic logics are complete with respect to the indicated classes of* $(n + 1)$-*ary relational frames:*

$G_n$ *All frames*

$G_n Con_n$ *Serial frames*

$G_n D_n$ *Serial frames*

$G_n T_n$ *Reflexive frames*

$G_n B_n$ *Symmetric frames*

$G_n 4_n$ *Transitive frames*

$G_n 5_n$ *Euclidean frames*

*Proof.* For the completeness of a logic L with respect to a class $\mathbb{C}$ of frames, it suffices to show that every L-consistent set of formulas is satisfiable in a model on a frame in class $\mathbb{C}$. In the case of a normal modal logic L, we need only show that its canonical model belongs to $\mathbb{C}$, for every L-consistent set of formulas is satisfiable in the canonical model according to the above corollary. (In the following, we use $\mathfrak{M}_L$ and $R_L$ for the canonical model and relation of the modal logic in context.)

For $G_n$. It suffices to note that the the canonical model of $G_n$ is an $(n + 1)$-ary relational frame.

For $G_n Con_n$. Let $x$ in $\mathfrak{M}_L$ be arbitrary. Since $[Con_n]$ is in $x$, we have by the fundamental theorem $\mathfrak{M}_L, x \models \Diamond \top^n$. Hence the canonical relation is serial.

For $G_n D_n$. Let $x$ in $\mathfrak{M}_L$ be arbitrary. Since both $[D_n]$ and $\Box \top^n$ are in $x$, we have $\Diamond \top^n$ in $x$ as well. Hence the canonical relation is serial.

For $G_n T_n$. To show that the canonical relation is reflexive, we assume $\Box(\alpha_1, \ldots, \alpha_n) \in x$, where $x$ in $\mathfrak{M}_L$, and formulas $\alpha_1, \ldots,$ and $\alpha_n$ are arbitrary. Since $[T_n]$ is in $x$, we have $\alpha_1 \vee \cdots \vee \alpha_n$ in $x$. Then at least one of $\alpha_1, \ldots, \alpha_n$ is in $x$. Hence $R_L xx \cdots x$ by the definition of the canonical relation.

For $G_n B_n$. We assume $R_L x y_1 \cdots y_i \cdots y_n$ where $x, y_1, \ldots, y_n$ in $\mathfrak{M}_L$ are arbitrary, and show that $R_L y_i x \cdots x$. This will follow if we can show that if $\alpha_1 \notin x, \ldots,$ and $\alpha_n \notin x$ then $\Box(\alpha_1, \ldots, \alpha_n) \notin y_i$. So assume $\alpha_1 \notin x, \ldots,$ and $\alpha_n \notin x$. Then $\neg \alpha_1 \in x, \ldots,$ and $\neg \alpha_n \in x$. Then $\neg \alpha_1 \wedge \cdots \wedge \neg \alpha_n \in x$. Since $[B_n] \in x$, we have $\Box(\bot^{i-1}, \Diamond(\neg \alpha_1, \ldots, \neg \alpha_n), \bot^{n-i}) \in x$. Given the assumption that $R_L x y_1 \cdots y_n$, we conclude $\Diamond(\neg \alpha_1, \ldots, \neg \alpha_n) \in y_i$, in other words, $\neg \Box(\alpha_1, \ldots, \alpha_n) \in y_i$. But this just means that $\Box(\alpha_1, \ldots, \alpha_n) \notin y_i$, which is what we want.

For $G_n 4_n$. We assume $R_L x y_1 \cdots y_i \cdots y_n$ and $R_L y_i z_1 \cdots z_n$ where $x, y_1, \ldots, y_n, z_1, \ldots, z_n$ are arbitrary points in $\mathfrak{M}_L$. To show that $R_L x z_1 \cdots z_n$, we argue that for any formulas $\alpha_1, \ldots, \alpha_n$, if $\Box(\alpha_1, \ldots, \alpha_n) \in x$, then $\alpha_j \in z_j$, for some $j$ where $1 \leq j \leq n$. So assume $\Box(\alpha_1, \ldots, \alpha_n) \in x$. Since $[4_n] \in x$, we have

$$\Box(\bot^{i-1}, \Box(\alpha_1, \ldots, \alpha_n), \bot^{n-i}) \in x.$$

Then $\Box(\alpha_1, \ldots, \alpha_n) \in y_i$, given that $R_L x y_1 \cdots y_n$. Then, as desired, we have $\alpha_j \in z_j$ for some $j$ such that $1 \leq j \leq n$, given that $R_L y_i z_1 \cdots z_n$.

For $G_n 5_n$. We assume that $R_L x y_1 \cdots y_i \cdots y_n$ and $R_L x z_1 \cdots z_n$ where $x, y_1, \ldots, y_n, z_1, \ldots, z_n$ are arbitrary. To show that $R_L y_i z_1 \cdots z_n$, we argue that for all formulas $\alpha_1, \ldots, \alpha_n$, if $\alpha_j \notin z_j$, where $j$ ranges from 1 to $n$, then $\Box(\alpha_1, \ldots, \alpha_n) \notin y_i$. So assume for all $j$ from 1 to $n$, $\alpha_j \notin z_j$. Since $R_L x z_1 \cdots z_n$, we have $\Box(\alpha_1, \ldots, \alpha_n) \notin x$, i.e. $\neg\Box(\alpha_1, \ldots, \alpha_n) \in x$, in other words,

$$\Diamond(\neg\alpha_1, \ldots, \neg\alpha_n) \in x$$

Then $\Box(\bot^{i-1}, \Diamond(\neg\alpha_1, \ldots, \neg\alpha_n), \bot^{n-i}) \in x$, given that $[5_n] \in x$. Then $\Diamond(\neg\alpha_1, \ldots, \neg\alpha_n) \in y_i$, given that $R_L x y_1 \cdots y_n$. In other words, $\Box(\alpha_1, \ldots, \alpha_n) \notin y_i$, as desired. $\qquad\square$

## 5.6   Diagonal Fragments of Normal Polyadic Modal Logics

We introduce the unary operator $\Box$ and its dual $\Diamond$ into the $n$-adic modal language $\mathcal{L}_n$ by the following identities:

$$\Box\alpha = \Box_n(\alpha, \ldots, \alpha) \qquad \Diamond\alpha = \Diamond_n(\alpha, \ldots, \alpha)$$

These unary operators can be described as 'diagonalization' of their $n$-ary counterparts: consider the set of $n$-tuples of formulas as an $n$-dimensional matrix, and the set of tuples whose coordinates are the same formula as a diagonal across such a matrix. The truth conditions for the diagonal operators are as follows:

$\mathfrak{M}, x \models \Box\alpha$ iff $\forall y_1, \ldots, y_n, Rxy_1 \cdots y_n \implies \exists y_i (1 \le i \le n):$ $\mathfrak{M}, y_i \models \alpha$.

$\mathfrak{M}, x \models \Diamond\alpha$ iff $\exists y_1, \ldots, y_n : Rxy_1 \cdots y_n$ & $\forall y_i (1 \le i \le n),$ $\mathfrak{M}, y_i \models \alpha$.

Let $\mathcal{L}_n \upharpoonright \Box$ be the set of $\mathcal{L}_n$-formulas that can be expressed by using only the unary $\Box$ and truth-functional connectives. We call the set of theorems of $G_n$ that can be so expressed, that is, the intersection of $G_n$ and $\mathcal{L}_n \upharpoonright \Box$, the diagonal fragment of $G_n$. This fragment has been shown to be axiomatized by the following system $K_n$. For details, see Jennings and Schotch (1984), Apostoli and Brown (1995), and Nicholson et al. (2000).

**Definition 9.** $K_n$ *has* PL, [RM], [RN], *and the following axiom:*

$$[K_n] \quad \Box p_1 \wedge \cdots \wedge \Box p_{n+1} \to \Box \bigvee_{i=1}^{n+1} \bigvee_{j=i+1}^{n+1} (p_i \wedge p_j).$$

Note that $K_1$ is just K. $K_n$ can be described as a 'weakly aggregative modal logic' since its aggregate principle $[K_n]$ is a weakening of the following principle of complete aggregation, which is a theorem of K.

$$\Box \alpha_1 \wedge \cdots \wedge \Box \alpha_n \to \Box(\alpha_1 \wedge \cdots \wedge \alpha_n).$$

$K_n$ can be extended by adding the familiar formulas [K], [Con], [T], [B], [4], and [5], and the resulting systems are called, respectively, $K_nK$, $K_nCon$, $K_nT$, $K_nB$, $K_n4$, and $K_n5$. Note that $K_nK$ is just $K_1$ or K, since $[K_n]$ is derivable from [K]. In the following, we list correspondence and determination results for these formulas and logics.

**Theorem 3.** *The following modal formulas correspond to the indicated first-order conditions:*

[K]    :  $(\forall x)(\forall \vec{y})(Rx\vec{y} \to (\exists y_i \in \vec{y})Rxy_i \cdots y_i)$

(Quasi-binarity)

[Con]   :  $(\forall x)(\exists \vec{y})Rx\vec{y}$                      (Seriality)

[T]    :  $(\forall x)Rxx \cdots x$                      (Reflexivity)

[B]    :  $(\forall x)(\forall \vec{y})(Rx\vec{y} \to (\exists y_i \in \vec{y})Ry_i x \cdots x)$    (Symmetry†)

[4]    :  $(\forall x)(\forall \vec{y}, \vec{z}_1, \ldots, \vec{z}_n)(Rx\vec{y} \wedge Ry_1\vec{z}_1 \wedge \cdots \wedge Ry_n\vec{z}_n \to$

$(\exists \vec{w} \subseteq \vec{z}_1 \cup \cdots \cup \vec{z}_n)Rx\vec{w})$           (Transitivity†)

[5]    :  $(\forall x)(\forall \vec{y}, \vec{z})(Rx\vec{y} \wedge Rx\vec{z} \to (\exists y_i \in \vec{y})Ry_i\vec{z})$ ·

(Euclideanness†)

*Note: In the condition of transitivity,* $\exists \vec{w} \subseteq \vec{z}_1 \cup \cdots \cup \vec{z}_n$ *means the following: there exists a* $\vec{w}$ *such that every* $w_k \in \vec{w}$ *belongs to the set of* $z_{i,j}$*'s where* $1 \leq i, j \leq n$.

Observe that the frame properties corresponding to [B], [4], and [5] are weaker than those corresponding to $[B_n]$, $[4_n]$, and $[5_n]$, which is to be expected since the former formulas are derivable from the latter ones. We distinguish the weaker properties from the stronger ones by the sign †.

**Theorem 4.** *The following diagonal logics are determined by the indicated classes of $(n + 1)$-ary relational frames:*

$K_n$ *All frames*

$K_n K$ *Quasi-binary frames*

$K_n Con$ *Serial frames*

$K_n T$ *Reflexive frames*

$K_n B$ *Symmetric† frames*

$K_n 4$ *Transitive† frames*

$K_n 5$ *Euclidean† frames*

# Six

---

# Preserving What?

GILLMAN PAYETTE AND PETER SCHOTCH

---

**Abstract**

In this essay Gillman Payette and Peter Schotch present an account of the key notions of level and forcing in much greater generality than has been managed in any of the early publications. In terms of this level of generality the hoary notion that correct inference is truth-preserving is carefully examined and found wanting. The authors suggest that consistency preservation is a far more natural approach, and one that can, furthermore, *characterize* an inference relation. But an examination of the usual account of consistency reveals problems that, in general, can be corrected by means of an auxiliary notion of inference (forcing) which relies upon a kind of generalization of consistency, called level. Preservation of the latter is shown to be another of the properties which characterize a logic and forcing is shown to preserve it. The essay ends with a sketch of a result which locates forcing among all possible level-preserving inference relations.

## 6.1   Introduction

The (classical) semantic paradigm for correct inference is often given the name 'truth-preservation.' This is typically spelled out to the awe-struck students in some such way as this:

85

> An inference from a set of premises, $\Gamma$, to a conclusion, $\alpha$,
> is correct, say *valid*, if and only if whenever all the members
> of $\Gamma$ are true, then so is $\alpha$.

This understanding of the slogan may be tried, but is it actually true? There is a problem: the way that 'truth' is used in connection with the premises is distinct from the way that it is used with the conclusion. In other words, this could be no better than a quick and dirty gloss. The chief virtue of the formulation is that of seeming correct to the naive and untutored.

But what of the sophisticates? They might well ask for the precise sense in which truth is supposed to be preserved in this way of unpacking. On the right hand side of the 'whenever' we are talking about the truth of a single formula while on the left hand side we are talking about the truth of a bunch of single formulas. Is it the truth of the whole gang which is 'preserved?'

Of course it is open to the dyed-in-the-wool classicalist to reply scornfully that we need only replace the set on the left with the conjunction of its members. In this way is truth preserved from single formula to single formula as homogeneously as anyone could wish.

It is open, but not particularly inviting. In the first place, this strategy forces us to restrict the underlying language to one with conjunction and conditional connectives – that must operate in something like the usual (which is to say classical) way. There are enough who would chafe under this restriction that a sensitive theorist would hesitate to impose it.

Apart from the objection, we are inclined to think of this business of coding up the valid inferences in terms of their 'corresponding conditionals'[1] as an accident of the classical way of thinking, and that it is no part of the *definition* of a correct account of inference. We also notice that on the proposal, we are restricted to finite sets.

Setting aside this unpalatable proposal then, we ask how is this notion of truth-preservation supposed to work? Since there is no gang on

---

[1] We think this usage was coined by Quine.

the right we seem to be talking about a different kind of truth, individual truth maybe, from the kind we are talking about on the left – mass truth perhaps. Looked at in that somewhat jaundiced way, there isn't any preserving going on at all, but rather a sort of transmuting.

The classical paradigm *really* ought to be given by the slogan 'truth transmutation.' In passing from the gaggle of premises to the conclusion, gaggle-truth is transmuted into single formula truth. It may be more correct to say that, but it makes the whole paradigm somewhat less forceful or even less appealing.

What we need in order to rescue the very idea of preservationism is to talk entirely about sets. So we shall have to replace the arbitrary conclusion $\alpha$ with the entire *set* of conclusions which might correctly be drawn from $\Gamma$. We even have an attractive name for that set – the *theory* generated by $\Gamma$ or the *deductive closure* of $\Gamma$. In formal terms this is

$$\mathbb{C}_X(\Gamma) = \{\alpha | \Gamma \vdash_X \alpha\}$$

Now that we have sets, can we say what it is that gets preserved – can we characterize classical inference, for instance, as that relation between sets of formulas and their closures such that the property $\Phi$ is preserved?

We can see that gaggle-truth would seem to work here in the sense that whenever $\Gamma$ is gaggle-true so must be $\mathbb{C}_X(\Gamma)$, at least for $\vdash_X$, the classical notion of inference. We are unable to rid ourselves, however, of the notion that gaggle-truth is somewhat lacking from an intuitive perspective. Put simply, our notion of truth is carried by a predicate which applies to *sentences* – or formulas if we are in that mood. These are objects which might indeed belong to sets but they aren't themselves sets. So however we construe the idea of a true set of sentences (or formulas), that construal will involve a stipulation or, more charitably, a new definition.

Generations of logic students may have been browbeaten into accepting 'A set of sentences is true if and only if each member of the set is true.' But it *is* a stipulation, and is no part of the definition of 'true.' It doesn't take very much imagination to think that somebody might actually balk at the stipulation. Somebody who is attracted to the idea of *coherence*, for instance, might well want to say that truth must be defined for (certain kinds of) sets first and that the sentential notion is derived from the set notion and not conversely. All of which is simply to say that a stipulation as to how we should understand the phrase 'true set of sentences' is unlikely to be beyond the bounds of controversy.[2]

It may gladden our hearts to hear then, that there is another property, perhaps a more natural one, which will do what we want. That alternative property is *consistency*.

## 6.2   Making a Few Things Precise

By a *logic* $X$, over a language $\mathcal{L}$ we understand the set of pairs $\langle \Gamma, \alpha \rangle$ such that $\Gamma$ is a set of formulas from the language $\mathcal{L}$ and $\alpha$ is a formula from that same language, and $\Gamma \vdash_X \alpha$. In the sequel we frequently avoid mention of the language which underlies a given logic, when no confusion will thereby be engendered.

This set of pairs is also referred to as the *provability* or *inference relation* of $X$. In saying this we expose our extensional viewpoint, according to which there is nothing to a logic over and above its inference relation. This has the immediate consequence that we shall take two logics $X$ and $Y$ which have the same inference relation to be the same logic.

When $X$ is a logic, we refer to the $X$-deductive closure of the set $\Gamma$ by means of '$\mathfrak{C}_X(\Gamma)$.'

Unless the contrary is specified, every logic mentioned below will be *compact*, which is say that whenever $\Gamma \vdash \alpha$ it follows that there must be some finite subset, say $\Delta$, of $\Gamma$, which proves $\alpha$.

---

[2]It may be helpful here to consider an analogy between sentences and numbers, taken to be *urelementen*. We can define the idea of a prime number easily enough but be puzzled about how to define a prime *set* of numbers. Somebody might be moved to offer 'Why not simply define a prime set of numbers to be a set of prime numbers?' The answer is likely to be 'Why bother?' Indeed the whole idea of a prime set of numbers seems bizarre and unhelpful. We can easily imagine circumstances in which we would require a set of prime numbers but the reverse is true when it comes to a prime set.

In mentioning consistency, we have in mind some previously given notion of inference, say $\vdash_X$. Each inference relation spawns a notion of consistency according to the formula

> $\Gamma$ is consistent, *in* or *relative to* a logic $X$ (alternatively, $\Gamma$ is $X$-consistent), if and only if there is at least one formula $\alpha$ such that $\Gamma \nvdash_X \alpha$.

To say this in terms of provability rather than non-provability we might issue the following definition:

> $\Gamma$ is *inconsistent* in a logic $X$ if and only if $\mathbb{C}_X(\Gamma) = \mathbb{S}$, where $\mathbb{S}$ is the set of all formulas of the underlying language of $X$.

> Where $X$ is a logic, the associated consistency predicate (of sets of formulas) for $X$, is indicated by CON$_X$.

We were interested in how an inference relation might be characterized in terms of preserving some property of sets. We have singled out consistency as a natural property of sets, and having done that we can see that preservation of consistency comes very naturally indeed. The time has come to state a little more exactly what we mean by 'characterized.' In order to do this we shall be making reference to the following three *structural* rules of inference:

[R] $\alpha \in \Gamma \implies \Gamma \vdash \alpha$,

[Cut] $\Gamma, \alpha \vdash \beta \ \& \ \Gamma \vdash \alpha \implies \Gamma \vdash \beta$,

[Mon] $\Gamma \vdash \alpha \implies \Gamma \cup \Delta \vdash \alpha$.

Unless there is a specific disavowal, every inference relation we consider will be assumed to admit these three rules. It should be noted that on account of [Mon], if the empty set $\varnothing$ is inconsistent in $X$, then the inference relation for that logic contains every pair $\langle \Gamma, \alpha \rangle$. In such a case we say that $X$ is the *trivial* logic over its underlying language. We shall take the logics we mention from now on to be non-trivial, barring a disclaimer to the contrary.

Let us say that an inference relation, say $\vdash_X$, *preserves consistency* if and only if:

> If $\Gamma$ is $X$-consistent (in the sense of the previous definition), then so is $\mathbb{C}_X(\Gamma)$.

It is easy to see that every inference relation with [Cut] and [Mon] must preserve consistency since if the closure of a set $\Gamma$ proves some formula, $\alpha$, then by compactness some finite sequence of [Cut] operations will lead to the conclusion that $\Gamma$ proves $\alpha$. It may be that we end up showing that some subset of $\Gamma$ proves $\alpha$, which is why we require [Mon] in this case.

We say that $X$ preserves consistency *in the strong sense* when the condition given above as necessary is also sufficient.

It is similarly easy to see that since every set is contained in its deductive closure by [R], and since inconsistency is preserved by supersets, given [Mon], every inference relation satisfying the three structural rules preserves consistency in the strong sense.

This is all very well, but we haven't really gotten to anything that would single out an inference relation from among a throng of such relations, all of which preserve consistency. In order to do that it will be necessary to talk about a logic $X$ preserving, in the strong sense, the consistency predicate of a logic $Y$.

A moment's thought will show us that when the preservation is mutual, when $X$ and $Y$ preserve each other's consistency predicates (which implies that they share a common underlying language), then they must agree on which sets are consistent and which are inconsistent.

For consider, if $\mathrm{CON}_X(\Gamma)$ and $Y$ preserves the $X$ consistency predicate, then $\mathrm{CON}_X(\mathbb{C}_Y(\Gamma))$. Suppose that $\Gamma$ is not $Y$-consistent, then $\mathbb{C}_Y(\Gamma) = \mathbb{S}$. By [R] $\mathbb{C}_X(\mathbb{C}_Y(\Gamma)) = \mathbb{C}_X(\mathbb{S}) = \mathbb{S}$, which is to say that $\mathbb{C}_Y(\Gamma)$ is not $X$-consistent, a contradiction. Similarly for the argument that $\Gamma$ is consistent in $Y$ and $X$ preserves the $Y$ consistency predicate.

When two logics agree in this way, that is, agree on the consistent and inconsistent sets, we shall say that they are *at evens*. Another moment's thought reveals that two logics which are at evens will preserve each other's consistency predicates. Assume $X$ and $Y$ are at evens and

$\text{CON}_X(\Gamma)$ but $\overline{\text{CON}_X}(\mathbb{C}_Y(\Gamma))$, where the overline indicates predicate negation. Then $\overline{\text{CON}_Y}(\mathbb{C}_Y(\Gamma))$ because $X$ and $Y$ agree on inconsistent sets. Hence by idempotentcy of $\mathbb{C}_Y$ $\Gamma$ is not consistent in $Y$, a contradiction. Thus we have the following:

**Proposition 1.** *Any two logics $X$ and $Y$ over a language $\mathcal{L}$ are at evens if and only if $X$ and $Y$ preserve each other's consistency predicates.*

This is nearly enough to guarantee that $X$ and $Y$ are the same logic. All we need is a kind of generalized negation principle:

---

**Definition 1.** *A logic $X$ is said to have* denial *provided that for every formula $\alpha$, there is some formula $\beta$ such that $\overline{\text{CON}_X}(\{\alpha, \beta\})$.*

---

In such a case we shall say that $\alpha$ and $\beta$ deny each other (in $X$, which qualification we normally omit when it is clear from the context). We will assume that any logic we mention has denial.

Clearly if a logic has classical-like negation rules then it has denial, since the negation of a formula will always be inconsistent with the formula. Of course classically, there are countably many other formulas which are inconsistent with any given formula – namely all those which are self-inconsistent. The generalized notion doesn't require that there be distinct[3] denials for each formula, only that there be some or other formula which is not consistent with the given formula.

Evidently, if two logics are at evens, then if one has denial, so does the other. In fact something stronger holds, namely:

**Proposition 2.** *If two logics $X$ and $Y$ are at evens, and $X$ has denial then, for every formula $\alpha$ there is some formula $\beta$ for which both $\overline{\text{CON}_X}(\{\alpha, \beta\})$ and $\overline{\text{CON}_Y}(\{\alpha, \beta\})$.*

Finally, we shall require of our logics that they satisfy the principle that denial commutes with provability in the right way:

[Den] $\Gamma \vdash_X \alpha \iff \overline{\text{CON}_X}(\Gamma \cup \{\beta\})$ where $\beta$ denies $\alpha$.

---

[3]Distinct up to logical equivalence, it goes without saying.

Now we are ready to state our result:

**Theorem 1.** *(Generalized Consistency Theorem) Two logics $X$ and $Y$ are at evens if and only if, $X$ and $Y$ are the same logic.*

*Proof.* For this argument we split the equivalence into its necessary and sufficient halves.

( $\Longrightarrow$ ) Assume $\mathbb{C}_X(\Gamma) = \mathbb{C}_Y(\Gamma)$ for every set $\Gamma$ – which is to say that $X = Y$. To say that $\overline{\text{CON}_X}(\Gamma)$ is to say that the $X$-closure of $\Gamma$ is $\mathbb{S}$. But then so must be the $Y$-closure of $\Gamma$. Similarly, to say that $\text{CON}_X(\Gamma)$ is to say that there is some $\alpha$ which is not in the $X$-closure of $\Gamma$, but then neither can $\alpha$ be in the $Y$-closure of $\Gamma$, hence $\text{CON}_Y(\Gamma)$. So $X$ and $Y$ are at evens.

($\Longleftarrow$) Suppose then that $X$ and $Y$ are at evens. Let $\Gamma$ be a consistent set, which means, by the assumption, that it is consistent in both logics. Assume for reductio that $\Gamma \vdash_X \alpha$ and $\Gamma \nvdash_Y \alpha$, and let $\beta$ deny $\alpha$. Thus, by [Den], $\overline{\text{CON}_X}(\Gamma \cup \{\beta\})$ and $\text{CON}_Y(\Gamma \cup \{\beta\})$, a contradiction.   $\square$

## 6.3   What's Wrong with This Picture?

To answer the question in the section heading, there really isn't anything wrong with an approach which characterizes inference in terms of preserving consistency. It's consistency itself, or at least many accounts of it, which casts a shadow over our everyday logical doings.

The way we have set things up, a set $\Gamma$ of formulas is either consistent in a logic $X$, or it isn't. But it doesn't take much thought to see that such an all-or-nothing approach tramples some intuitive distinctions. In particular, we may find the *reason* for the inconsistency to be of interest.

In the logic $X$, for example, there may be a single formula $\delta$ which is, so to speak, inconsistent *by itself*. In other words $\overline{\text{CON}_X}(\{\delta\})$. Formulas of this dire sort are sometimes described as being *self-inconsistent* (in $X$) or *absurd* in $X$. By [Mon] any set of formulas which contains a self-inconsistent formula is bound to be inconsistent.

Thinking of the possible existence of absurd formulas leads us to sharpen our previous notion of denial:

---

**Definition 2.** *We shall say that X has* non-trivial *denial if and only if for every non-absurd formula* α *there is at least one non-absurd formula* β *which is not X-consistent with* α.

---

We are now struck by the contrast between $X$-inconsistent sets which contain $X$-absurdities and those which do not. Isn't there an important distinction between these two cases? If we think of consistency as a desirable property which we are willing to trouble ourselves to achieve, then the trouble will be light indeed if all we need to do is reject absurdities. On the other hand, an entire lifetime of angst may await those who wish to render consistent their beliefs or their obligations.[4] There is a great deal more that one could say on this topic and some of the current authors have said much of it. For now, we shall take it that the need for a distinction has been established and our job is to construct an account of consistency which allows it.

We have in mind building upon what we have already discovered instead of pursuing a slash-and-burn policy. This means, among other things, that the predecessor account should appear as a special (or limiting) case of the new proposal. The intuitive distinction bruited above is clearly a distinction between different kinds of inconsistency or, perhaps, different degrees. We might think of one kind being *worse* than the other, which leads to a rather natural way of classifying inconsistency.

## 6.4 Speak of the Level

The account of inconsistency which we propose is a generalization of the one first suggested in the twentieth century in the work of Jennings and Schotch,[5] namely the idea of a *level* (of incoherence, or inconsistency). The basic idea is that we can provide an intuitive measure of how inconsistent a set is by seeing how finely it must be divided before

---

[4] In saying this, we assume that nobody is obliged to bring about anything impossible and that whatever is self-inconsistent cannot truly be a belief.

[5] See especially Schotch and Jennings (1980a, 1989).

all of the divisions are consistent. What in the earlier account is stated in terms of classical provability, we now state in terms of arbitrary inference relations that satisfy the minimal conditions given in the earlier section.

It all begins with the notion of a certain kind of indexed collection of sets being a *logical cover* for a set $\Gamma$ of formulas, in the logic $X$. First we need a special kind of indexed family of sets (of formulas).

---

**Definition 3.** $A(\Delta) = \{a_0, a_1, \ldots, a_\xi\}$ *is an indexed set* starting with $\Delta$, *provided $a_0 = \Delta$ and all the indices $0 \ldots \xi$ are drawn from some index set $I$.*

---

**Definition 4.** *Let $\mathfrak{F}$ be an indexed set starting with $\varnothing$. $\mathfrak{F}$ is said to be a* logical cover *of the set $\Sigma$, relative to the logic $X$, indicated by* $\mathrm{COV}_X(\mathfrak{F}, \Sigma)$, *provided that*

*for every element a of the indexed family,* $\mathrm{CON}_X(a)$ *and*

$$\Sigma \subseteq \bigcup_{i \in I} \mathbb{C}_X(a_i).$$

---

So an $X$-logical cover for $\Gamma$ is an indexed family of sets starting with the empty set, such that there are enough logical resources in the cover to prove, in the logic $X$, each member of $\Gamma$. Evidently, given the rule [R], $\{\varnothing, \Gamma\}$ will always be a logical cover of $\Gamma$ if the latter set is $X$-consistent, although it won't, in general, be the least.

If $\mathfrak{F}_\Sigma$ is a logical cover for the set $\Sigma$, the cardinality $|I| - 1$, where $I$ is the index set for $\mathfrak{F}_\Sigma$, is referred to as the *width* of the cover, indicated by $w(\mathfrak{F}_\Sigma)$.

In the special circumstance that all the members of a logical cover of $\Sigma$ are disjoint, the cover is said to *partition* $\Sigma$.[6]

---

[6]This should be contrasted with a covering family *being* a partition. We can recover the latter notion from this one by intersecting the covered set with each of the disjoint sets in the logical cover.

And finally we introduce the notion which we have hinted at since the start of this section.

---

**Definition 5.** *The* level *(relative to the logic X) of the set* $\Gamma$ *of formulas of the underlying language of X, indicated by* $\ell^X(\Gamma)$, *is defined as*

$$\ell^X(\Gamma) = \begin{cases} \min\limits_{w(\mathfrak{F})} [\mathrm{COV}_X(\mathfrak{F}, \Gamma)] & \textit{if this limit exists} \\ \infty & \textit{otherwise.} \end{cases}$$

---

In other words: the $X$-level (of incoherence or inconsistency) of a set $\Sigma$ in a logic $X$ is the width of the narrowest $X$-logical cover of $\Sigma$, if there is such a thing, and if there isn't, the level is set to the symbol $\infty$.

One might think that there will fail to be a narrowest logical cover when there is more than one – when several are tied with the least width, but this is a misreading of the definition. There might indeed be several distinct logical covers but there can only be one least width (which they all share). The uniqueness referred to in the definition attaches to the width so to speak, not to the cover.

The only circumstance in which there might fail to be a narrowest logical cover, is one in which $\Sigma$ has no logical covers at all. In this circumstance $\Sigma$ must contain what we earlier called an absurd formula.

This notion satisfies both the requirement that it distinguish between inconsistent sets which contain absurd formulas and those which don't, and the requirement that the predecessor notion of consistency relative to $X$ appear as a special case. For it is clear that if $\Gamma$ is an $X$-consistent set of formulas which does not consist entirely of $X$ theorems, then a narrowest logical cover of $\Gamma$ is $\{\varnothing, a_1\}$ where $\Gamma \subseteq \mathbb{C}_X(a_1)$ and $\mathrm{CON}_X(a_1)$. So at least part of the earlier notion of $\mathrm{CON}_X(\Gamma)$ is captured by $\ell^X(\Gamma) = 1$.

There is even an interesting insight which comes out of this new idea. For there are *two* levels of $X$-consistency, 0 and 1. In our earlier naive approach, we thought of consistency as an entirely monolithic affair, but once we give the matter some thought we see that the empty set does indeed occupy a unique position in the panoply of $X$-consistent sets. If we know only that $\Gamma$ and $\Sigma$ are both $X$-consistent, nothing at all follows about the $X$-consistency of $\Gamma \cup \Sigma$. But we may rest assured that both $\Sigma \cup \varnothing$ and $\Gamma \cup \varnothing$ are $X$-consistent. And the same goes for the $X$-consequences of the empty set, namely $X$-theorems. By our definition, $\ell^X(\Delta) = 0$ if $\Delta$ is empty or any set of $X$-theorems, and of course such sets are consistent with any $X$-consistent set of formulas. It is tempting to call these level 0 sets *hyperconsistent*.

## 6.5   Level Preservation

So now that we have the concept of an $X$-level, should we be concerned about preserving such a thing? Perhaps there is no need for such concern, since it is at least possible that the logic $X$ preserves its own level, isn't it? Well, in a word, no. It is not in general true that $X$ preserves level beyond, of course, the levels 0 and 1 of $X$-consistency. All the logics we consider not only do that, but are characterized by doing that.

Suppose the set $\Gamma$ contains not only the formula $\alpha$ but also a denial $\beta$ of $\alpha$, although it does not contain any $X$-absurdities. Now, since $X$ has the rule [R], $\Gamma$ must $X$-prove both $\alpha$ and $\beta$. If $X$ permits the arbitrary conjunction of conclusions, then $\Gamma$ will prove an $X$-absurd formula, namely $\alpha \wedge \beta$. Hence by the meaning of closure, that absurdity belongs to the $X$-closure of $\Gamma$, which must thus have $X$-level $\infty$. This amounts to a massive failure to preserve level.

The obvious question to raise is this: given that $\ell^X$ is a generalization of $\mathrm{CON}_X$, is it the case that level characterizes logics in the same way that preserving consistency (in the strong sense) does? If not, then it seems that the generalization is not perhaps as central a notion as the root idea upon which it generalizes. Fortunately for supporters of the general notion, we may prove the following generalization of the Generalized Consistency Theorem.

**Theorem 2.**  *(Level Characterization Theorem) Suppose that $X$ and $Y$ are inference relations over the same language $\mathcal{L}$ and let $\ell^X$ and $\ell^Y$ be the level functions associated with the respective inference relations.*

*Then*

$$[\ell^X(\Gamma) = \ell^Y(\Gamma) \text{ for every set } \Gamma \text{ of formulas of } \mathcal{L}] \iff X = Y.$$

*Proof.* The proof depends upon the Generalized Consistency Theorem.

( $\Longrightarrow$ ) Assume that $\ell_X(\Gamma) = \ell_Y(\Gamma)$ for every set $\Gamma$ of formulas of $\mathcal{L}$. Then by definition the two agree on which sets have level 1 and level 0. But this is to say that $X$ and $Y$ agree on which sets are consistent. But by the Generalized Consistency Theorem, any two such logics (logics which we say are at evens) must be identical.

( $\Longleftarrow$ ) Assume that $X = Y$ and suppose that for some arbitrary set $\Gamma$ of formulas of $\mathcal{L}$ $\ell^X(\Gamma) = \xi$, for $\xi$ some cardinal. Then, by the definition, there is a narrowest $X$-logical cover $\mathfrak{F}_\Gamma$ such that $w(\mathfrak{F}_\Gamma) = \xi$. Since $X = Y$, it must be the case by the Generalized Consistency Theorem that the two logics agree on consistency (in the strong sense). Further, by definition each $a_i \in \mathfrak{F}_\Gamma$ is such that $\mathrm{CON}_X(a_i)$. But then, since $X$ and $Y$ are at evens, $\mathrm{CON}_Y(a_i)$. Thus, $\mathfrak{F}_\Gamma$ must be a $Y$-logical cover of $\Gamma$ of width $\xi$. Moreover, this must be the narrowest such logical cover or else, by parity of reasoning, there would be an $X$-logical cover of cardinality less than $\xi$, contrary to hypothesis. Since $\Gamma$ was arbitrary it follows that $\ell^X$ and $\ell^Y$ must agree on all sets of formulas of the language $\mathcal{L}$. $\square$

This suggests that level is worth preserving, that it is a sort of natural logical kind, but doesn't show how the preservation may be carried out. It is time to repair that lack.

Perhaps the most straightforward route to preserving $X$-level is to define a new inference relation based on $X$. Evidently the definition in question must also connect somehow with the notion of $X$-level and thus ultimately to $\mathrm{CON}_X$ (from now on we shall mostly drop reference to the background logic, like $X$, when no confusion will result). The process might have been informed by the ancient joke:

*Question*: How do you get down from an elephant?

*Answer*: You don't get down from an elephant, you get down from a duck.

Except in our case the question and answer would go like this:

*Question*: How do you reason from inconsistent sets?

*Answer*: You don't reason from inconsistent sets, since every formula follows in that case, you reason from consistent *subsets*.

In other words, an inconsistent set is one for which the distinction between what follows and what doesn't has collapsed. This lack of meaningful contrast means that it no longer makes sense to talk about inferring conclusions from such a set. In order to regain the distinction we are going to have to drop back to the level of consistency, and the only way to do that is to look at consistent subsets of the original set.

Absent the notion of level, there are different ways to do this. The one suggested in Quine and Ullian (1970) to deal with inconsistent sets of beliefs involves two stages: At the first stage we discover the smallest subset of the inconsistent set which still exhibits the inconsistency. At the second stage we discard the member of the inconsistent subset with the least evidence, and repeat as necessary until the set is consistent. Having thus cleansed the belief set, we may now draw conclusions as we did before.[7]

We don't say that this process can't work. We do say that it doesn't seem to work in every case. There is a clear difficulty here when the two conditions on rational belief – consistency (which we might call the external condition) and evidential support (the internal condition) – pull us in different directions.

In the lottery paradox, for instance, we seem to have good evidence for each one of the lottery beliefs (ticket 1 won't win, ticket 2 won't win, ..., ticket $n$ won't win), and we can make the evidence as strong as we like by making the lottery ever larger. Now conjoin the beliefs and we get 'No ticket will win,' which contradicts fairness. We could get consistency by throwing out the belief that the lottery is fair, but that would be cheating. The problem is that each of the lottery beliefs

---

[7]This procedure was intended to apply to classical inference, but the method obviously generalizes to cover cases in which the base inference is $X$.

has exactly the same support as the others. They stand or fall as one, it would seem. If we let them all fall, then the rationality, or at least the non-irrationality of buying a lottery ticket would seem to follow. But isn't it true that it isn't rational, according to the accepted canons at least, to buy a lottery ticket?[8]

Leaving aside the possibly controversial issue of the lottery paradox, take any situation in which we are unable to find a rationale for discarding one member of an inconsistent subset rather than another. Quine seems to suggest that in this situation, the counsel of prudence is to wait until we do find some way to distinguish among the problematic beliefs. Those with less patience seem to regard random discarding until at last we get to consistency, to be the path of wisdom.[9] We are inclined to reply to Quine that patience, for all that it is a virtue, is sometimes also a luxury we cannot afford or even a self-indulgence that we do well to deny ourselves.

To the others we say consistency is not a virtue which trumps everything else. Suppose we might achieve consistency by throwing away one of $\alpha$ or $\beta$ though we have no reason to prefer one over the other. Flipping a coin is a method for determining which goes to the wall, but we have no way of knowing if we have determined the correct one. We have left ourselves open to having rejected a truth and accepted a falsehood. 'Yes, but at least we now have consistency!' won't comfort us much if the consequences of picking the wrong thing to throw away are unpleasant enough.

Let us take up level once more.[10] In saying the level of the set $\Sigma$ is $k$, we are saying two things. First, that there is a way to divide the logical resources of $\Sigma$ into $k$ distinct subsets, each of which is consistent. From now on we shall refer to these consistent subsets as *cells*. Second, that any way of thus dividing $\Sigma$, must have at least $k$ cells. Here we have got to the level of consistency not once, but $k$ times. Not only might

---

[8] Not for nothing have lotteries long been known as 'a tax on fools.'

[9] This seems to be the route advocated by some of those in computing science who have devised so-called truth-maintenance systems.

[10] We realize that the Quinean suggestion is not the only one, though it might be the most well-known, to deal with inconsistent sets of formulas. We do not, however, intend this essay as a survey of all of so-called paraconsistent logic.

we wonder which of the $k$ cells is the 'real' one, the one which best represents 'the way things really are,' but there may be lots and lots of distinct ways to form the $k$ cells. Which of the possibly many ways should we privilege?

At this point, we cannot answer these questions, which means that we must treat the cells on an equal footing along with the various ways of producing them.[11] In saying this, we say that we shall count as a consequence of $\Sigma$ in the derived inference relation, whatever formula follows (in the 'underlying' logic, say $X$) from at least one cell in every way of dividing $\Sigma$ into $k$ cells.

When the underlying logic is $X$, the derived inference relation is called $X$-level forcing, which relation in indicated by $\lceil \Vdash_X$. We can give the precise definition as follows:

---

**Definition 6.**

$\Gamma \lceil \Vdash_X \alpha$ *if and only if, for every division of* $\Gamma$ *into* $\ell^X(\Gamma)$ *cells, for at least one of the cells* $\Delta$, $\Delta \vdash_X \alpha$

---

It is easy to see that

**Proposition 3.** *If* $\Gamma \lceil \Vdash_X \alpha$ *then* $\ell^X(\Gamma) = \ell^X(\Gamma \cup \{\alpha\})$.

*Proof.* Suppose the condition obtains and let $\ell^X(\Gamma) = k$. It follows from the definition that every division of $\Gamma$ into $k$ cells results in at least one cell that $X$-proves $\alpha$. But then we could add $\alpha$ to the cell in question without losing the cell property since $X$ is a logic which preserves consistency. In such a case, after adding $\alpha$ we would have a division of $\Gamma \cup \{\alpha\}$ into $k$ cells. Moreover, there couldn't be a division of $\Gamma \cup \{\alpha\}$ into fewer than $k$ cells without there being a similar division of $\Gamma$ which would contradict the hypothesis.                □

It obviously follows directly from this that

**Corollary 1.** $\lceil \Vdash_X$ *preserves* $X$-*level, in the sense that* $\ell^X(\Gamma) = \ell^X(\mathbb{C}_{\lceil \Vdash_X}(\Gamma))$.

---

[11]Which is not to say that there is no way to. Elsewhere one might find suggestions which narrow the range of ways of dividing up our initial set. In this connection see the discussion of A-forcing in chapter 9.

## 6.6 Yes, But Is It *Inference*?

To be perfectly honest, or at least honest enough for practical purposes, all we have shown is that $X$-level forcing is a relation that preserves $X$-level. There is a gulf between this, and the assertion that $\lceil \Vdash_X$ is an inference relation which preserves X-level. The obvious problem for anybody wishing to assert such a thing resides in the fact that we haven't, for all our efforts at precision, actually *said* which relations count as inference relations. What we *have* said is that we assume that the inference relations we mention admit certain rules. Shall we take the collection of these rules to be constitutive of inference?

We shall not, because some, at least, of the rules which the underlying logic admits simply don't make sense for the derived relation. This should not come as a surprise. It is our palpable annoyance with the underlying logic which leads us to propose $\lceil \Vdash_X$. How silly then to require that the derived logic inherit everything from the underlying logic, since that would make the derived logic another source of irritation rather than the balm for which we hope.

Although it is easy to check that $\lceil \Vdash_X$ inherits from its underlying inference relation $X$ both [R] and [Cut], we can see that it fails to admit the rule [M] of monotonicity, which we would do better to label the rule of *unrestricted* monotonicity from now on. But this is one of those cases in which the rule ought not to apply to the derived relation. If we are allowed to dilute premise sets in an arbitrary way, there is nothing to prevent us from raising the $X$-level of such sets. But raising the level gives us, in general, (logically) weaker cells in each logical cover. What used to $X$-follow from at least one cell of every such cover might no longer do so, as we are cut off from vital logical resources by the finer division.[12]

This is not to say that no form of monotonicity makes sense for the derived relation. Quite the contrary, in fact, what most emphatically

---

[12]Here is a concrete example where the underlying logic is classical. The premise set $\{\alpha, \alpha \supset \beta\}$ has the classical-level forcing consequence $\beta$ since it has level 1. If we add the formula $\neg\beta$ the resulting set has level 2, and now there is a logical cover, $\{\varnothing, \{\alpha, \neg\beta\}, \{\alpha \supset \beta\}\}$, no cell of which classically proves $\beta$. Thus $\beta$ is not a classical-level forcing consequence of the diluted set.

*does* make sense is that X-level forcing consequence must survive any dilution which preserves the level of the premise set. Such a restricted version of monotonicity manifestly is a rule for $X$-level forcing, as is trivial to verify.

Along with level-preserving dilution, there are certain consequences which must survive any dilution at all, whether or not the $X$-level of the premise set increases. These are the consequences which dilution cannot affect, and we can say precisely which they are: The consequences, according to $X$, of the empty set and of any unit set will remain $X$-consequences of at least one cell of every logical cover of any set which contains any of these privileged sets. In earlier work these sets were called *singular*.

The other properties which we have been mentioning for the underlying logics are non-triviality and having denial. It should be clear that when the underlying logic is non-trivial so will be its derived forcing relation. In fact, keeping to our original definition of consistency, in passing from an underlying logic $X$ to its derived $\lceil \Vdash_X$, many of the $X$-inconsistent sets fail to be $\lceil \Vdash_X$-inconsistent, which is, after all, the whole point of the derived relation.

Which brings us to denial. If the underlying logic has denial, nothing follows about the derived forcing relation, which is not necessarily a bad thing. This is because in the underlying logic, inconsistent sets are (typically) relatively easy to come by, but in the derived logic, the only inconsistent sets have inconsistent unit subsets, or what we called $X$-absurd formulas. Having denial doesn't imply having absurdities. So the derived logic will have denial only if the underlying logic has absurd formulas, but in no case will the derived logic have non-trivial denial.

And since $\beta$ denies $\alpha$ in the derived logic if and only if one or both of the two are absurd in the underlying logic, the principle [Den] must hold of the derived relation, but it is much less interesting there than it is in the underlying logic.

So, for the derived relation, we would seem to be on solid ground when we require [R], [Cut], and the restricted version of monotonicity. Those we might well regard as the hallmarks of inference, or at least of *derived* inference. And let us not forget that the derived relation agrees exactly with the underlying relation $X$ on the consequences of the $X$-consistent sets. So for this reason alone, we ought to admit the forcing relation into the fold.

Perhaps we should put it this way: Anybody who thinks that $X$ is fine and dandy except for its failure to be properly sensitive to the varieties of inconsistent sets, *must* think that $X$-level forcing is an adequate account of inference. This is because when premise sets are $X$-consistent, $X$-level forcing just *is* $X$. And while it surely isn't $X$ for (some) $X$-inconsistent sets, in those cases $X$ isn't an inference relation. $X$ has abdicated, throwing up its hands and retiring from the inferential struggle, offering the hopeful reasoner nothing beyond a contemptuous 'Whatever!'

## 6.7 Forcing in Comparison with Other Level-Preserving Relations

Finally, we consider the place of the $X$-level forcing relation compared with other possible relations which preserve $X$-level. We cannot claim uniqueness here, for there may be plenty of relations, even inference relations, which preserve $X$-level. What we can claim, however, is inclusiveness, in a sense to be made precise.

That precision will require another property[13] of the underlying logic $X$.

---

**Definition 7.** *A logic $X$ will be said to be* productival *if and only if for every finite set $\Gamma$ there is some formula $\pi$ such that*

$\pi \vdash_X \gamma$ *for every $\gamma \in \Gamma$, and*

$\Gamma \vdash_X \pi$.

---

[13] If we regard deductive systems as categories, then to call a logic productival is simply to say that the category (logic) $X$ has products. The first condition amounts to the assertion of canonical projections while the second amounts to the universal mapping property of products.

Evidently being productival is another of those properties more honoured at the level of underlying logics. If a productival logic $X$ has denial, then $X$-level forcing will certainly not be productival. But of course at the underlying level, products are useful. For instance:

**Theorem 3.** *If $X$ is productival then for any pair $\Gamma, \alpha$ with $\Gamma$ a finite set of formulas and $\alpha$ a formula, if $Y$ preserves $X$-level and admits level-preserving monotonicity, then $\Gamma \vdash_Y \alpha \implies \Gamma \lceil \Vdash_X \alpha$.*

*Proof.* We shall content ourselves with a sketch only – a fuller treatment can be found in 'Level Compactness' by Payette and d'Entremont (2006). Assume for indirect proof that $\Gamma \vdash_Y \alpha$ and that $\Gamma$ fails to X-level force $\alpha$. From the latter we know that $\Gamma$ has finite level, say $k$, and that there is a logical cover of $\Gamma$ of width $k$ such that none of the $k$ cells $X$-proves $\alpha$. Where $\beta$ (non-trivially) denies $\alpha$ add $\beta$ to each cell and then form each of the $k$ products of the cells. The set of these products must have $X$-level $k$ but the $Y$ closure of the set must have $X$-level $k + 1$. So $Y$ fails to preserve $X$-level, contrary to hypothesis.     □

The restriction to finite premise sets will chafe us only until we see its removal in the more general result referenced above.

So while there may be many inference relations which preserve $X$-level, $X$-level forcing is the largest of them.

# Seven

# Preserving Logical Structure

GILLMAN PAYETTE

**Abstract**

In this paper Gillman Payette looks at various structural properties of the underlying logic $X$, and ascertains if these properties will hold of the forcing relation based on $X$. The structural properties are those that do not deal with particular connectives directly. These properties include the structural rules of inference, compactness, and compositionality among others. The presentation of the logic $X$ is carried out in the style of algebraic logic; thus, a description of the resulting 'forcing algebras' is given. The paper concludes with a discussion of first-order classical forcing as a particular instance of these properties.

## 7.1   Introduction

Faced with the possibility of logical pluralism, if not the reality of it, one should follow a methodology of research which is sensitive to the plurality of logics. What has not been dealt with so sensitively is the question of how best to deal with inconsistent sets if we don't want to trivialize inference in every one of these cases.

In classical and intuitionistic logic the sets $\{P \wedge \neg P\}$ and $\{P, \neg P\}$ have the same deductive closure: Everything! In Latin the rule of inference is phrased as *ex falso quodlibet*, which may be translated as 'from

105

the false whatever.' This is the notion of inconsistency first presented by Post and used throughout this volume and elsewhere. For sets of formulas this general definition of inconsistency has it that a set is inconsistent just when everything follows from it.[1] It should not escape our keen attention that the definition is mute on the subject of falsity in general, and that there is likewise no mention in particular of the negation connective.

The paraconsistent 3-valued logic of Priest, the logic of paradox (LP), uses the same language as classical logic, and has all of the same theorems.[2] Thus, it has $(P \wedge \neg P) \supset Q$ as a theorem so, in a sense, it rings true that from the necessarily false, that is, the absurd, everything follows in LP. However, the two sets above do not have trivial closures in LP. So, this logic can, in its way, deal with inconsistency. However, falsity and truth apply to sentences. Only by type raising do they apply to sets. What has happened, historically speaking, is a running together of absurdity, inconsistency, and falsity. LP still runs together absurdity and inconsistency; it merely renders the two inert.

Although the sets above have the same closure in classical logic (and LP respectively) there is an obvious difference in the composition of the two: one contains what is often taken to be an absurd formula and the other does not. One might ask, 'Is there a logic that can distinguish between these two kinds of set?' But this question may be wrongheaded. Inconsistency, as well as consistency, is a relative notion; it is relative to a particular logic. Therefore, when a logic like LP says that $\{P, \neg P\}$ does not explode, it says that this set is not LP-inconsistent. Lacking another notion of inconsistency, we see that some paraconsistent logics merely regard what are inconsistent sets in other logics as consistent.

This shifts the ground by proposing what was called in chapter 2 a *replacement* of the original theory (logic), but it leaves the originating problem untouched. Think of it this way: Axiomatic set theory does not fix naive set theory – the latter remains paradoxical. Neither does LP fix the classical account of inconsistency – we are still unable, classically, to distinguish inferentially between classically inconsistent sets which

---

[1] Such sets are often said to *explode* (inferentially).
[2] See Avron (1994).

contain an absurd formula and those which do not.

In opting for a replacement strategy, what happens is that the rules of the game have changed to solve the problem. Of course this may be entirely respectable – it may even be the only way to proceed. We change the rules all of the time. But when the rules have changed in logic, it seems that the meanings of the connectives involved change as well. And that may be a problem.

Consider a set that we regard as consistent. In that case the logic does not permit us to treat that set as classically consistent. We must continue according to the rules unless we are constantly changing the meanings of the connectives to suit our desires. But that seems wrong.

A different solution is possible. There are many logics which suffer under the iron yoke of *ex falso*. Thus, it would make sense to develop – rather than a new logic to deal with the classical account of inconsistency – a method of determining, for a whole class of logics which have this problem, a notion of *derived* consequence that enables the distinction we want without having to construct a whole new logic in each case. We seek a method which we can apply to a logic $X$ described quite generally so long as we can represent $X$'s notion of inconsistency as the explosive Postian kind. This may be considered a method of paraconsistentizing the logic.[3] The notion of forcing à la Schotch and Jennings (1989), which is the subject of this volume, is what shall be used, but massaged into the framework of algebraic logic.

Just what constitutes a good way of constructing such a derived inference relation is obviously crucial. The Quinean idea of minimal mutilation is what we take to be an obvious criterion for 'goodness.' The more of a logic that can be kept the better. What is of interest here is how the 'structural properties' of an underlying logic $X$ may be transferred to the forcing relation $\lceil \Vdash_X$. We call properties 'structural' when they don't have a direct relation to particular connectives. These are properties like compactness, preservation of consequence by substitutions, and the structural rules of inference. The compositionality of a logic, that is, the meaning of the whole is given by the meaning of the

---

[3]This term was used first by Alexandre Costa-Leite in his dissertation (2007). However, the method that appears here is different from his approach.

parts, is also a structural property since it does not deal with *particular* connectives. I will also make a few comments on how the existence of certain kinds of formulas, like denials,[4] may affect these structural properties.

The present study makes up part of the justification of the forcing relation as an acceptable notion of paraconsistent consequence. The point is to see that much of the general structure of a logic $X$ can be preserved by the forcing relation. The other part involves the idea of level preservation which is taken up in detail in chapter 6 of this volume. We also show where the forcing relation sits amongst other similar relations on $X$. The final discussion concerns first-order classical logic as an instance of many of the properties mentioned above.

## 7.2   Definitions

This study is diverse and long. Therefore I will present many definitions to give some background to what follows. In what follows there is a minor departure from previous work; this will be pointed out where necessary. The reason for the departure is the focus on the semantic presentation of a logic, rather than the syntactic. We will begin with the definition of a logic.

### Logics

---

**Definition 1.** *A logic $X$ is given by a tuple $\langle \mathbb{S}_X, \vdash_X, M_X, \models_X \rangle$ such that*

1. *$\mathbb{S}_X$ is the set of formulas.*

2. *$\vdash_X$ is the provability relation, thus the proof-theoretic consequence. This may not exist for some logics.*

3. *$M_X$ is the class of models, whatever it may be. Models of a logic will be denoted by $\mathcal{M}, \mathcal{R}$.*

---

[4]In the sense of that term introduced in chapter 6 of this volume.

> 4. $\models_X$ *is the satisfaction relation between models and formulas.*

Note that $\models$ is not semantic consequence. Semantic consequence, or entailment, is defined in the usual way using $\models$, that is, $\Gamma \models \alpha$ iff for all $\mathcal{M} \in M$, $\mathcal{M} \models \Gamma \implies \mathcal{M} \models \alpha$. I will follow the convention and use the $\models$ symbol for both relations. Also, when $\mathcal{M} \models \varphi$ for every $\mathcal{M} \in M$, we write $\models \varphi$ which means $\varphi$ is a truth or theorem of the logic. Relative to each logic there is a consistency predicate $\mathrm{CON}_X$ which holds of $\Gamma$ when there is at least one model of $\Gamma$.

An important part of the algebraic presentation of logic is the meaning function $mng$. The algebras of a logic are the focus of study in algebraic logic, and these algebras depend on the meaning functions. I will present a candidate for the meaning function of the derived forcing relation, and show some properties which it inherits from the meaning function for the original logic. So in what follows a logic is given with a meaning function right from the start.

> **Definition 2.** *A meaning function for a logic $X$ is a map*
> $mng : M_X \times \mathbb{S}_X \to H$ *where $H$ is some class. A function $mng$ is*
> *a meaning function for a logic $X$ – subscripts omitted – just when*
> $(\forall \mathcal{M} \in M \psi, \varphi \in \mathbb{S})[mng(\mathcal{M}, \psi) = mng(\mathcal{M}, \varphi) \implies \mathcal{M} \models$
> $\varphi \iff \mathcal{M} \models \psi]$.

There could be many meaning functions for a logic, but there are canonical examples. The composition of the set $H$ is left undefined in general; it will vary from logic to logic as the composition of $M$ does. In the case of first-order logics the meaning of a formula, relative to a model, is given as the set of variable assignments that satisfy that formula in that model. For the usual 2-valued propositional logic the models are just the truth-value assignments and the meaning functions are their extensions to all of the formulas.

A meaning function will only be of use if its image of the formulas forms an algebra. An algebra is a set $A$ (often called the underlying set of the algebra) along with a set of functions from $A^n$ to $A$ for various natural numbers $n$ (including zero).[5] A logic is said to 'have connectives' when for any $n$-tuple of formulas $\psi_1, ..., \psi_n$ and any $n$-ary connective $\triangle$ in the set Cn of connectives of the language of $X$, the formula $\triangle(\psi_1, ..., \psi_n)$ is also part of the language. The set of formulas can then be seen as an algebra called the 'formula algebra,' denoted $\mathring{A}_X$. Recursively generated sets of formulas will produce formula algebras. In that case, the underlying set is just the set of all formulas generated, and the functions are the connectives.

A function (or map) $h : \langle A, *_A \rangle \longrightarrow \langle B, *_B \rangle$ is a homomorphism when $h(a *_A b) = h(a) *_B h(b)$, and if $h : A \longrightarrow A$, then $h$ is an endomorphism. Homomorphisms are structure-preserving maps. When the meaning function of a logic is a homomorphism for each model, the logic is called compositional. We can give a nice mathematical definition of compositionality as follows. The subscripts for the logic $X$ are omitted where confusion is unlikely.

---

**Definition 3.** *A logic $X$ is compositional just when the meaning of compound formulas depend on the meanings of the component formulas. More precisely, let $\psi_1, ..., \psi_n$ and $\varphi_1, ..., \varphi_n$ be $n$-tuples of formulas from $\mathbb{S}$, and $\triangle$ an $n$-ary connective in the language of $X$ then given a model $\mathcal{M} \in M$, if for each $1 \leq i \leq n$ $mng_\mathcal{M}(\psi_i) = mng_\mathcal{M}(\varphi_i)$, then*

$$mng_\mathcal{M}(\triangle(\varphi_1, ..., \varphi_n)) = mng_\mathcal{M}(\triangle(\psi_1, ..., \psi_n))$$

---

When a logic's meaning function is a homomorphism for each model, we can generate a meaning algebra for a logic. That is what it means for the image of a meaning function to form an algebra.

There are two interesting sets that deserve mention.

---

[5]This is the $n$-ary cartesian product of $A$.

**Definition 4.** *Let $K \subseteq M$ and $\Sigma \subseteq \mathbb{S}$.*

1. *The 'theory of $K$' is $Th(K) = \{\psi \in \mathbb{S} : \mathcal{M} \models \psi \ \forall \mathcal{M} \in K\}$, i.e., the set of formulas modelled by every model in $K$.*

2. *The 'models of $\Sigma$' is the class $Mod(\Sigma) = \{\mathcal{M} \in M : \mathcal{M} \models \psi \ \forall \psi \in \Sigma\}$, which is the class of models which model all the formulas in $\Sigma$.*

The aim of this essay is to discuss the properties which carry over to the forcing relation. In furtherance of this aim we introduce some important properties of consequence relations. The substitution property comes in two flavours, namely, weak and strong. A substitution $s$ is a morphism from the set of atomic formulas to the set of all formulas which can be extended uniquely to a homomorphic endomorphism of the formula algebra. So a substitution $s$ on a propositional language maps each atom to a formula which is not necessarily atomic. Then one can reconstruct formulas with the substituted atoms.

**Definition 5.** *The substitution properties for a logic $X$ are,*

1. *(Weak) If $\models \psi$ then $\models \psi(P/s(P))$ where $\psi(P/s(P))$ is the uniform substitution of $s(P)$ for $P$ in $\psi$, with $P$ an atom and $s$ a substitution.*

2. *(Strong) If $\Gamma \models \psi$, then $\Gamma^s \models \psi^s$ where $\Gamma^s$ is $\{\varphi^s : \varphi \in \Gamma\}$ and $\varphi^s$ is $\varphi(P/s(P))$ for each atom mentioned in $\varphi$.*

A logic which obeys the substitution properties preserves consequences under uniform substitutions of the atoms in the formulas. The strong property implies the weak property by letting $\Gamma = \varnothing$. The weak property asserts that theorem-hood or truth-hood is preserved by uniform substitutions.

There are logics that have what are called 'structural rules' of inference. Such logics are not called 'structural logics'; however, every structural logic must have these rules. A common presentation of the structural rules goes like this (I omit the subscripts on the $\vdash$):

[R] for reflexivity; if $\psi \in \Gamma$ then $\Gamma \vdash \psi$,

[M] for monotonicity; if $\Gamma \vdash \psi$, and $\Gamma \subseteq \Delta$ then $\Delta \vdash \psi$ and

[Cut-1]; if $\Gamma \vdash \psi$ and $\Gamma, \psi \vdash \varphi$ then $\Gamma \vdash \varphi$.

The first two rules are fine; however, there are many formulations of [Cut]. The formulation we shall use is the following:

[Cut]: Let $\Gamma \vdash \delta$ for all $\delta \in \Delta' \subseteq \Delta$ and $\Delta \vdash \psi$ then $\Gamma, \Delta - \Delta' \vdash \psi$. Where $\Delta - \Delta'$ is the set of members of $\Delta$ not in $\Delta'$.

This version of the rule is slightly more general than the one above. It is also more general than the following version:

[Cut-2]$\Gamma \vdash \delta$ for all $\delta \in \Delta$ and $\Delta \vdash \alpha$ then $\Gamma \vdash \alpha$.

But the previous version is a bit too strong for our purposes in this paper; thus we use [Cut]. There is a very interesting fact to be noticed about the last formulation of the rule.

**Proposition 1.** [R] *and* [Cut-2] *imply* [M].

Thus, only in certain situations will the three rules really 'come apart'; forcing is, as will be shown, one of those situations.

---

**Definition 6.** *A logic X is structural if and only if it obeys both the strong substitution property above and the structural rules of inference (with [Cut-2] in place of [Cut]).*

---

## Covers, Models, and Levels

Essential to forcing are the notions of *cover* and *level*.

A cover $\mathbb{C}$ in $X$, or an $X$-cover, is a function $\mathbb{C} : \xi + 1 \twoheadrightarrow K \subseteq \mathcal{P}(\mathbb{S})$, where $K$ is a set of sets of formulas. Note that the function is surjective. We can think of the covers as tuples (possibly infinite) of sets of formulas indexed by some ordinal $\xi + 1$:

$$\mathbb{C} = \langle \Delta_i : i \in \xi + 1 \ \& \ \Delta_0 = \varnothing \rangle$$

such that for each $i \in \xi + 1$, $\mathrm{CON}_X(\Delta_i)$ where $\mathrm{CON}_X$ is the consistency predicate for $X$. The $\xi$ from the index ordinal of $\mathbb{C}$ is referred to as the *width* of the cover $\mathbb{C}$ and denoted $w(\mathbb{C})$. Each $\Delta_i$ in the image of $\mathbb{C}$, indicated by a pardonable abuse of notation as '$\Delta_i \in \mathbb{C}$', is called a cell. The collection of $X$-covers will be referred to as $M^*$. This notion of cover departs from the definitions in the literature, for example, Schotch and Jennings (1989), Brown and Schotch (1999), and the present volume, but it will help avoid technical problems later. Since a cover is defined as an ordered tuple of length less than or equal to $\omega$,[6] the condition for two covers $\mathbb{C}, \mathbb{C}^*$ to be equal is $w(\mathbb{C}) = w(\mathbb{C}^*) = \xi$ and $\forall i \leq \xi \ \Delta_i = \Delta_i^*$, where $\Delta_i \in \mathbb{C}$ and $\Delta_i^* \in \mathbb{C}^*$. So covers may have repetitions of cells, and two covers with different orderings of the same sets are *not* equal.

---

**Definition 7.** $\mathbb{C} : \xi + 1 \twoheadrightarrow K \subseteq \mathcal{P}(\mathbb{S})$ *is a cover of* $\Gamma$, *that is,* $\mathbb{C} \vDash^* \Gamma$), *when*

1. $\mathbb{C}(0) = \Delta_0 = \varnothing$,

2. $\mathrm{CON}_X(\mathbb{C}(i) = \Delta_i)$, $\forall i \in \xi + 1$,

3. *For each* $\gamma \in \Gamma$ *there is a* $i \in \xi + 1$ *such that* $\mathbb{C}(i) = \Delta_i \vdash \gamma$, *and*

4. *If the constant symbol* $a$ *or free variable* $x$ *of the language of* $X$ *is mentioned in* $\Delta_i$ *for some* $i \in \xi + 1$, *then it is mentioned in* $\Gamma$.

---

[6]$\omega$ is the first countable ordinal, or the order type of the natural numbers.

> 5. $\xi$ is referred to as the width of the cover, $w(\mathbb{C})$.

For a symbol $t$ to be mentioned in a set means that for some formula in the set $t$ appears in that formula.

It is easy enough to see that a cover covers a single formula $\gamma$ when there is a cell in the cover that entails that formula. In such case it is written $\mathbb{C} \models^* \gamma$. The condition on terms and constant symbols will be of use when we discuss first order logic. As the definition stands it is only a small divergence from the one found in earlier literature.

This notion of cover can be interpreted as something like a model; it is a kind of model for certain inconsistent sets relative to the logic $X$, though not all $X$-inconsistent sets will have these kinds of models. To see that the $\mathbb{C}$'s function in this way, suppose $\mathbb{C} \models^* \psi$. Thus, there is some cell $\Delta_i$ in $\mathbb{C}$ that $X$-entails $\psi$, and $\mathrm{CON}_X(\Delta_i)$ by the definition of cover. We call a formula absurd when its unit set is inconsistent. An absurd formula does not have any models, nor does it have any covers. Consider an absurdity $\alpha$. If $\alpha$ had a cover, then there would be a $\mathbb{C}$ and $\Delta_i \in \mathbb{C}$ such that $\Delta_i \models \alpha$, but that would require that $\overline{\mathrm{CON}_X}(\Delta_i)$, because $X$ has [Cut], which contradicts the second condition in the definition cover. Thus, sets like $\{\alpha\}$ have no covers and the converse of this also holds. Thus it can be shown that:

**Proposition 2.** $\Gamma$ does not have a cover iff $\Gamma$ contains an absurdity.

Note that it must be assumed that the logic $X$ is not trivial, that is, the $X$-closure of the empty set is not everything. A related fact is that the minimal cover for a set is a cover just when there are covers for a set. The minimal cover of $\Gamma$ is $\mathbb{C}_\Gamma^m = \langle \varnothing, \{\gamma\} : \gamma \in \Gamma \rangle$. $\mathbb{C}_\Gamma^m$ is minimal in two senses. The cover $\mathbb{C}_\Gamma^m$ is the finest partition one can make of the set $\Gamma$; it is 'contained' in any other cover of the set. It is contained in the sense that, for any cover $\mathbb{C}$ of a set $\Gamma$, if $\mathbb{C}_\Gamma^m \models^* \alpha$ then $\mathbb{C} \models^* \alpha$. This cover will be of use when discussing infinite levels.

A level function relative to $X$, $\ell_X$, is defined using the notion of cover. The codomain, or range, of the level function will depend on the size of $\mathbb{S}$. We restrict the cardinality of $\mathbb{S}$ to the countable cardinal for this essay; thus, $|\mathbb{S}| = \omega$.

---

**Definition 8.** *The $X$-level (that is, level relative to the logic $X$) of the set $\Gamma$ of formulas of the underlying language of $X$, indicated by $\ell_X(\Gamma)$, is defined as follows:*

$$\ell_X(\Gamma) = \begin{cases} \min_{w(\mathbb{C})} [\mathrm{COV}_X(\mathbb{C}, \Gamma)] & \textit{if this limit exists} \\ \infty & \textit{otherwise} \end{cases}$$

---

Thus, the level of a set is determined by the minimum width of the collection of covers of a set $\Gamma$. This is of course a function, and under the assumptions made in this paper its domain is $\omega \cup \{\omega\} \cup \{\infty\}$. Level actually induces a kind of measure on the set $\Gamma$. Level measures how inconsistent a set is. One must use more classically consistent sets to cover $\{P \wedge Q, \neg P \wedge R, \neg R \wedge \neg Q\}$ than to cover $\{P, \neg P, Q, R\}$. And one cannot cover $\{P \wedge \neg P\}$; it has level $\infty$! This is how we can finally see the difference between inconsistency and absurdity. An inconsistent set may have a level, but absurdity does not.

Also note that if there are theorems, then any set of theorems has level 0. Since the cover $\mathbb{C} = \langle \varnothing \rangle$ is a cover for a set of theorems, $w(\mathbb{C}) = 0$ because $\mathbb{C}$ is indexed over the ordinal $1=0+1=\xi + 1$. With level we can define the forcing inference relation on $\mathcal{P}(\mathbb{S}) \times \mathbb{S}$.

---

**Definition 9.** [Forcing] $\Gamma \llbracket \Vdash_X \psi \iff (\forall \mathbb{C})[(\mathbb{C} \vDash^*$
$\Gamma \,\&\, w(\mathbb{C}) = \ell_X(\Gamma)) \implies \mathbb{C} \vDash^* \psi]$.

---

This is read '$\Gamma$ level forces $\psi$, relative to $X$.'[7] A set will force a conclusion, $\psi$, just when every cover of $\Gamma$ of width 'level of $\Gamma$' is a cover of $\psi$. This relation in some cases will collapse into precisely

---

[7]This relation is slightly different from the one contained elsewhere. It is based on the entailment relation and not the proof relation. Why this is so will become apparent. The $\llbracket \Vdash$ relation will be the same when the logic in question is complete.

what follows from the unit sets, but not always, and, considering the size of $\mathcal{P}(\mathbb{S})$, one may say only half of the time.

What is needed to fill out the algebraic approach to forcing is a meaning function. However, meaning functions are semantic entities; they take models as one input and formulas as the other and spit out something. If the derived meaning function for forcing is to depend on the underlying logic it will, ideally, depend on the models of the underlying logic. The models for the forcing relation are, as mentioned above, covers. Thus, what must be constructed are covers, not out of sets, but, rather, out of models. This can be accomplished by the following construction.

---

**Definition 10.** *A semantic cover $\mathfrak{F}$ of a set $\Gamma$, written $\mathfrak{F} \models^* \Gamma$, is a surjection $\mathfrak{F} : \xi \twoheadrightarrow K \subseteq M$ (M is the class of models). In essence, a cover is a tuple of models $\langle \mathcal{M}_i : i \in \xi \rangle$, $\xi$ an ordinal, such that for any $\gamma \in \Gamma$ there is an $\mathcal{M}_i = \mathfrak{F}(i)$ such that $\mathcal{M}_i \models \gamma$.*

---

Again, the $\xi$ in the definition above will be referred to as the width of the cover, and covering a single formula is to cover its unit set. The level of a set of formulas according to semantic covers is defined thus:

$$\ell^X(\Gamma) = \begin{cases} 0 \text{ if } \Gamma \subseteq \mathbb{C}_X(\varnothing) \\ \min_{w(\mathfrak{F})} \{\mathfrak{F} \models^* \Gamma\} & \text{if this limit exists} \\ \infty \quad \text{otherwise} \end{cases}$$

Of course a forcing relation can then be defined relative to this notion of cover in an analogous way.

---

**Definition 11.** $\Gamma \lceil \models \alpha$ *if and only if*
$$\begin{cases} \models \alpha, \text{if } \ell^X(\Gamma) = 0, \text{or} \\ \forall \mathfrak{F}, \mathfrak{F} \models^* \Gamma \text{ such that } w(\mathfrak{F}) = \ell^X(\Gamma), \mathfrak{F} \models^* \alpha. \end{cases}$$

---

But, do these two notions of cover give rise to the same forcing relation, extensionally speaking? The short answer is yes.

**Lemma 1.** *If $\mathbb{C}$ is a (syntactic) cover of $\Gamma$ then there is a semantic cover of $\Gamma$ of the same width, and vice versa.*

*Proof.* Suppose that $\mathbb{C} \vDash^* \Gamma$, and $w(\mathbb{C}) = \xi$. Then for any $\gamma \in \Gamma$ there is $\Delta_i \in \mathbb{C}$ such that $\Delta_i \vDash \gamma$. Thus if $\mathcal{M} \in Mod(\Delta_i)$ then $\mathcal{M} \vDash \gamma$. Each $Mod(\Delta_i) \neq \varnothing$ by definition of cover, so let $\mathfrak{F}_{\mathbb{C}} : \xi \twoheadrightarrow K$ where $\mathfrak{F}_{\mathbb{C}}(j) = \mathcal{M}_i$, $j \in \xi$ for some $\mathcal{M}_i \in Mod(\Delta_i)$ $i \neq 0$. So the width of $\mathfrak{F}$ is that of $\mathbb{C}$, and every member of $\Gamma$ is modelled by some member of $\mathfrak{F}$. The opposite direction follows by making up $\mathbb{C}_{\mathfrak{F}}$ from $\varnothing$ and $\Delta_i = Th(\mathcal{M}_i)$, for $\mathcal{M}_i \in \mathfrak{F}$. $\qquad\square$

And what about the different types of level?

**Lemma 2.** *For all $\Gamma \subseteq \mathbb{S}$, $\ell_X(\Gamma) = \ell^X(\Gamma)$.*

*Proof.* Suppose that $\ell_X(\Gamma) = 0$. Obviously $\ell^X(\Gamma) = 0$, and vice versa. If $\ell_X(\Gamma) = \xi$, then let $\mathbb{C} \vDash^* \Gamma$ and $w(\mathbb{C}) = \xi$. If the levels were different, then we could generate a semantic cover, or regular cover, with the $Mod$ and $Th$ operators respectively to derive a contradiction. If $\ell_X(\Gamma) = \infty$ then there are no covers of $\Gamma$ of either kind, because $\Gamma$ must contain an absurdity. This is the case with either definition of cover. $\qquad\square$

Then we can prove the result that we want.

**Theorem 1.** *For any $\Gamma$ and $\alpha$, $\Gamma \lceil \Vdash \alpha \iff \Gamma \lceil \vDash \alpha$.*

*Proof.* Suppose $\Gamma \lceil \nVdash \alpha$. Then suppose $\mathbb{C} \nvDash^* \alpha$. Construct a semantic cover out of $\mathbb{C}$ as in lemma 1. By lemma 2 this cover has the same width, which is the $\ell^X(\Gamma)$, as $\mathbb{C}$ and it is a semantic cover of $\Gamma$. So $\Gamma \lceil \vDash \alpha$. For the other direction, the dual argument as in lemma 1 is used and the definition of the $Th$ operator. $\qquad\square$

With the two notions of cover and forcing amounting to the same thing from two different directions I will use whichever notion is appropriate for the context.

## 7.3 Substitutions

Recall definition 5. There are two versions of a logic being syntactically substitutional. One is strong, the other weak. Given that $X$ is structural, the forcing relation is weakly substitutional (proof omitted), and only obeys a qualified version of the strong substitutional property.[8]

Recall that the logics considered are ones that obey the three structural rules mentioned above. In what follows I will use the syntactic version of forcing since I am discussing a syntactic notion of substitution.

---

**Definition 12.** *A 'partition cover' of* $\Gamma$ *is a cover* $\mathfrak{C}$ *such that* $w(\mathfrak{C}) \geq \xi = \ell_X(\Gamma)$ *and* $\bigcup_{i \in w(\mathfrak{C})} \mathfrak{C}(i) = \Gamma$. *Further, if* $\Delta_i$ *and* $\Delta_k$ $(i, k \leq w(\mathfrak{C}))$ *are distinct members of* $\mathfrak{C}$ *then* $\Delta_i \cap \Delta_k = \varnothing$.

---

This definition says that the image of $\mathfrak{C}$ is a partition of the set $\Gamma$. It is the kind of partition in which each cell is a consistent set relative to $X$. Such a thing is not unique in general, but there is always the possibility of having such a partition if the set's level is not $\infty$.

**Lemma 3.** *Partition Cover Lemma. If* $\ell(\Gamma) = \xi \in \omega$, *then, given a cover* $\mathfrak{C}$ *of* $\Gamma$, *there is a partition cover* $\mathfrak{C}'$ *which one can construct from* $\mathfrak{C}$.

*Proof.* Assume that $\ell(\Gamma) = \xi$. Then let $\mathfrak{C}$ be a cover whose width is $\xi$. We shall construct the partition cover out of $\mathfrak{C}$. First, let $\Delta_i' = \mathfrak{C}_X(\Delta_i) \cap \Gamma$ for all $1 \leq i \leq \xi$. Note that $i$ does not start at 0. Once the construction has finished, we add $\varnothing$ to the rest of the sets to get the $\mathfrak{C}'$ wanted. Let $\Delta_{ij} = \Delta_i' \cap \Delta_j'$ where $i \neq j$. Further, define

$$\Delta_k^* = \bigcup_{m=1}^{k-1} (\Delta_k' - (\Delta_k' \cap \Delta_m'))$$

---

[8]An interesting side note to this point is that forcing will also have the interpolation property if the underlying logic does.

for $k \leq \xi$. Since $\mathfrak{C}$ is well ordered by its width ordinal one can speak of the 'first $\Delta_i$ such that ...' In a sense the $\Delta^*$'s 'check' to see if they are disjoint with all of the sets 'before' them.

Claim: These $\Delta_k^*$'s are all disjoint, and $\Gamma = \bigcup_{k \leq \xi} \Delta_k^*$. Suppose $i \neq j$, and $\psi \in \Delta_i^* \cap \Delta_j^*$. Assume that $i < j$. Since $\psi \in \Delta_i^*$, it must be that $\psi \notin \Delta_k'$ for all $k < i$, but $\psi \in \Delta_i'$. So, $\psi \in \Delta_i' \cap \Delta_j'$. However, by the construction of $\Delta_j^*$ it is impossible that $\psi \in \Delta_i^*$ since $i < j$. By parity of reasoning assuming $j < i$ also leads to a contradiction. Thus, $\psi \notin \Delta_i^* \cap \Delta_j^*$.

It is clear that $\bigcup_{k \leq \xi} \Delta_k^* \subseteq \Gamma$ so assume that $\psi \in \Gamma$. Then for some $\Delta_i \in \mathfrak{C}$, $\psi \in \mathfrak{C}_X(\Delta_i)$, but that means $\psi \in \Delta_i'$. We may assume that $i$ is the smallest such index, since there must be one. If $\psi \notin \Delta_i^*$, then there would have to be a smaller $j$ such that $\psi \in \Delta_j'$, which is not possible. Thus, $\psi \in \Delta_i^* \subseteq \bigcup_{k \leq \xi} \Delta_k^* \subseteq \Gamma$; therefore, $\Gamma = \bigcup_{k \leq \xi} \Delta_k^*$. Let $\mathfrak{C}'(0) = \varnothing$ and $\mathfrak{C}'(i) = \Delta_i^*$ where $1 \leq i \leq \xi$. Then $\mathfrak{C}^*$ is clearly a partition cover of $\Gamma$. $\qquad\square$

The next lemma allows us to restrict which covers we must consider of the collection of covers of a set $\Gamma$. Notice that although this lemma is proved for the forcing case it will work in the $X^*$ case since in the latter case all covers are considered. Only covers whose width is the level of the set $\Gamma$ are considered in forcing. Thus the obvious extension will suffice for that case.

**Lemma 4.** *For $\ell_X(\Gamma) > 0$, $\Gamma[\Vdash \psi \iff \forall \mathfrak{C}$ a partition cover of $\Gamma$ of width $\ell_X(\Gamma)$, $\mathfrak{C} \vDash^* \psi$.*

*Proof.* ( $\Longrightarrow$ ) If $\Gamma[\Vdash \psi$, then all covers of $\Gamma$ of appropriate width will cover $\psi$. Partitions are covers of $\Gamma$, so they must cover $\psi$.

( $\Longleftarrow$ ) By contrapositive. If $\Gamma[\nVdash \psi$ then there is a cover $\mathfrak{C}$ of $\Gamma$, of width $\ell_X(\Gamma)$, which does not cover $\psi$. Let $\mathfrak{C}^*$ be a partition cover of $\Gamma$ associated with $\mathfrak{C}$ as in the partition cover lemma 3 above. Notice that $\Delta_i^* \subseteq \mathfrak{C}_X(\Delta_i)$ for $\Delta_i \in \mathfrak{C}$. This is because $\Delta_i^* \subseteq \Delta_i'$, and $\Delta_i' = \mathfrak{C}_X(\Delta_i) \cap \Gamma$. Thus, $\mathfrak{C}_X(\Delta_i^*) \subseteq \mathfrak{C}_X(\Delta_i)$ by assumptions on $X$ which transfer to $\mathfrak{C}_X$. So, $\psi \notin \mathfrak{C}_X(\Delta_i)$ for all $\Delta_i \in \mathfrak{C}$, and $\psi \notin \mathfrak{C}_X(\Delta_i^*)$ for each $\Delta_i^* \in \mathfrak{C}^*$. Thus, $\mathfrak{C}^* \nVdash^* \psi$. $\qquad\square$

The case where $\ell_X(\Gamma) = 0$ and $\Gamma$ is non-empty will not have any partition covers of width 0 since the only cover of width 0 is $\langle\varnothing\rangle$. However, this poses no problem because if a set of theorems forces something then that something is also a theorem. But forcing is weakly substitutional.

We can see that strong substitution does not hold for forcing by considering the following counterexample. Let $\Gamma = \{P, \neg Q\}$. Let the substitution $s$ be the function which takes $P \mapsto P$ and $Q \mapsto P$. As we shall see in the next section, forcing is just like the underlying logic $X$ when the sets are consistent; thus, $\Gamma[\Vdash P \wedge \neg Q$. Notice, however, $\Gamma^s = \{P, \neg P\}$ and $s(P \wedge \neg Q) = P \wedge \neg P$. But then $\Gamma^S[\nVdash P \wedge \neg P$ since forcing is level preserving (see theorem 6). Although the underlying logic may be substitutional, the forcing relation is not. However, if we restrict the class of substitutions, we can derive a substitution theorem for substitutions from that class.

**Theorem 2.** *Suppose that $s$ is a substitution from the set of atoms to the set of all formulas such that $s \in \{g \in \mathbb{S}^A : \ell_X(\Gamma^g) = \ell_X(\Gamma)\}$, that is, all of the substitutions which are level-preserving. If $X$ is such that for any pair $\langle\Gamma, \varphi\rangle$ and any substitution $s'$, $\Gamma \vDash \varphi \implies \Gamma^{s'} \vDash \varphi^{s'}$; then $\Gamma[\Vdash \varphi \implies \Gamma^s[\Vdash \varphi^s$.*

*Proof.* By contraposition. Assume that for some level-preserving substitution $s$, $\Gamma^s[\nVdash \psi^s$. $X$ has been assumed to obey the substitution property which is equivalent to the following: if $\Delta^s \nvDash \varphi^s$ then $\Delta \nvDash \varphi$. Let $\mathbb{C}$ be a partition of $\Gamma^s$ such that $\mathbb{C} \nvDash^* \psi$, which exists by definition.

Then for each $\Delta_i \in \mathbb{C}$, $\Delta_i \nvDash \psi^s$. Consider the sets $s^{-1}[\Delta_i]$: the inverse image of the $\Delta_i$'s from $\mathbb{C}$. If $s$ is applied to these sets the $\Delta_i$ is returned, since each member of the inverse image gets mapped to some element of $\Delta_i$, and since $\Delta_i \subset \Gamma^s$, there must be something which was mapped to each element of $\Delta_i$. Thus, $(s^{-1}[\Delta_i])^s = \Delta_i$. Let $\Delta_i^* = s^{-1}[\Delta_i] \cap \Gamma$.

Claim $\Delta_i^* \nvDash \psi$. Suppose that $\Delta_i^* \vDash \psi$. Then, by the assumption that $X$ has the substitution property, $(\Delta_i^*)^s \vDash \psi^s$. But $\Delta_i = (\Delta_i^*)^s$. So $\Delta_i \vDash \psi^s$, but it does not. Thus, $\Delta_i^* \nvDash \psi$. This implies $\mathrm{CON}_X(\Delta_i^*)$ for all $\Delta_i \in \mathbb{C}$.

Claim $\Gamma \subseteq \bigcup \Delta_i^*$. Each element of the $\Delta_i$'s is an image of some element of $\Gamma$, so all of $\Gamma$ is recovered in the inverse images of the $\Delta_i$'s. We don't get more than $\Gamma$ since we restrict the inverse images to $\Gamma$ in the construction of the $\Delta_i^*$'s. Let $\mathbb{C}^*(0) = \varnothing$, and $\mathbb{C}^*(i) = \Delta_i^* : \Delta_i \in \mathbb{C} - \varnothing$. This is clearly a cover of $\Gamma$, and not a cover of $\psi$. But there are only as many $\Delta_i^*$'s as there are $\Delta_i$'s; thus, $\mathbb{C}^*$ has the same width as $\mathbb{C}$. But the width of $\mathbb{C}$ is the level of $\Gamma^s$, that is, it is equal to $\ell_X(\Gamma)$. So $\Gamma \lceil \not\Vdash \psi$, which is what is wanted. □

Thus not all is lost, but there must be some room given for failures to balance out the gains.

## 7.4 Algebraic Concerns

There are two types of algebras which are of particular interest to the algebraic logician. These algebras arise from a logic through the application of the meaning function. The first type of algebra is the meaning algebra, and the second is the Lindenbaum-Tarski algebra. The meaning algebra is derived directly from the meanings of the formulas of the logic. Lindenbaum-Tarski algebras are made up of equivalence classes of formulas. Forcing has many of the necessary properties that make it susceptible to algebraic methods, but it fails in a crucial place. To begin this study some definitions are needed.

---

**Definition 13.** *[Algebra, subuniverse] An algebra* $\mathbf{A} = \langle A, \Omega_A \rangle$ *is a set $A$ with a collection of (finitary) operators*
$\Omega_A = \{ f_{i,k} : i \in \xi, k \in \zeta \}$. *The $\Omega$ is referred to as the 'type' of the algebra and $A$ as the 'universe' or 'carrier' of the algebra.*
*A subuniverse $\mathbf{B}$ of an algebra $\mathbf{A}$ is a subset $B$ of $A$ such that $B$ is closed under the operations in $\Omega_A$.*

---

The important definitions for algebraic logic are as follows:

---

**Definition 14.** *A Lindenbaum-Tarski (LT) algebra is given with respect to a class of models K. The LT-algebras are all the algebras isomorphic to a quotient algebra of the formula algebra $\mathring{A}_X$ modulo the equivalence relation $\sim_K$ for some class of models K. $\sim_K$ is given by the following: $\psi \sim_K \varphi$ iff $mng_{\mathcal{M}}(\psi) = mng_{\mathcal{M}}(\varphi)$ for all $\mathcal{M} \in K$.*

---

The class of LT-algebras is denoted $Alg_{LT}(L)$.[9]

---

**Definition 15.** *The meaning algebra relative to a model $\mathcal{M}$ is denoted $mng(\mathcal{M})$. It is the set $\{mng_{\mathcal{M}}(\varphi) : \varphi \in \mathbb{S}\}$. The type of $mng(\mathcal{M})$ is the interpretation of the connectives of the language in the models of $X$. The class of meaning algebras for L is denoted as $Alg_m(L)$.*

---

With these definitions in place it is time to construct meaning functions for forcing.

### Meaning Functions and $X^*$

Meaning functions have less to do with the consequence relation and more with the relation between the class of models and formulas. For the rest of this section we will assume that $M$ is a set and not a proper class. The idea now is to, somehow, define a meaning function for $X^*$ from the meaning function for the logic $X$. The one presented may not be the only one available, but it does do enough of the work we would want it to. In this section I will use the semantic version of cover.

Recall that the 'models' of $X^*$ are (semantic) covers so the meaning function will have to be a function which takes cover-formula pairs to some set. Let $\mathfrak{F} : \xi \twoheadrightarrow K = \{\mathcal{M}_i : i \in \xi\}$ and $\varphi \in \mathbb{S}$. Then,

$$mng^*_{\mathfrak{F}}(\varphi) = \prod_{i \in \xi} \{mng_{\mathfrak{F}(i)}(\varphi)\}$$

---

[9]The class of LT-algebras does not have to be made up of merely the quotient algebras, but also includes all the algebras isomorphic to such quotient algebras.

So for two instances of $mng^*_{\mathfrak{F}}$ to be equal, at $\psi$ and $\varphi$ say, means that for each $\mathcal{M}_i \in \mathfrak{F}$, $mng_{\mathcal{M}_i}(\varphi) = mng_{\mathcal{M}_i}(\psi)$.

Before proceeding it must be proved that this $mng^*$ is a meaning function. The reader should recall definition 2.

**Theorem 3.** *$mng^*$ is a meaning function for $X^*$. That is, for $\psi, \varphi \in \mathbb{S}$ and any cover $\mathfrak{F}$, if $mng^*_{\mathfrak{F}}(\psi) = mng^*_{\mathfrak{F}}(\varphi)$, then*
$$\mathfrak{F} \vDash^* \psi \iff \mathfrak{F} \vDash^* \varphi.$$

*Proof.* Let $mng^*_{\mathfrak{F}}(\psi) = mng^*_{\mathfrak{F}}(\varphi)$, for some $\psi, \varphi$, and $\mathfrak{F}$. Suppose $\mathfrak{F} \vDash^* \varphi$. By definition there is some $\mathcal{M}_i \in \mathfrak{F}$ such that $\mathcal{M}_i \vDash \varphi$. By hypothesis, $mng_{\mathcal{M}_i}(\psi) = mng_{\mathcal{M}_i}(\varphi)$. Since $mng$ is a meaning function for $X$, $\mathcal{M}_j \vDash \psi \iff \mathcal{M}_j \vDash \varphi$ for all $\mathcal{M}_j \in \mathfrak{F}$, that is, it does so for $\mathcal{M}_i$. Thus, $\mathfrak{F} \vDash^* \psi$. And similarly from the assumption that $\mathfrak{F} \vDash^* \psi$. $\square$

Thus $mng^*$ is a meaning function. What can be said about compositionality?

**Theorem 4.** *If a logic $X$ is compositional, then the derived $X^*$ will also be compositional relative to the meaning function $mng^*$.*

*Proof.* Suppose that $X$ is compositional. Then suppose there is an $n$-ary connective $\triangle$, and some $n$-tuples of formulas as in definition 3 such that given a cover $\mathfrak{F} \in M^*$, for each $1 \le i \le n$, $mng^*_{\mathfrak{F}}(\psi_i) = mng^*_{\mathfrak{F}}(\varphi_i)$. These assumptions imply that, given $\mathcal{M}_i \in \mathbb{C}$ and $\psi_j$ and $\varphi_j$, one has

$$mng_{\mathcal{M}_i}(\psi_j) = mng_{\mathcal{M}_i}(\varphi_j).$$

This implies that one has

$$mng_{\mathcal{M}_i}(\psi_1) = mng_{\mathcal{M}_i}(\varphi_1), ..., mng_{\mathcal{M}_i}(\psi_n) = mng_{\mathcal{M}_i}(\varphi_n).$$

By hypothesis $mng$ is a compositional meaning function so it follows that

$$mng_{\mathcal{M}_i}(\triangle(\psi_1, ..., \psi_n)) = mng_{\mathcal{M}_i}(\triangle(\varphi_1, ..., \varphi_n))$$

for each $\mathcal{M}_i$. So, $mng^*_{\mathfrak{F}}(\triangle(\psi_1, ..., \psi_n)) = mng^*_{\mathfrak{F}}(\triangle(\varphi_1, ..., \varphi_n))$, which is what is wanted. $\square$

## Algebras

What can this information do for this study? It is clear that a meaning algebra can be formed relative to any semantic cover $\mathfrak{F}$. But one can also form the quotient algebras relative to covers as well. So, one can generate both LT and meaning algebras. Indeed, it is possible, but what can be said about the resulting algebras given knowledge of the underlying algebras?

Actually, more than one may expect. In the case of meaning algebras, which is the more complex case, the meaning algebra relative to a cover is a subuniverse of a product of meaning algebras. Recall that $mng^*_{\mathfrak{F}}(\alpha)$ is a tuple of meanings of the underlying logic. That means it is a member of the direct product of the meaning algebras in $\mathfrak{F}$. That is,

$$mng^*_{\mathfrak{F}}(\alpha) \in \prod_{\mathcal{M}_i \in \mathfrak{F}} mng(\mathcal{M}_i)$$

However, it is not clear that $mng^*(\mathfrak{F})$ is the product. The product of $mng(\mathcal{M}_1) \times mng(\mathcal{M}_2) \times mng(\mathcal{M}_3)$ will be all of the triples of $\langle mng_{M_1}(\alpha_1), mng_{M_2}(\alpha_2), mng_{M_3}(\alpha_3) \rangle$ where the $\alpha_i$'s may be distinct. However, in $mng^*(\mathfrak{F})$ all of the $\alpha_i$'s must be identical. Thus, there may be many elements which are not in $mng\mathfrak{F}$. However, the meaning algebra relative to $\mathfrak{F}$ is a subset of the product which is closed under the operations on the product, that is, $mng(\mathfrak{F})$ is a *subuniverse* of the product. $mng\mathfrak{F}$ can easily, in this case, be turned into a subalgebra by taking the restrictions of the functions in the type of the product algebra, which corresponds to the set of connectives for the logic. Of course, if one knows more about the class of meaning algebras of $X$ then one can say more about the meaning algebras of $X^*$. For instance it is well known that the class of meaning algebras of classical propositional logic is a variety. This means that it is closed under products and subalgebras, among other operations on the class. Thus, for such logics, the forcing meaning algebra is a member of the class of meaning algebras for the original logic.

Consider the LT-algebras. These are made of quotients of the formula algebra. If the definition of an LT-algebra is scrutinized something very interesting pops out. Let $K$ be a class of semantic covers. Then consider the equivalence relation relative to $K$, $\sim_K$, given by

$$\varphi \sim_K \psi \iff mng^*_{\mathfrak{F}}(\varphi) = mng^*_{\mathfrak{F}}(\psi) \ \forall \mathfrak{F} \in K.$$

Breaking this definition down further we can see that what really matters is that the meanings relative to the models in $\mathfrak{F}$ are equal. So $mng^*_{\mathfrak{F}}(\varphi) = mng^*_{\mathfrak{F}}(\psi)$ when $mng_{\mathcal{M}_i}(\varphi) = mng_{\mathcal{M}_i}(\psi)$ for all $\mathcal{M}_i \in \mathfrak{F}$.

Take $K$ a class from $M^*$, and $K_m = \{\mathcal{M} : \mathcal{M} \in \mathfrak{F}\}$ for each $\mathfrak{F} \in K$, then $\alpha \sim_K \beta \iff \alpha \sim_{K_m} \beta$. In this way every forcing LT-algebra corresponds to an LT-algebra of $X$. But does it go the other way too?

**Theorem 5.** *The Lindebaum-Tarski algebras for forcing and the logic $X$ are the same.*

*Proof.* The comments above imply that the forcing LT-algebras are a subclass of the LT-algebras for $X$. Take a set of models of $X$ say $U$. For each $\mathcal{M} \in U$ generate the unit cover $\mathfrak{F}$ where $\mathfrak{F}(0) = \mathcal{M}$. Then the collection of these unit covers forms a class of covers. The LT-algebra corresponding to that class of covers is of course a forcing LT-algebra. $\square$

## 7.5 Denials

A denial of a formula $\varphi$ is a formula $\psi$ such that $\overline{CON_X}(\varphi, \psi)$ (the pair set is inconsistent). According to this definition of denial, a logic which has only $\bot$ – with its usual meaning – as the only denial will be said to have denials. Formulas like $\bot$ are called *absurd* formulas. A logic $X$ has *non-trivial* denial when there are denials of formulas other than absurdities. A formula is contingent when it is neither absurd nor a theorem (or logical truth). Suppose that $\varphi$ is a contingent formula, and there is another contingent formula $\psi$ such that the pair set is inconsistent. These will be called 'contingent denials.' The next definition is more complex.

**Definition 16.** *Let $\alpha$ be a contingent formula of a logic $X$ and $\beta$ be a denial of $\alpha$. $\beta$ is a negation-denial of $\alpha$ (ND) if and only if*

1. *$\beta$ is contingent,*

2. *$\overline{CON_X}(\alpha, \beta)$, and*

3. *if $\overline{CON_X}(\alpha, \delta)$ then $\delta \vdash_X \beta$.*

We have chosen the term 'ND' rather than 'negation' since it may be the case that a logic has a connective in its language which is commonly called negation, but where there may also be a derived connective which satisfies the definition of ND.[10] A derived connective is a formula schema that does the work of a connective. A formula does the work of another when the inferential relationships of the two are the same. For instance, in a classical system with only $\wedge$ and $\neg$, the derived connective $\neg(\neg A \wedge \neg B)$ does the work of $\vee$. The formula $\neg(\neg A \wedge \neg B)$ obeys the same truth conditions as $A \vee B$ and it will obey the same introduction and elimination rules in some calculi.[11]

Notice that ND is not a symmetric relationship. For instance, the negation of intuitionistic logic (IL) satisfies this formulation, but $A$ is not an ND of $\neg A$ in IL because, although $A \supset \neg\neg A$ is a theorem, the implication does not go in the other direction.

In the sequel we make the following assumption about the logic $X$: Suppose that $\overline{CON_X}(\Gamma, \beta)$. Then there is a denial $\delta$ of $\beta$ such that $\Gamma \vdash_X \delta$. If one further assumes that ND is a symmetric relationship then the logic $X$ will have the following property:

$$[\text{Den*}] \; \forall \Gamma, \alpha, \beta [\beta ND \alpha \implies (\Gamma \vdash_X \alpha \iff \overline{CON_X}(\Gamma, \beta))].$$

Note that $ND$ is used to represent the relation of negation-denial.

---

[10]Consistency preservation can characterize a logic under certain assumptions on denials. For details see Payette and Schotch (2007).

[11]See the Fitch-style system in Schotch (2004).

**Proposition 3.** *Given that a logic $X$ has the following properties,*

1. *If $\overline{\text{CON}_X}(\Gamma, \beta)$ then there is $\delta$ such that $\overline{\text{CON}_X}(\delta, \beta)$ and $\Gamma \vdash_X \delta$, and*

2. *$X$ has symmetric ND's,*

*then the logic satisfies* [Den*].

*Proof.* Suppose that ND is symmetric for $X$, and assumptions 1 and 2 hold of $X$. Then assume $\beta ND \alpha$. Suppose that $\Gamma \vdash_X \alpha$. Then, of course, $\overline{\text{CON}_X}(\Gamma, \beta)$, since $\beta$ is a denial of $\alpha$. Now suppose that $\overline{\text{CON}_X}(\Gamma, \beta)$. Then there is some denial of $\beta$, $\gamma$, such that $\Gamma \vdash_X \gamma$ by assumption. Since $ND$ is symmetric, $\alpha ND \beta$. By the definition of an ND, it follows that $\gamma \vdash_X \alpha$, and by [Cut] $\Gamma \vdash_X \alpha$. $\qquad\square$

## 7.6 Forcing and Preservationism

The theme of this volume is to investigate inference relations according to the property or properties they preserve. The obvious question that one might ask is, What does this new forcing relation preserve? As mentioned elsewhere in this volume forcing preserves level. To see this note that the level function is monotonic, that is, if $\Gamma \subseteq \Delta$ then $\ell_X(\Gamma) \leq \ell_X(\Delta)$. This follows from $\text{CON}_X$ being downward monotonic – I omit the proof.

**Theorem 6.** *If $\ell_X(\Gamma) = \xi$ then $\ell_X(\mathbb{C}_{[\Vdash}(\Gamma)) = \xi$.*

*Proof.* Again the level $\infty$ case is trivial. Suppose $\ell_X(\Gamma) = \xi \neq \infty$. Then let $\mathbb{C}$ be a cover of $\Gamma$ such that $w(\mathbb{C}) = \ell_X(\Gamma)$. Suppose that $\psi \in \mathbb{C}_{[\Vdash}(\Gamma)$. Then, by definition, $\mathbb{C} \models^* \psi$ for all $\mathbb{C}$, of appropriate width, which cover $\Gamma$. However, $\psi$ was arbitrary, as was $\mathbb{C}$. Thus, one can see that $\mathbb{C}$ is a cover of $\mathbb{C}_{[\Vdash}(\Gamma)$, and has width $\xi$. Thus $\ell_X(\mathbb{C}_X(\Gamma))$ has level at most $\xi$, but $\ell_X$ is monotonic, and $\Gamma \subseteq \mathbb{C}_{[\Vdash}(\Gamma)$; therefore, $\ell_X(\mathbb{C}_{[\Vdash}(\Gamma)) = \xi$. $\qquad\square$

The relation of forcing as a paraconsistent inference relation is 'nice' in the sense that one does not lose out on consequences that other relations based on covers may have to give up. If it is the case that a set of premises is $X$-consistent then the forcing closure is the closure of the set relative to the logic $X$. Notice that I am now using syntactic covers.

**Theorem 7.** *If $\ell_X(\Gamma) = \xi$, $\xi \in \{0, 1\}$ then $\mathfrak{C}_X(\Gamma) = \mathfrak{C}_{[\Vdash}(\Gamma)$.*

*Proof.* Assume that $\alpha \in \mathfrak{C}_{[\Vdash}(\Gamma)$. Then for any partition $\mathfrak{C}$ there is $\Delta_i \in \mathfrak{C}$ such that $\Delta_i \vDash \alpha$. Then, $\Delta_i \subseteq \Gamma$, and, by monotonicity of $X$, it follows that $\alpha \in \mathfrak{C}_X(\Gamma)$.

Now suppose that $\ell_X(\Gamma) = 0$, then $\langle \varnothing \rangle$ is a cover of $\Gamma$. In fact it is the only cover, since it is the only cover of width 0. So $\mathfrak{C}_X(\Gamma) \subseteq \mathfrak{C}_{[\Vdash}(\Gamma)$. Now assume that $\ell_1(\Gamma) = 1$. One may restrict the investigation of the covers of $\Gamma$ to the partition covers by lemma 4. Thus, all one must consider is the cover $\mathfrak{C} = \langle \varnothing, \Gamma \rangle$, then $\mathfrak{C}_X(\Gamma) \subseteq \mathfrak{C}_{[\Vdash}(\Gamma)$. The result follows. $\qquad\square$

So for consistent sets the relation collapses into the underlying logic.

What about other levels beyond the finite into the transfinite? The level function can assign the level $\omega$ to a set under the assumptions which have been made. And of course the forcing closure will preserve that level, but can we say anything about what that closure will be? Recall that the language which we are working with is denumerable at most.

**Proposition 4.** *If $\ell_X(\Gamma) = \omega$ then $\mathfrak{C}_{[\Vdash}(\Gamma) = \bigcup_{\gamma \in \Gamma} \mathfrak{C}_X(\{\gamma\})$.*

*Proof.* Assume that $\ell_X(\Gamma) = \omega$. Then the largest the cardinality of $\Gamma$ can be is $\omega$. Thus, the cover $\mathfrak{C}_\Gamma^m$ is a cover of width $\omega$, the level of $\Gamma$. Clearly $\mathfrak{C}_\Gamma^m \subseteq \mathfrak{C}_{[\Vdash}(\Gamma)$. Let $\alpha \in \mathfrak{C}_{[\Vdash}(\Gamma)$. Then for every cover $\mathfrak{C}$ of width the level of $\Gamma$, $\mathfrak{C} \vDash^* \alpha$. Thus, $\alpha \in \mathfrak{C}_\Gamma^m$. $\qquad\square$

Until now, the only assumptions used are that the consequence relations and/or operators obey [M], [R], and [Cut]. No concerns about compactness or connectives have been addressed except that the logic $X$ has connectives and is compositional. Now it is time to ask these questions. Namely, what structural rules are preserved in the 'move up' and what can be said about compact logics and the effects of connectives on forcing?

## 7.7 Structural Rules and Compactness

Continuing with the study of the properties inherited from the underlying logic one might ask if the forcing relation has [R], [M], and [Cut]. That forcing has [R] is perfectly obvious, but that it has [Cut] is not. Before [Cut] is discussed we must discuss [M]. There is a problem with [M]. If $\Gamma\lceil \Vdash \alpha$ then it is possible that the level will rise if one adds a set to it. For instance, if the underlying logic is classical then $\{A, B\}$ will force $A \wedge B$, but $\{A, B, \neg B\}$ will not force $A \wedge B$, since it has level 2, and $\{\varnothing, \{B\}, \{A, \neg B\}\}$ is a partition of width 2. But that cover will not cover $A \wedge B$. This is the downfall of forcing. It is not monotonic, but it is not anti-monotonic. With a caveat it is monotonic. That restriction is that the set being added must not make things worse. This means that when one adds a set of premises, the new set must not be more inconsistent. The level of the superset must not change, that is, $\ell_X(\Gamma) = \ell_X(\Gamma \cup \Delta)$. The new version of [M], $[M^*]^{12}$ is, If $\ell_X(\Gamma) = \ell_X(\Gamma \cup \Delta)$, and $\Gamma\lceil \Vdash \alpha$ then $\Gamma \cup \Delta\lceil \Vdash \alpha$. However, this is not something assumed about forcing; it follows from the definition.

**Proposition 5.** *The forcing relation* $\lceil \Vdash$ *has* [M*], *given that X has* [M].

*Proof.* Assume $\ell_X(\Gamma) = \ell_X(\Gamma \cup \Delta)$, and $\Gamma\lceil \Vdash \alpha$. Then, let $\mathfrak{C} \models^* \Gamma \cup \Delta$, and $w(\mathfrak{C}) = \ell_X(\Gamma \cup \Delta)$. Then $\mathfrak{C} \models^* \Gamma$, so by definition $\mathfrak{C} \models^* \alpha$, since $w(\mathfrak{C}) = \ell_X(\Gamma)$. Hence $\Gamma \cup \Delta\lceil \Vdash \alpha$, since $\mathfrak{C}$ was an arbitrary cover of the proper width. $\square$

Given [M*], one can see that the version of [Cut] given in the section above is not satisfied in all cases. However, the formulation of [Cut] as, If $\Gamma \vdash \delta$ for all $\delta \in \Delta$ and $\Delta \vdash \alpha$ then $\Gamma \vdash \alpha$, is also not satisfied. As already noted in the section above, the version of [Cut] just mentioned gives the correlation between the consequence operator and the consequence relation. Consider the following counter example: Let $\Delta = \{A, B\}$ and $\Gamma = \{A, B, C, \neg C, D\}$. Then, although any cover of $\Gamma$ of width 2 is a cover of $\Delta$, it may not cover $\Delta$ properly. The set $\Delta$ forces $A \wedge B$, but $\Gamma$ does not. Thus [Cut] cannot be satisfied, at least on

---

[12]This is also known as $X$-level-preserving monotonicity in Payette and d'Entremont (2006).

the formulation that has been chosen. But not all is lost, just most of it. A different, but not finitist version can be satisfied. In fact this principle has been used implicitly many times over in the proofs above. It goes as follows: If $\Gamma \vdash \delta$ for all $\delta \in \Delta$ and $\Gamma, \Delta \vdash \alpha$ then $\Gamma \vdash \alpha$. This will be known as [Cut*].

**Proposition 6.** *If the relation $\vDash$ of $X$ has* [R], [M], *and* [Cut] *then* $\big[\Vdash$ *has* [Cut*]. *That is, if* $\Gamma\big[\Vdash \delta$ *for all* $\delta \in \Delta$ *and* $\Gamma, \Delta\big[\Vdash \alpha$ *then* $\Gamma\big[\Vdash \alpha$.

*Proof.* Assume $\Gamma\big[\Vdash \delta$ for all $\delta \in \Delta$, and $\Gamma, \Delta\big[\Vdash \alpha$. Then assume that $\mathfrak{C} \vDash^* \Gamma$, and $w(\mathfrak{C}) = \ell_X(\Gamma)$. $\Delta \subseteq \mathfrak{C}_{[\Vdash}(\Gamma)$ so $\mathfrak{C} \vDash^* \Delta$ by definition because $\mathfrak{C} \vDash^* \Gamma$. Since $\ell_X(\Gamma) = \ell_X(\mathfrak{C}_{[\Vdash}(\Gamma))$, proposition 6, it must be that $\ell_X(\Gamma \cup \Delta) = \ell_X(\Gamma)$. Thus $\mathfrak{C}$ is a cover of $\Gamma \cup \Delta$ of the right width to be a cover of $\alpha$ by definition of forcing. Since $\mathfrak{C}$ is an arbitrary cover of $\Gamma$ of the right width, $\Gamma\big[\Vdash \alpha$.                    $\square$

It would be at best misleading and at worst cowardly to omit mention of some rather odd results that flow from the definition of forcing. Forcing can take a logic $X$ that does not have [Cut][13] and give it [Cut*]. Because of this peculiarity, for the logic and its derived forcing relation to agree on consistent sets, the logic must obey the structural rules. However, the same cannot be said about the rule [R]. The case of [M*] is similar to that of [Cut*]. The restricted version of monotonicity may hold even though $X$ does not have [M]. But we place these problems out of bounds because the logics we are considering are 'structural' as given in definition 6.

The preservation of compactness is not from the logic to forcing, but, rather, from the logic to the level function. The forcing relation is compact given the compactness of $X$, albeit in an uninteresting way. If $\Gamma\big[\Vdash \psi$ then take a partition cover of $\Gamma$, $\mathfrak{C}$. By definition of forcing there is a $\Delta_i \in \mathfrak{C}$ such that $\Delta_i \vDash \psi$. By the compactness of $X$ we get a $\Delta_i' \subseteq_\omega \Delta_i$ such that $\Delta_i' \vDash \psi$. Here $\subseteq_\omega$ is the finite subset of relation. However, $\Delta_i' \subseteq_\omega \Gamma$ so we satisfy compactness. Level compactness is much more interesting.

---

[13]Although, strictly speaking, some might wish to argue that there is no such thing as a logic which fails to have [Cut].

Here we correct the demonstration given in Payette and d'Entremont (2006) of level compactness. Assume for this section that the consequence relation of the logic $X$ is compact. That means that the $\mathrm{CON}_X$ predicate is also compact. This demonstration follows from a general theorem about partitions and a use of Rado's selection lemma. First a definition.

---

**Definition 17.** *Let $P$ be a property of sets, and $n \in \omega$. An $(n, P)$-partition of a set $\Gamma$ is a partition of $\Gamma$ into n cells such that each cell has the property $P$.*

---

The theorem that we prove here is a variation on the Set Partition Theorem from Cowen et al. (2002, p. 214). The version of Rado's lemma used here can be found in that paper, and a proof of it can be found in Cowen (1972).

**Lemma 5.** *Rado's Selection Lemma. Let $I$ be an infinite set, and the set $\{A_v : v \in I\}$ where each $A_v$ is finite, is index by $I$. Assume that for each $W \subseteq_\omega I$ there is a function $f_W$ with domain $W$ and for every $v \in W$, $f_W(v) \in A_v$. Then there is a function $f$ with domain $I$ such that for every $W \subseteq_\omega I$, there is a $W' \subseteq_\omega I$ an extension (maybe not proper) of $W$ such that for any $v \in W$ $f(v) = f_{W'}(v)$.*

**Theorem 8.** *$(n, P)$-partition Theorem. If every $\Delta \subseteq_\omega \Gamma$ has at most an $(n, P)$-partition, $\Gamma$ has at most an $(n, P)$-partition, provided $P$ is a compact property of sets and is downward monotonic. (i.e., $P(\Gamma)$ iff $\forall \Delta \subseteq_\omega \Gamma P(\Delta)$ and if $\Delta \subseteq \Gamma$ and $P(\Gamma)$ then $P(\Delta)$.)*

*Proof.* Of course we assume that $\Gamma$ is infinite. Let each $\Delta \subseteq_\omega \Gamma$ have at most an $(n, P)$-partition. Let $\{A_v : v \in I\}$ be $\{A_\varphi : \varphi \in \Gamma\}$ where each $A_\varphi = \{1, \ldots, n\}$. Let $\Delta \subseteq_\omega \Gamma$. Then there is a $(k, P)$-partition ($k \leq n$), thus we can define a function $f_\Delta : \Delta \to \{1, \ldots, k\}$ since we can take the partition of $\Delta$ and enumerate the cells. Then $f_\Delta(\varphi) = i$ iff $\varphi \in \Delta_i$ of the enumeration of the partition. Then composing $f_\Delta$ with the inclusion function from $\{1, \ldots, k\}$ to $\{1, \ldots, n\}$ we get a function $f_\Delta : \Delta \to \{1, \ldots, n\}$. Since all $A_\varphi$ are $\{1, \ldots, n\}$, $f_\Delta(\varphi) \in A_\varphi$. Since the function is defined using the $(n, P)$-partition of $\Delta$ each $f_\Delta^{-1}(i)$ $1 \leq i \leq n$ has the property $P$.

Now we can apply Rado's lemma to get a function $f$ from $\Gamma$ to $\{1, \ldots, n\}$ with the special property that for every $\Delta \subseteq_\omega \Gamma$, there is $\Delta' \subseteq_\omega \Gamma$ that extends $\Delta$ and for each $\varphi \in \Delta$ $f_{\Delta'}(\varphi) = f(\varphi)$. Define a partition of $\Gamma$ as $\{f^{-1}(i) : 1 \leq i \leq n\}$. This is a partition since $f$ is a function, what remains to be seen is that $f^{-1}(i)$ has the property $P$. Since $P$ is compact we show this by showing every finite subset of $f^{-1}(i)$ has $P$. Let $\Delta \subseteq_\omega f^{-1}(i)$. So there is $\Delta'$ that extends $\Delta$ such that $f_{\Delta'}(\varphi) = f(\varphi)$, if $\varphi \in \Delta$. So $f_{\Delta'}(\varphi) = i$ since $f(\varphi) = i$ when $\varphi \in \Delta$. But that means that $\Delta \subseteq f_{\Delta'}^{-1}(i)$. Since the way that we defined the $f_{\Delta'}$ guarantees that $P(f_{\Delta'}^{-1}(i))$, by monotonicity of $P$ it follows that $P(\Delta)$. So any finite subset of $f^{-1}(i)$ has $P$, and by compactness of $P$, $f^{-1}(i)$ has $P$. $\qquad\square$

To get the important theorem the following equivalence is needed.

**Theorem 9.** *The following are equivalent when $\ell_X(\Gamma) < \omega$ and $\text{CON}_X$ is compact (the subscripts will be omitted):*

1. *For all $n$, $\ell(\Gamma) \leq n \iff \forall \Gamma' \subseteq \Gamma$ that are finite, $\ell(\Gamma') \leq n$.*

2. *For all $n$, if $\ell(\Gamma) = n$ then $\exists \Gamma' \subseteq \Gamma$, which is finite, such that $\ell(\Gamma') = n$.*

3. *For all $n$, if there is a finite subset $\Gamma^*$ of $\Gamma$ such that for any other finite $\Gamma' \subseteq \Gamma$, $\ell(\Gamma') \leq \ell(\Gamma^*)$ and $\ell(\Gamma^*) = n$, then $\ell(\Gamma) = n$.*

*Proof.* We proceed by showing the equivalence in a triangle. All $n, m, k$ etc. are elements of $\omega$.

$1 \Rightarrow 2$. Assume 1 and assume for reductio that $\ell(\Gamma) = n$ and that there is no finite subset of $\Gamma$ which has level $n$. We know by monotonicity of level that all of the subsets of $\Gamma$ must have level less than that of $\Gamma$, so there is an upper bound. This upper bound will also apply to finite sets. Call this upper bound $m$. This $m$ is strictly less than $n$ because otherwise there would be a finite subset of level $n$ which there isn't. With 1 it follows that $\ell(\Gamma) \leq m < n$, which is a contradiction.

$2 \Rightarrow 3$. Assume 2, the existence of a $\Gamma^*$, as in the antecedent of 3, and so $\ell(\Gamma^*) = n$. There must be, by 2, a finite $\Gamma' \subseteq \Gamma$ with $\ell(\Gamma') = \ell(\Gamma) = m$, but then $m = \ell(\Gamma) = \ell(\Gamma') \leq \ell(\Gamma^*) = n$. By monotonicity of $\ell$, $n = \ell(\Gamma^*) \leq \ell(\Gamma) = m$; hence, $\ell(\Gamma^*) = \ell(\Gamma)$, i.e., $m = n$.

$3 \Rightarrow 1$. Assume 3. The only if direction of 1 follows from monotonicity of $\ell$; thus, assume that for every finite $\Gamma' \subseteq \Gamma$ $\ell(\Gamma') \leq n$. Let $m = max\{k | \ell(\Gamma') = k$ & $\Gamma' \subseteq_\omega \Gamma\}$. This must exist since there is an upper bound, namely $n$. Let $\Gamma^* = \Gamma'$ such that $\ell(\Gamma') = m$. Then the conditions for 3 are satisfied; thus, $\ell(\Gamma^*) = \ell(\Gamma) = m \leq n$. $\square$

With theorems 8 and 9 we can prove the following:

**Theorem 10.** *Finite Level Compactness. If $\Gamma$ is a set of formulas with $\ell(\Gamma) < \omega$ and $\mathrm{CON}_X$ is compact then, $\ell(\Gamma) \leq n$, if and only if for all finite subsets $\Gamma'$ of $\Gamma$, $\ell(\Gamma') \leq n$.*

*Proof.* The result follows by showing 3 from theorem 9. Assume there is a $\Gamma^* \subseteq_\omega \Gamma$ whose level, $n$, is a bound for the levels of all finite subsets of $\Gamma$. Using theorem 8, letting $\mathrm{CON}_X$ be the property $P$, we have an $(n, \mathrm{CON}_X)$-partition of $\Gamma$, which can be made into a cover of $\Gamma$. Thus we have that the level of $\Gamma$ can be at most $n$, but using the assumption that there is a finite subset of level $n$, namely $\Gamma^*$, the level of $\Gamma$ is $n$. $\square$

Notice the crucial restriction to finite levels in these two theorems. The level of a set is bounded by its cardinality. If a set has a level that is not $\infty$ then $\mathbb{C}_\Gamma^m$ is a cover. But, $w(\mathbb{C}_\Gamma^m) = |\Gamma|$. If $\Gamma$ had a level greater than its cardinality, $\mathbb{C}_\Gamma^m$ could not be a cover. So $\ell_X(\Gamma) \leq |\Gamma|$. If $\ell_X(\Gamma) = \omega$, for example, then there is no finite subset that could have level $\omega$ since the set can have at most a finite level. What this means is that any set with level $\omega$ will have a subset of every finite level.

To conclude the general look at properties that are preserved in the move to forcing, consider a particular example of a logic that meets these properties: classical first-order logic.

## 7.8   First-Order Logic and Forcing

The properties studied thus far can be used to judge the value of this method of paraconsistentizing a logic. However, they are not just idle properties; they have applications that give us more reasons to think that forcing is a good method.

I will show this in two steps. First I will give the general case then a specific case: first-order logic. What I want to show is that forcing under certain conditions will be the largest relation that can be defined that has many of the aforementioned properties. In particular the key properties will be the restricted versions of the structural rules and level preservation. To accomplish this we must introduce some new concepts.

---

**Definition 18.** $\Gamma^+$ *is a maximal level-preserving extension* (MLPE) *of* $\Gamma$ *if and only if*

*1.* $\Gamma \subseteq \Gamma^+$,

*2.* $\ell(\Gamma^+) = \ell(\Gamma)$, *and*

*3. for any formula* $\psi$, *if* $\ell(\Gamma^+ \cup \{\psi\}) = \ell(\Gamma^+)$ *then* $\psi \in \Gamma^+$.

---

It follows, with the help of theorem 10 above, that any set with finite level can be extended to an MLPE. We can show this by considering the following result about partial orders.

---

**Definition 19.** *A partially ordered set* $\langle S, \leq \rangle$ *is a set* $S$ *with a relation* $\leq$ *such that for* $a, b, c \in S$,

*1.* $a \leq a$ *(reflexivity),*

*2. if* $a \leq a$ *and* $b \leq c$ *then* $a \leq c$ *(transitivity),*

*3. if* $a \leq b$ *and* $b \leq a$ *then* $a = b$ *(anti-symmetry).*

---

A monotone operator on a partial order, say $\langle S, \leq \rangle$, is an operator, $\Phi : S \longrightarrow S$ such that if $a \leq b$ then $\Phi(a) \leq \Phi(b)$. Given a set $T \subseteq S$ one says that $T$ has an upper bound if there is an $a \in S$ such that for all $t \in T$, $t \leq a$. A least upper bound for $T$ is an upper bound $a$ of $T$, such that for any other upper bound $b$, $a \leq b$. An element $m \in S$ is maximal when, for any $a \in S$, if $m \leq a$, then $m = a$. A fixed point of the operator $\Phi$ is an $a \in S$ such that $\Phi(a) = a$. A 'chain' in $S$ is a set $C \subseteq S$ such that for each $a, b \in C$, either $a \leq b$ or $b \leq a$. A smallest member of $S$ is a $b \in S$ such that, for any $a \in S$, $b \leq a$. With this terminology in mind the following can be shown.

**Theorem 11.** *Let $\langle S, \leq \rangle$ be a partial order such that $S$ has a smallest member, every non-empty set of members of $S$ which has an upper bound has a least upper bound, and $\Phi$ is a monotone operator on $S$. Suppose every chain in $S$ has an upper bound. Then, if $a \in S$ is such that $a \leq \Phi(a)$ then there is a maximal fixed point of $\Phi$, call it $b$, such that $a \leq b$.*

For a proof of theorem 11 see Fitting (1986, 78–9). In the logics we are considering, all of the suppositions of the theorems above are satisfied, save the condition on chains. For a compact logic the chain condition follows immediately. However, this theorem applies very easily to some propositional logics. But for first-order logics it is not so clear; a maximally consistent extension may not correspond to a model in some cases. There may be need of something more, but that would take us off track. What I want to show is that a partial order can be made out of sets so that a MLPE will be a maximal item.

Consider a set $\Delta$ with a finite level relative to the compact logic $X$. Define the set $L_\Delta$ as the set of all level preserving supersets of $\Delta$. That is,

$$L_\Delta = \{ \Gamma \cup \Delta : \ell_X (\Gamma \cup \Delta) = \ell_X(\Delta) \}.$$

**Proposition 7.** $\langle L_\Delta, \subseteq \rangle$ *is a partial order which satisfies the conditions in theorem 11.*

*Proof.* Any non-empty set $D$ of $L_\Delta$ that has an upper bound $\Gamma'$ will be such that $\ell_X(\Delta \cup \Gamma') = \ell_X(\Delta)$. Also, since $\bigcup D \subseteq \Gamma'$, and level is monotonic, $D$ has a least upper bound, $\bigcup D$.

That unions of chains have upper bounds follows from the Finite Level Compactness theorem, since, if the union of the chain $C$, $\bigcup C$, has the property that $\ell_X(\bigcup C \cup \Delta) > \ell_X(\Delta)$, then there is a finite subset of this set that has $\ell_X(\bigcup C \cup \Delta)$, or there is some finite subset that has a level greater than $\ell_X(\Delta)$ if the level of $\bigcup C \cup \Delta$ is infinite. Either way that finite set would be contained in some set in the chain, but that is impossible. The monotone operator is the forcing closure operator. This operator is not monotone in general, but, since it has [M*], it is monotone on $L_\Delta$.                                              □

Thus the expected result:

**Lemma 6.** *If $\Gamma$ has level $m \in \omega$, then it can be extended to a* MLPE $\Gamma^+$.

*Proof.* For any $\Gamma \subseteq \mathbb{S}$ it is the case that $\Gamma \subseteq \mathbb{C}_{[\Vdash}(\Gamma)$. Apply proposition 7. It is clear that the maximal sets will be the maximal upper bounds we get from this theorem. Every upper bound must be in $L_\Delta$ so they are level-preserving supersets, which takes care of the first and second conditions. The third condition holds because of the maximality of these sets in $L_\Delta$: if something could be added to the set that maintained the level, the set would not be maximal in $L_\Delta$. The result holds. □

Notice that if the level of $\Delta$ is $\omega$ then the extensions will be everything except those formulas which have level $\infty$.

We can then define the relation which will be the largest on a compact logic, even for sets of infinite levels. Notice that for any MLPE the following holds: $\Gamma^+[\Vdash \psi \iff \psi \in \Gamma^+$. This follows at once since forcing obeys [R], and forcing is level-preserving. The largest relation, regardless of underlying logic $X$, can be defined as follows:

$$\Gamma \vdash_{\text{MLPE}} \varphi \Leftrightarrow \varphi \in \bigcap_{\Gamma^+ \in \text{MLPE}} \Gamma^+$$

where MLPE stands for the class of maximal level-preserving extensions of $\Gamma$.[14] We abbreviate the right hand side as $\bigcap \Gamma^+$.

---

[14]The general case will have to obey some other condition if the logic is first-order; namely, like the one found in the completeness theorem of Henkin. That is, one only considers formulas which occur in the original language of $\Gamma$, not the extensions.

**Proposition 8.** *Given a compact logic $X$ and a relation $Y$ which obeys* [Cut*], [R], *and* [M*] *and preserves $X$-level, it follows that for all $\Gamma$* $\mathbb{C}_Y(\Gamma) \subseteq \bigcap \Gamma^+$.

*Proof.* Assume for reductio that $\varphi \in \mathbb{C}_Y(\Gamma)$, but $\varphi \notin \bigcap \Gamma^+$. Then there is an MLPE of $\Gamma$, call it $\Gamma_\varphi^+$, such that $\varphi \notin \Gamma_\varphi^+$. By definition $\ell(\Gamma_\varphi^+ \cup \{\varphi\}) > \ell(\Gamma_\varphi^+) = \ell(\Gamma)$. And since $\Gamma \subseteq \Gamma_\varphi^+$, by hypothesis on $Y$, it follows that $\mathbb{C}_Y(\Gamma) \subseteq \mathbb{C}_Y(\Gamma_\varphi^+)$ by [M*]. Thus $\varphi \in \mathbb{C}_Y(\Gamma_\varphi^+)$, and so $\ell(\mathbb{C}_Y(\Gamma_\varphi^+)) > \ell(\Gamma_\varphi^+)$. Therefore, $Y$ does not preserve $X$-level, or $Y$ does not obey [M*]; either option is contrary to hypothesis. $\square$

The next question to raise is whether a sufficient and/or necessary condition for forcing to agree with this 'largest' relation $\bigcap \Gamma^+$ can be established. It can indeed be shown that there is a sufficient condition, but to establish this the object language of the logic $X$ requires consideration. The next theorem holds for logics said to be productival or said to have products. The definition of such a logic is as follows:

---

**Definition 20.** *A logic $X$ is productival iff, given any finite set $\Gamma$, there is a formula $\varphi$ such that $\varphi \vdash_X \psi$ for each $\psi \in \Gamma$ and $\Gamma \vdash_X \varphi$.*

---

This notion of a product is like that of a denial. A product will be some derived connective which will allow one to satisfy the conditions above. It is worth noticing that if a logic has binary products, then it has all finite products. This is a well-known theorem from category theory.

Somebody might be tempted to say 'Oh I see, products are just a kind of conjunction!' but that would be to put the matter backwards. In particular, a logic may have products without its underlying language having any explicit connectives at all. Or if it has connectives it might not have an explicit conjunction. Classical logic with $\vee$ and $\neg$ as the only primitive connectives serves as an example. The product of $\alpha$ and $\beta$ is $\neg(\neg\alpha \vee \neg\beta)$. The further assumption needed about logics is that they have symmetric negation denials. The reader should recall the definition 16. Then we have the following:

**Theorem 12.** *Maximal Forcibility Theorem. Let X be a compact, productival logic, which has symmetric negation denials, so obeys* [Den*], *and let $\ell_X(\Gamma) \in \omega$. Then, $\Gamma\big[\Vdash \psi$ if and only if, for each MLPE $\Gamma^+$ of $\Gamma$, $\Gamma^+\big[\Vdash \psi$.*

*Proof.* ($\Rightarrow$) (I will omit the subscript $X$s.) Suppose $\Gamma\big[\Vdash \psi$. Then let $\Gamma^+$ be an MLPE of $\Gamma$. So, by definition $\ell(\Gamma) = \ell(\Gamma^+)$. Suppose that $\mathfrak{C}$ covers $\Gamma^+$ and has width $\ell(\Gamma)$. Then $\mathfrak{C}$ is also a cover of $\Gamma$ because $\Gamma \subseteq \Gamma^+$. But the width of $\mathfrak{C}$ is also the level of $\Gamma$, so $\mathfrak{C}$ is a cover of $\Gamma$ of the appropriate width for there to be a $\Delta_i \in \mathfrak{C}$ such that $\Delta_i \vDash \psi$ by the definition of forcing. This follows because $\mathfrak{C}$ was arbitrary $\Gamma^+\big[\Vdash \psi$.

($\Leftarrow$) By contrapositive. Assume $\Gamma\big[\nVdash \psi$ and $\ell(\Gamma) = m$. Then there is a $\mathfrak{C}$ which is a partition cover of $\Gamma$ of width $m$ where $\forall \, \Delta_i \in \mathfrak{C}$, $\Delta_i \nvDash \psi$. Thus, by [Den*], $\mathrm{CON}(\Delta_i \cup \{\psi'\})$ for each $i$, where $\psi'$ is a ND of $\psi$. For each $\Delta_i \neq \Delta_j$, $\Delta_i \cap \Delta_j = \varnothing$, and $\overline{\mathrm{CON}}(\Delta_i \cup \Delta_j)$. By compactness of CON, for each pair of cells there are finite sets $\Delta_i'$ and $\Delta_j'$, contained in $\Delta_i, \Delta_j$ respectively, which are inconsistent with one another. Thus, form their respective products and get $\varphi_{ij}$ and $\varphi_{ji}$. So it follows that $\overline{\mathrm{CON}}(\{\varphi_{ij}\} \cup \{\varphi_{ji}\})$.

There are only finitely many of these $\varphi_{ij}$s for each $i$; thus, there is a product for each $i$, call it $\varphi_i$, such that $\varphi_i \vDash \varphi_{ij}$ for each $j \neq i$. The $\varphi_i$s are clearly consistent, by the definition of products, with the $\Delta_i$s, and any two distinct $\varphi_i$s are inconsistent. Use the fact that $\mathrm{CON}(\Delta_i \cup \{\psi'\})$ to form the product of $\{\varphi_i, \psi'\}$ to get $\varphi_i^*$ for each $i$, which will also be consistent with each $\Delta_i$. Form the cover $\mathfrak{C}'(0) = \varnothing$ and

$$\mathfrak{C}'(i) = \Delta_i \cup \{\varphi_i^*\} : \ \Delta_i \in \mathfrak{C}, \ \& \ 1 \leq i \leq m;$$

$\mathfrak{C}'$ is a cover of $\Gamma \cup \{\psi'\}$ of width $m$. Let $\Gamma^* = \Gamma \cup \{\varphi_i^* : 1 \leq i \leq m\}$. By monotonicity of level it follows that $\ell(\Gamma^*) = \ell(\Gamma \cup \{\varphi_i^* : 1 \leq i \leq m\}) = \ell(\Gamma)$. This new set $\Gamma^*$ will have a MLPE $\Gamma^+$. By definition, $\Gamma^+$ will have level $m$, and, since each $\varphi_i^*$ entails $\psi'$ and must be contained in a different cell, $\psi$ cannot be added to $\Gamma^+$ without increasing its level. But that is to say $\Gamma^+\big[\nVdash \psi$ with $\Gamma \subseteq \Gamma^+$. $\qquad \square$

What this theorem implies is that for logics satisfying the specified properties what is forced by a given set is what ends up in every MLPE of the set. Thus forcing agrees with $\bigcap \Gamma^+$, and $\bigcap \Gamma^+$ is the biggest relation there is that fits our description.

The reason for assuming symmetric NDs and products is to guarantee that the extensions will be able to exclude a given formula – the one which is not to follow from the set. The set $\{A, \neg A\}$ does not force $\neg B$, but without the ability to make the formulas, $\neg A \wedge B$ and $A \wedge B$, one may be able to add $\neg B$ to the set without raising the level. The symmetric NDs are needed so that entailment and consistency will commute in the right way, that is, so that non-provability will imply that the set is consistent with an ND. This will of course fail for intuitionistic logic. The general problem is that, depending on the logic, the maximal extension may include things that do not follow from the sets. In IL there are formulas that are consistent with a set, make it into every maximal extension, but are never proved by the original set. These restraints, if absolutely necessary, greatly limit the number of logics for which forcing is the largest relation, but they do not exclude all except classical logic. The Łukasiewicz many-valued $Ł_n$ logics all have conjunctions, and have a type of bar negation which act as a symmetric ND.

Next comes a particular example of these properties. As was the case with the maximal Henkin-extensions of first-order logic used to prove completeness, we need a more complex extension for forcing.

---

**Definition 21.** *An $\Omega$-MLPE $\Gamma^+$ of a set $\Gamma$ is such that it is an MLPE; and if $\Gamma^+\lceil \Vdash (\exists x)\psi$, then $\Gamma^+\lceil \Vdash \psi(a)$. That is, every existential claim is witnessed.*

---

**Theorem 13.** *If $\vDash$ is the relation of CFL, then for all $\Gamma, \varphi \subseteq \mathbb{S}$, with finite level, $\Gamma\lceil \Vdash \varphi \iff \Gamma^+\lceil \Vdash \varphi$ for all $\Omega$-MLPEs $\Gamma^+$ such that $\Gamma \subseteq \Gamma^+$.*

To prove this we need another extension lemma, one that says that each $\Gamma$ can be extended to an $\Omega$-MLPE. Here the reader should also recall definition 7.

**Lemma 7.** *Each $\Gamma$ with CFL-level $n \in \omega$ can be extended to an $\Omega$-MLPE.*

*Proof.* Let $\ell_{CFL}(\Gamma) = n \in \omega$. Let $\psi_1, ..., \psi_k, ...$ such that $k \in \omega$ be an enumeration of the formulas of the language. Form sets $\Sigma_n$ for $n \in \omega$ by

$$\Sigma_0 = \Gamma$$

$$\Sigma_n = \begin{cases} \Sigma_{n-1} \cup \{\psi_n\} & \text{if } \ell(\Sigma_{n-1} \cup \{\psi_n\}) = \ell(\Gamma) \\ \Sigma_{n-1} \cup \{\psi_n\} \cup \{\varphi(a)\} & \text{if } \ell(\Sigma_{n-1} \cup \{\psi_n\}) = \ell(\Gamma) \\ & \text{and } \psi_n = (\exists x)\varphi \\ \Sigma_{n-1} & \text{otherwise} \end{cases}$$

Where $a$ is not mentioned in $\Sigma_{n-1} \cup \{\psi_n\}$.

Let $\Gamma^+ = \bigcup_{n \in \omega} \Sigma_n$. Claim: this set is an $\Omega$-level-preserving maximal extension of $\Gamma$. By the recursive construction and compactness $\ell(\Gamma^+) = \ell(\Gamma)$.

First it must be established that for each clause of the construction $\ell(\Sigma_n) = \ell(\Sigma_{n-1})$. For the first clause it is simple; it follows by monotonicity of level. Similarly for the third clause. The second clause is more complicated. Assume the result holds.

There are three cases, if $\ell(\Gamma^+) \neq \ell(\Gamma)$:

1. $\ell(\Gamma^+) = \infty$

2. $\ell(\Gamma^+) \geq \omega$

3. $\omega > \ell(\Gamma^+) > \ell(\Gamma)$

If 1, then an absurd formula was added which cannot be covered, which is impossible since that would have occurred at some stage $k$ and would raise the level from the previous stage. If 2, then for any $n \in \omega$, there is a finite subset of $\Gamma^+$ of level $n$. If there were a finite upper bound on the levels of the finite subsets of $\Gamma^+$ then the compactness theorem, theorem 10, says the whole set would have that finite level, which is contrary to assumption. So choose $n = \ell(\Gamma) + 1$; the finite subset of level $n$ will be contained in some $\Sigma_k$ so $\ell(\Sigma_k) > \ell(\Gamma)$, which is impossible. Finally, if 3, there was a finite set which was the culprit, and it would be contained in some $\Sigma_n$, which is also impossible. Thus $\ell(\Gamma^+) = \ell(\Gamma)$.

Claim: $\Gamma^+$ is an MLPE. Suppose $\ell(\Gamma^+ \cup \{\varphi\}) = \ell(\Gamma^+)$, then either $\varphi \in \Gamma$ or, if not, $\varphi = \psi_n$ for some $n \in \omega$. If the former then $\varphi \in \Gamma^+$ *a fortiori*. If the latter, then $\varphi$ was considered for membership at stage $n$, and since adding it to $\Gamma^+$ does not change its level, adding $\varphi$ to $\Sigma_{n-1}$ does not change the level of $\Sigma_{n-1}$ since $\ell(\Sigma_n) = \ell(\Gamma) = \ell(\Gamma^+)$. Thus, $\varphi$ was added at stage $n$. Therefore, $\varphi \in \Gamma^+$.

Claim: $\Gamma^+$ is $\Omega$-complete. Suppose that $\Gamma^+[\, \Vdash \, (\exists x)\varphi$. Then $\ell(\Gamma^+ \cup \{(\exists x)\varphi\}) = \ell(\Gamma^+)$, because by the previous result $(\exists x)\varphi \in \Gamma^+$. And for some $k \in \omega$, $(\exists x)\varphi = \psi_k$. Thus $\psi_k$ was added at stage $k$, but then so was $\varphi(a)$ for some constant $a$, by the construction. Therefore $\Gamma^+[\Vdash \varphi(a)$ *a fortiori*. This completes the proof. $\qquad\square$

**Lemma 8.** *The second clause of the construction preserves level.*

*Proof.* This uses theorem 10 essentially. Let $\Sigma_n = \Sigma_{n-1} \cup \{\psi_n\} \cup \{\varphi(a)\}$ with $\psi_n = (\exists x)\varphi$ as is stipulated. By assumption $\ell(\Sigma_{n-1} \cup \{\psi_n\}) = \ell(\Sigma_{n-1}) = k \in \omega$. For any $\Sigma' \subseteq_\omega \Sigma_{n-1} \cup \{(\exists x)\varphi\}$, $\ell(\Sigma') \leq k$ by monotonicity of $\ell$. Note that for any $\Sigma' \subseteq_\omega \Sigma_{n-1} \cup \{(\exists x)\varphi\}$ the level of $\Sigma' \cup \{(\exists x)\varphi\}$ must also be $\leq k$.

Claim: For all $\Sigma' \subseteq_\omega \Sigma_{n-1} \cup \{(\exists x)\varphi\}$, $\ell(\Sigma' \cup \{\varphi(a)\}) \leq k$. Suppose not, then there is some $\Sigma' \subseteq \Sigma_{n-1} \cup \{(\exists x)\varphi\}$, such that for each cover $\mathfrak{C} = \langle \varnothing, \Delta_1, \ldots \Delta_k \rangle$ with $w(\mathfrak{C}) = k$, we have $\overline{\text{CON}_{CFL}}(\Delta_i, \varphi(a))$ for each $1 \leq i \leq k$. If there wasn't, then by compactness the result would follow since each finite subset would have level $\leq k$. However, CFL obeys [Den*]; thus, one has $\Delta_i \vDash \neg\varphi(a)$ for $1 \leq i \leq k$. Note that $a$ is not mentioned in any $\Delta_i$, since $\mathfrak{C}$ is an elementary cover, and $a$ is not mentioned in $\Sigma_{n-1} \cup \{(\exists x)\varphi\}$ by hypothesis, so $\Delta_i \vDash (\forall x)\neg\varphi(x)$ by the rules for classical logic. But that means $\Delta_i \vDash \neg(\exists x)\varphi(x)$ also, by classical logic.

But, some $\Delta_i$ must entail $(\exists x)\varphi$ because $\mathfrak{C}$ is a cover of $\Sigma' \cup \{(\exists x)\varphi\}$. So, for some $\Delta_i$, $\overline{\text{CON}_{CFL}}(\Delta_i)$, which is contrary to the hypothesis that $\mathfrak{C}$ is a cover. Therefore, each finite subset of $\Sigma_{n-1} \cup \{(\exists x)\varphi\} \cup \{\varphi(a)\}$ has level $\leq k$, and, by compactness, that is, theorem 10, the whole set must have level $\leq k$. However, $\ell(\Sigma_{n-1}) = k$, and $\Sigma_{n-1} \subseteq \Sigma_{n-1} \cup$

$\{(\exists x)\varphi\} \cup \{\varphi(a)\}$ so by monotonicity of level, $\ell(\Sigma_n) = \ell(\Sigma_{n-1})$. Which is what is wanted. $\qquad\qquad\qquad\qquad\qquad\qquad\qquad\qquad\qquad\square$

Using these results the proof of theorem 13 follows easily.

*Proof of theorem 13.* Assume that $\Gamma$ has finite level. Then suppose that $\Gamma[\Vdash \psi$. If so, every $\Omega$-MLPE will force it, since it must contain $\psi$. Suppose that $\Gamma[\nVdash \psi$, then proceed as in theorem 12 by conjoining the proper finite sets with the negation of $\psi$. Then by lemma 7 extend this new set to an $\Omega$-MLPE which will not force $\psi$ since it would raise its level to do so. $\qquad\qquad\qquad\qquad\qquad\qquad\qquad\qquad\qquad\square$

This concludes the study of forcing as an approach to paraconsistent logic that derives a paraconsistent relation from an inconsistency intolerant logic $X$.[15]

## 7.9   Conclusion

The purpose of this chapter was to display the many properties that can be preserved by the move to the forcing version of some underlying logic (which is assumed to have the properties). Even when the full version of the property fails (which is guaranteed since the whole point of a forcing relation is to fix perceived problems with the underlying relation) there are usually restricted versions of the properties which hold for forcing. In fact the restricted versions can be seen to make more sense for a paraconsistent relation, which is certainly the case for monotonicity and substitutionality (in the strong sense). The hope is that these considerations may persuade the reader that this method is, from a technical standpoint, the right way to go. What is important to recognize is that the method does not completely change the rules of the game. It recognizes a failing, and then offers a solution. It does not change the meaning of logical constants; it merely does not permit one to use those constants in certain contexts: namely inconsistent contexts. In all of the consistent contexts one may proceed as one always does using the logic one wants.

---

[15]Please note that theorem 9, theorem 10, proposition 8, and theorem 12 were originally published in Payette and d'Entremont (2006).

What happens in the inconsistent contexts is that something has gone awry. But we want to keep as much as possible of the original way of doing things, because we presumably have some strong motivation for doing so. Forcing allows us to keep within sight of the familiar even while straying into unexplored logical territory.

# Eight

# Representation of Forcing

DORIAN NICHOLSON AND BRYSON BROWN

**Abstract**

This essay shows how the forcing relation with underlying logic $X$ might be represented in a way which more closely resembles an axiomatic approach. Following the initial result we take up the problem of representing the forcing relation in the case where the underlying logic $X$ allows sets to the the right of $\vdash_X$. This requires us to redefine the notion of $X$-level forcing to take into account the 'handedness' of sets. We must also expand the definition of $X$-level to take this difference into account.

## 8.1  Introduction

Once it is realized that $X$-level forcing[1] inherits only some of the principles of the underlying logic $X$, and in particular that an abridgement of the structural rule [Mon] of monotonicity is required,[2] the question of alternative presentations of the relation naturally arises. The goal is to give something like an axiomatization of the relation, and once that has been accomplished, we can, those of us who were worried, heave a sigh

---

[1] See 'Preserving What?' in this volume for the definitive account.

[2] In fact many otherwise well-intentioned folk have gone so far as to equate monotonicity with deduction, in the sense that if a relation is not monotonic, then it can't be deductive inference.

of relief. The project is not so urgent as the corresponding problem in so-called $n$-ary modal logic, but that shouldn't be regarded as an excuse for not undertaking it.

## 8.2  Background

We consider logics $X$ which satisfy the usual structural rules:

[R] $\alpha \in \Gamma \implies \Gamma \vdash_X \alpha$,

[Cut] $\Gamma, \alpha \vdash_X \beta \ \& \ \Gamma \vdash_X \alpha \implies \Gamma \vdash_X \beta$, and

[Mon] $\Gamma \vdash_X \alpha \implies \Gamma \cup \Delta \vdash_X \alpha$.

For these logics, we understand the notion of consistency in the manner of Post.

$\Gamma$ is consistent, *in* or *relative to* a logic $X$ (alternatively, $\Gamma$ is $X$-consistent) if and only if there is at least one formula $\alpha$ such that $\Gamma \nvdash_X \alpha$.

Where $X$ is a logic, the associated consistency predicate (of sets of formulas) for $X$ is indicated by $\text{CON}_X$.

Having a notion of consistency allows us to define a certain relation between pairs of formulas (of the underlying language of the logic $X$ – after this we won't bother to keep mumbling that particular mantra) which we term *non-trivial denial*.

$X$ has *non-trivial* denial if and only if for every non-absurd formula $\alpha$ there is at least one non-absurd formula $\beta$ which is not $X$-consistent with $\alpha$. Two formulas which are related in this way are said to deny each other. We also say each is *a denial* of the other.

There are, in addition, two properties which we may require of a logic $X$:

We shall say of the logic $X$ that it is *productival* (or that it *has products*), which is to say two things:

($\Pi_1$) For every finite set $\Sigma$ there is a formula $\Pi(\Sigma)$ such that $\Pi(\Sigma) \vdash_X \sigma_i$ for every $\sigma_i \in \Sigma$, and

($\Pi_2$) $\Sigma \vdash_X \Pi(\Sigma)$.

We say of the logic $X$ that it is *coproductival* (or that it has co-products) when it satisfies these two conditions:

($\coprod_1$) For every finite set of formulas $\Sigma$ there is a formula $\coprod(\Sigma)$ such that, for every $\sigma \in \Sigma, \sigma \vdash_X \coprod(\Sigma)$.

($\coprod_2$) If, for any formula $\beta, \sigma \in \Sigma \implies \sigma \vdash_X \beta$ then $\coprod(\Sigma) \vdash_x \beta$.

When the logic $X$ enjoys all of these, it will be said to have a *full* set properties.

Given a set $\Gamma$ of formulas drawn from the language of the logic $X$, we say that an indexed family of sets (starting with $\varnothing$), is an *X-logical cover* of $\Gamma$ provided:

For every element $a$ of the indexed family, $\text{CON}_X(a)$, and

$$\Gamma \subseteq \bigcup_{i \in I} \mathbb{C}_X(a_i),$$

where $\mathbb{C}_X(a_i)$ is the $(X)$ logical closure of $a_i$, which is to say,

$$\{\beta | a_i \vdash_X \beta\}.$$

When $\mathfrak{F}$ is an $(X)$ logical cover for $\Gamma$ we write

$$\text{COV}_X(\mathfrak{F}, \Gamma).$$

Mention of the particular logic $X$ is often suppressed when no confusion is thereby engendered. We shall refer to the size of the index set of the indexed family in this definition as the *width* of the logical cover, indicated by $w(\mathfrak{F})$.

And now for the central idea. The *level* (relative to the logic $X$) of the set of formulas $\Gamma$, indicated by $\ell^X(\Gamma)$, is defined as follows:

$$\ell^X(\Gamma) = \begin{cases} \min_{w(\mathfrak{F})} [\text{COV}_X(\mathfrak{F}, \Gamma)] & \text{if this limit exists,} \\ \infty & \text{otherwise.} \end{cases}$$

In other words, the $X$-level (of incoherence or inconsistency) of a set $\Sigma$ in a logic $X$ is the width of the narrowest $X$-logical cover of $\Sigma$, if there is such a thing, and if there isn't, the level is set to the symbol $\infty$.

Finally, we define the relation of $X$-level forcing, which, as its name suggests, is derived from some underlying logic $X$. The relation is defined as follows:

$\Gamma[\Vdash_X \alpha$ if and only if, for every division of $\Gamma$ into $\ell^X(\Gamma)$ cells, for at least one of the cells $\Delta$, $\Delta \vdash_X \alpha$.

## 8.3  Representation

In order to *represent*, as we shall say, the relation $[\Vdash_X$ of $X$-level forcing, we shall provide another relation to be called simply $X$-forcing, indicated by $[\vdash_X$ and eventually show that the two are the same relation. In doing this we axiomatize, in a certain sense, the relation of $X$-level forcing for a variety of logics $X$.

### $X$-forcing.

We describe $[\vdash_X$ by saying first that it connects to $X$ by means of the *singular* sets of formulas in this manner:

[Sing] If $\Gamma$ is singular then

$\Gamma[\vdash_X \alpha \iff \Gamma \vdash_X \alpha,$

where a set is singular if it cannot be broken up by logical covers. In this case the empty set is singular, along with all unit sets.

As a result of this bridge rule, we should notice the following consequence:

$[\Pi] \{\gamma\} [\vdash_X \{\alpha\} \ \& \ \{\gamma\} [\vdash_X \{\beta\} \implies \{\gamma\} [\vdash_X \Pi \{\alpha.\beta\}.$

Next we stipulate that $X$-forcing satisfies [Ref] and [Cut] but only a restricted form of monotonicity (or dilution) which has two parts:

[M1] If $\Gamma[\vdash_X \alpha$ then $\Gamma \cup \Gamma^*[\vdash_X \alpha$
provided $\ell^X(\Gamma) = \ell^X(\Gamma \cup \Gamma^*)$

[M2] If $\Gamma[\vdash_X \alpha$ then
$\Gamma \cup \Gamma^*[\vdash_X \alpha$ if $\Gamma$ is singular.

We shall have need of bunches of products as well as coproducts of such bunches. To maximize the ease of displaying such conglomerations of formulas we define as follows:

---

**Definition 1.** $\Gamma_{ij}$ for $\Gamma \setminus \{\gamma_i, \gamma_j\}$.

---

**Definition 2.** PAIRS$(\Gamma)$ for the set of pairs of elements of $\Gamma'$.

---

For example, if our set is $\{x, y, z\}$,
then PAIRS$(\{x, y, z\}) = \{\{x, y\}, \{y, z\}, \{x, z\}\}$.

---

**Definition 3.** PPAIRS$(\Gamma)$ for the set of products of pairs of elements of $\Gamma$.

---

For example, PPAIRS$(\{x, y, z\}) = \{\Pi\{x, y\}, \Pi\{y, z\}, \Pi\{x, z\}\}$. With the aid of this notation, we can now state two rules of inference for $[\vdash_X$:

[RPig]$\Gamma[\vdash_X \alpha_1 \quad \& \ldots \& \quad \Gamma[\vdash_X \alpha_k \implies$
$\Gamma[\vdash_X \bigsqcup\{\text{PPAIRS}(\{\alpha_1, \ldots \alpha_k\})\}$

[LPig] $\Gamma_{i,j}, \Pi\{\gamma_i, \gamma_j\}[\vdash_X \alpha \; \forall \{\gamma_i, \gamma_j\} \in \text{PAIRS}(\Gamma) \implies$
$\Gamma, \bigsqcup\{\text{PPAIRS}(\Gamma)\}[\vdash_X \alpha,$

where 'Pig' suggests 'Pigeonhole.' The assumption of the two rules is that the cardinality of $\Gamma$ exceeds the $X$-level of $\Gamma$.

The soundness of [RPig] is no serious issue since it is simply a way of stating the pigeonhole principle. The soundness of [LPig] requires a bit more than just seeing however. The requirement is provided by the following:

**Lemma 1.** *Let* $\Gamma_{ij}^* = \Gamma_{ij} \cup \{\Pi(\gamma_i, \gamma_j)\}$. *Then* $\ell(\Gamma_{ij}^*) = \ell(\Gamma)$, *when* $\gamma_i, \gamma_j \in \Gamma$ *and there is some* $X$-*cover of* $\Gamma$ *which is a cover of their product.*

*Proof.* Suppose that $\mathfrak{F}$ is an $X$-cover of $\Gamma$ and $w(\mathfrak{F}) = \ell(\Gamma)$, and $\mathfrak{F}$ is a cover of $\Pi\{\gamma_i, \gamma_j\}$ for some $\gamma_i, \gamma_j \in \Gamma$. Suppose further that $\ell(\Gamma) = k$. Now let $\mathfrak{F} = \{\Delta_0, \ldots \Delta_k\}$, and for some $\Delta_i \in \mathfrak{F}$, $\Delta_i \vdash_X \Pi(\gamma_i, \gamma_j)$, as in the hypothesis. Let $\Delta_i^* = \Delta_i \cup \{\Pi\{\gamma_i, \gamma_j\}\}$, and form $\mathfrak{F}^* = \{\Delta_0, \ldots, \Delta_i^*, \ldots, \Delta_k\}$. This is clearly an $X$-cover of $\Gamma_{ij}^*$; thus, $\ell(\Gamma_{ij}^*) \leq \ell(\Gamma)$.

Suppose for reductio that $\ell(\Gamma_{ij}^*) < \ell(\Gamma)$. By definition there is $\mathfrak{F}'$ that covers $\Gamma_{ij}^*$ with width $w(\mathfrak{F}') = \ell(\Gamma_{ij}^*) < \ell(\Gamma)$. Let $\mathfrak{F}' = \{\Delta_0, \ldots, \Delta_m\}$, and $m < k$.

We want to show that $\mathfrak{F}'$ is a cover of $\Gamma$. There is some $\Delta_i \in \mathfrak{F}'$ that proves $\Pi(\gamma_i, \gamma_j)$ since it is a cover of $\Gamma_{ij}^*$. By definition of product, the product must prove both $\gamma_i$ and $\gamma_j$. And there must be a cell that proves the product, so by [Cut] on the underlying logic it follows that that cell, $\Delta_i$, must prove both $\gamma_i$ and $\gamma_j$. But $\Gamma - \Gamma_{ij}^* = \{\gamma_i, \gamma_j\}$. So that makes $\mathfrak{F}'$ a cover of $\Gamma$. However, that means $\ell(\Gamma) \leq w(\mathfrak{F}') < \ell(\Gamma)$, and that is a contradiction. Therefore $\ell(\Gamma_{ij}^*) = \ell(\Gamma)$.                    $\square$

**Lemma 2.** [LPig] *holds for* $\llbracket \Vdash_X$.

$$\Gamma_{ij}, \Pi\{\gamma_i, \gamma_j\}\llbracket\Vdash_X \alpha \vee \{\gamma_i, \gamma_j\} \in \text{PAIRS}(\Gamma) \implies$$
$$\bigcup_{\{\gamma_i, \gamma_j\}\in\text{PAIRS}(\Gamma)} \Gamma_{ij}, \coprod\{\text{PPAIRS}(\Gamma)\}\llbracket\Vdash_X \alpha$$

*Proof.* Arguing indirectly, we show is that there is some $\Gamma_{ij}, \Pi(\gamma_i, \gamma_j)$ that does not $X$-level force $\alpha$, given that the consequent of [LPig] fails. We do this by showing that there is a cover, of appropriate width, of $\Gamma_{ij} \cup \{\Pi(\gamma_i, \gamma_j)\}$ that does not cover $\alpha$.

By assumption, the antecedent of the conclusion does not $X$-level force $\alpha$, so there must be a cover of $\Gamma$, of width $\ell(\Gamma)$, that does not cover $\alpha$. Since the cardinality of $\Gamma$ exceeds the $X$-level of $\Gamma$, by pigeonhole reasoning, there must be a cell in this cover with at least two elements. Take the $\Gamma_{ij} \cup \{\Pi\{\gamma_i, \gamma_j\}\}$ relative to those two elements and that set will not $X$-level force $\alpha$. What needs to be shown to give us that conclusion is that the level of this set is the same as the level of $\Gamma$. That way the cover that we construct has the right width to act as an $X$-level forcing cover for $\Gamma_{ij} \cup \{\Pi(\gamma_i, \gamma_j)\}$. This follows at once from the previous lemma. $\qquad\square$

## 8.4   The Representation Theorem

With all this under our belt, we are finally ready to prove the Representation Theorem for $X$-level forcing. We assume that $X$ enjoys a full set of properties.

**Theorem 1.** (Representation Theorem for $X$-level Forcing). *For every set $\Gamma$ of formulas and every formula $\alpha$,* $\Gamma[\Vdash_X \alpha \iff \Gamma[\vdash_X \alpha$

*Proof.* The proof is by induction on the cardinality of the premise set $\Gamma$. The basis of the induction is the case in which the cardinality in question is less than or equal to the $X$-level of the premise set. In this case, since there will be at least one logical cover of the premise set in which each cell contains no more than one formula, there must be an $X$-inference of the form $\{\gamma\}[\Vdash_X \alpha$, and thus the result follows at once by [Sing].

In the induction step, the hypothesis of induction is that the cardinality of the premise set is n+1, and that the result holds for all premise sets of cardinality up to and including n. To avoid loss of generality we must take n to be greater than the $X$-level of $\Gamma$.

Assume $\Gamma[\Vdash_X \alpha$. It is easy to see that $\Gamma_{i,j}, \Pi\{\gamma_i, \gamma_j\}[\Vdash_X \alpha$ for every pair $\{\gamma_i, \gamma_j\}$ in PAIRS($\Gamma$). Since the cardinality of each of the premise sets is less than the cardinality of $\Gamma$, by the hypothesis of induction we may replace $[\Vdash_X$ by $[\vdash_X$ in each of the inferences. But by now invoking the rule [LPig] we get $\Gamma, \bigsqcup\{\text{PPAIRS}(\Gamma)\}[\vdash_X \alpha$. But $\Gamma[\vdash_X \bigsqcup\{\text{PPAIRS}(\Gamma)\}$ by [RPig], so the result follows at once by [Cut]. $\square$

## 8.5   More Definitions and Motivation

It would be an exaggeration, although a pardonable one, to say that the most general way to do proof theory is to take an inference relation to be a relation between *sets* of formulas.[3] This is different from studying the relation between a set of premises and its closure, which is simply gathering together all of the single formulas which follow from the premises. In this new approach we, in effect, draw a distinction between two *kinds* of sets (of formulas).

We could label the two kinds *premise* sets and *conclusion* sets, but that terminology invites a confusion between the notion of deductive closure, which is after all a set of conclusions, and the new species which we now consider. For the most part, we call the sets that appear on the left side of the provability symbol l-sets while those on the right are r-sets.

Perhaps the easiest way to think of what is going on here is as a kind of *dualism*; r-sets and l-sets are dual to one another in a sense that we shall try to illuminate as we go.

First we shall formulate our basic structural rules, generalizations of the rules which we have already seen, which apply to all the logics we discuss unless we issue an explicit disclaimer.

[R] $\Delta \cap \Gamma \neq \varnothing \implies \Gamma \vdash \Delta$.

[Cut] $\Gamma, \alpha \vdash \Delta \ \& \ \Gamma \vdash \alpha, \Delta \implies \Gamma \vdash \Delta$.

[Mon] $\Gamma \vdash \Delta \implies \Gamma \cup \Sigma \vdash \Delta \cup \Lambda$.

In previous work we took the notion of consistency as central. Alas, this is peculiar to l-sets, which is to say that it doesn't translate to r-sets. Of course, this is what we ought to expect. What we shall require is a more general notion, which we call *triviality*, which comprehends both sides of the provability relation. Here it is for l-sets:

---

[3]Those who favour Gentzen-style proof theory, also known as *sequent calculus*, would argue that sequents are more general than sets since the latter, in effect, build in a number of structural rules rather than making them explicit.

A set $\Gamma$ is said to be $(X)$ *l-trivial*, indicated by $\text{TRIV}_{XL}(\Gamma)$, if and only if $\Gamma \vdash_X \varnothing$.

Notice that, since we are assuming that $\vdash_X$ satisfies [Mon], this amounts to saying that $\Gamma$ proves every set, which is simply a way of saying that there is no distinction between what $\Gamma$ proves in $X$ and what it doesn't. Whatever notion of $X$-provability has interested us thus far can interest us no longer, when it comes to $\Gamma$.

For r-sets, we must take the dual formulation:

A set $\Delta$ is said to be $(X)$ *r-trivial*, indicated by $\text{TRIV}_{XR}(\Delta)$, if and only if $\varnothing \vdash_X \Delta$.

Of course l-triviality is merely inconsistency in sheep's clothing while r-triviality seems much more radical or even gratuitous. An r-trivial unit set, say $\{\alpha\}$, which we would normally write $\alpha$, is what others would call a *theorem* of the logic in question. So, far from being trivial, these are the whole point of a logic, aren't they?

In a word, no. Logic is about inference, and the r-trivial sets trample the distinction, dual to the one offended by inconsistency, between what proves some set and what doesn't. Once again, given [Mon], *every* set proves an r-trivial one.

In general terms we might say this in defence of our derogatory terminology: In so far as an inference relation draws a distinction between those kinds of reasoning which are correct and those which aren't, both kinds of triviality are well named. In both cases there is no longer a distinction. In the l-case we have lost the distinction between what a set proves and what it fails to prove and in the r-case the dual distinction between what it would take to prove a set and what it would take not to prove it. There is no reason to reject one sort of trampling while embracing its dual. And while we are at it, let us not forget that 'tautology' is indeed a term of derogation, often prefixed by some such qualifier as 'mere.'

First, we define an ambidextrous predicate:

---

**Definition 4.** *Relative to a logic $X$, a set $\Sigma$ is said to be $X$-consistent, indicated by $\mathrm{CON}_X(\Sigma)$, if and only if $\overline{\mathrm{TRIV}}_R(\Sigma)$ if $\Sigma$ is on the right, and $\overline{\mathrm{TRIV}}_L(\Sigma)$ if $\Sigma$ is on the left.*

---

Here the overline indicates predicate negation.

Having increased the scope of the consistency predicate to cover both kinds of sets, we carry over our earlier definitions of logical cover and level which have become similarly ambidextrous.

Level applies to both flavours of set, but rather than use explicit notation to display which kind of level is at issue, we shall let the context determine whether we are dealing with left-level or right. It ought to go without saying that one and the same set will not in general have the same level on both sides of the inference relation.[4]

Having level functions for both left- and right-handed sets permits us to define two derived inference relations. The first is just X-level forcing, while the second, more exotic one we shall dub *inverse* X-level forcing. Once the second relation is defined, the aptness of the name we have chosen will become apparent.

$X$-level forcing:

$\Gamma[\Vdash_X \alpha$ if and only if, for every division of $\Gamma$ into $\ell^X(\Gamma)$ cells, for at least one of the cells $a, a \vdash_X \alpha$.

Inverse $X$-level forcing:

$\alpha[\Vdash_X \Delta$ if and only if, for every division of $\Delta$ into $\ell^X(\Delta)$ cells, for at least one of the cells $a, \alpha \vdash_X a$.

Although the inverse case looks a bit unusual, both these relations preserve level, though we need to specify what that means in the inverse case. Here we must define, for every conclusion-set $\Sigma$, the *inverse X-theory* of $\Sigma$, indicated by $\mathbb{C}_X^{-1}(\Sigma)$:

---

[4]A significant exception is $\varnothing$ which has the same level on the left as it does on the right, namely 0.

---

**Definition 5.** $\mathbb{C}_X^{-1}(\Sigma) = \{\sigma | \sigma \vdash_X \Sigma\}$

---

To say that $X$-level forcing preserves level is to say that

$$\ell^X(\Gamma) = \ell^X(\mathbb{C}_X(\Gamma))$$

and to say that inverse $X$-level forcing preserves level is to say the same thing except for inverse closure, namely,

$$\ell^X(\Delta) = \ell^X(\mathbb{C}_X^{-1}(\Delta)).$$

This in turn means that neither left- nor right-handed sets can be trivial unless the set in question contains an absurd formula.

Just as we earlier showed how to represent $X$-level forcing, we can now do the same for the inverse relation.

### Inverse $X$-Forcing

It is relatively easy to see that what we could do by way of representing the relation of $X$-level forcing, we can also do with the relation of inverse $X$-level forcing, by 'dualizing.'

This certainly applies to the syntactical presentation of the relation we call inverse $X$-forcing. We say, as before, that it connects to $X$ by means of the *singular* sets of formulas in this manner:

[Sing] If $\Gamma$ is singular then, $\alpha[\vdash_X \Gamma \iff \alpha \vdash_X \Gamma$

where a set is singular if it cannot be broken up by logical covers (once again the empty set is singular, along with all unit sets).

Next we stipulate that inverse $X$-forcing satisfies [Ref] and [Cut] but these rules should be stated:

[Ref] $\alpha \in \Gamma \implies \alpha[\vdash_X \Gamma$

[Cut] $(\alpha[\vdash_X \Gamma, \beta \,\&\, \beta[\vdash_X \Gamma) \implies \alpha[\vdash_X \Gamma$

The restricted form of monotonicity (or dilution) still has two parts, namely the duals of the previous ones:

[M1] If $\alpha\big[\vdash_X \Gamma$ then $\alpha\big[\vdash_X \Gamma \cup \Gamma^*$
provided $\ell^X(\Gamma) = \ell^X(\Gamma \cup \Gamma^*)$

[M2] If $\alpha\big[\vdash_X \Gamma$ then
$\alpha\big[\vdash_X \Gamma \cup \Gamma^*$ if $\Gamma^*$ is singular.

Using the notation we introduced for $X$-forcing, we can state the dual pigeonhole principles which hold for the inverse relation.

[LPig]$\alpha_1\big[\vdash_X \Gamma \quad \& \ldots \& \quad \alpha_k\big[\vdash_X \Gamma \implies$
$\Pi\{\text{COPPAIRS}(\{\alpha_1, \ldots \alpha_k\})\}\big[\vdash_X \Gamma$

[RPig] $\alpha\big[\vdash_X \Gamma_{i,j}, \bigsqcup\{\gamma_i, \gamma_j\} \; \forall \{\gamma_i, \gamma_j\} \in \text{PAIRS}(\Gamma) \implies$
$\alpha\big[\vdash_X \Gamma, \Pi\{\text{COPPAIRS}(\Gamma)\}$

The assumption of the two rules is that the cardinality of $\Gamma$ exceeds the $X$-level of $\Gamma$.

We use the expression $\text{COPPAIRS}(\Sigma)$, by analogy with $\text{PPAIRS}$, to represent the set of coproducts of pairs of elements of $\Sigma$.

We can argue for the soundness of the 'Pig' rules, and for the representation of inverse $X$-level forcing by inverse $X$-forcing, by simply reusing the original arguments for the representation of $X$-level forcing, in dual form.

We now consider the proper way to characterize the set-set version of forcing.

## 8.6   $\Gamma\big[\vdash_X \Delta$

We start by describing the relation $\big[\vdash_X$, called $X$-forcing, based upon the underlying (multiple conclusion) logic $X$. Our aim is to show that this relation is the same as the multiple-conclusion $X$-level forcing that we describe below. It will turn out that there are two ways to accomplish this – as we have been calling it – *representation* result, and that the two theorems are equivalent.

We shall stipulate that $X$ satisfy the structural rules already mentioned and be *productival*.

We shall also, as we expect from the earlier account, want $X$ to be *coproductival*, which we may now define more elegantly than we did earlier:

($\bigsqcup$ 1) For every finite set $\Delta$, there is a formula $\bigsqcup \Delta$ such that for every $\delta \in \Delta, \delta \vdash_X \bigsqcup \Delta$, and

($\bigsqcup$ 2) $\bigsqcup \Delta \vdash_X \Delta$.

We describe $[\vdash_X$ by saying first that it connects to $X$ by means of the *singular* sets of formulas as we have done earlier.

[Sing] If $\Gamma$ and $\Delta$ are singular then $\Gamma[\vdash_X \Delta \iff \Gamma \vdash_X \Delta$

The notion of singularity need suffer no change from the earlier concept so that the empty set is singular, along with all unit sets.

As a result of this bridge rule, we should notice the consequences:

[$\Pi$] $\{\gamma\}[\vdash_X \{\alpha\}$ & $\{\gamma\}[\vdash_X \{\beta\} \implies \{\gamma\}[\vdash_X \Pi\{\alpha, \beta\}$

Next we stipulate that $X$-forcing satisfies the multiple conclusion form of [Ref] and [Cut] but again, only a restricted form of monotonicity (or dilution) which has two parts:

[M1] If $\Gamma[\vdash_X \Delta$ then $\Gamma \cup \Gamma^*[\vdash_X \Delta \cup \Delta^*$, provided $\ell^X(\Gamma) = \ell^X(\Gamma \cup \Gamma^*)$ and $\ell^X(\Delta) = \ell^X(\Delta \cup \Delta^*)$

[M2] If $\Gamma[\vdash_X \Delta$ then $\Gamma \cup \Gamma^*[\vdash_X \Delta$ if $\Gamma$ is singular, and $\Gamma[\vdash_X \Delta \cup \Delta^*$ if $\Delta$ is singular.

Finally, we must expand our collection of pigeonhole principles:

[RPigL]$\Gamma[\vdash_X \alpha_1, \Delta$ & ... & $\Gamma[\vdash_X \alpha_k, \Delta \implies$ $\Gamma[\vdash_X \bigsqcup \text{PPAIRS}(\{\alpha_1, \dots \alpha_k\}), \Delta$

[LPigL] $\Gamma_{i,j}, \Pi\{\gamma_i, \gamma_j\}[\vdash_X \alpha, \Delta \; \forall \{\gamma_i, \gamma_j\} \in \text{PAIRS}(\Gamma) \implies$ $\Gamma, \bigsqcup \text{PPAIRS}(\Gamma)[\vdash_X \alpha, \Delta$

[RPIGR]$\Gamma[\vdash_X \Delta_{i,j}, \bigsqcup\{\delta_i, \delta_j\} \; \forall \{\delta_i, \delta_j\} \in \text{PAIRS}(\Delta) \implies$ $\Gamma[\vdash_X \Delta, \Pi\text{COPPAIRS}(\Delta)$

[LPIGR]$\Gamma, \delta_1 [\vdash_X \Delta$ or ... or $\Gamma, \delta_k [\vdash_X \Delta \implies$
$\Gamma, \Pi\text{COPPAIRS}(\{\delta_1, \ldots, \delta_k\}) [\vdash_X \Delta$

In the statement of these principles, we assume that the cardinality of the sets $\Gamma$ and $\Delta$ are strictly greater than their corresponding levels.

## 8.7   $\Gamma[\Vdash_X \Delta$

We shall say that $\Gamma[\Vdash_X \Delta$ provided that for every pair $\mathfrak{F}\Gamma$, $\mathfrak{F}\Delta$ of logical covers of the premise set and the conclusion set respectively, that there is a simple logical relation between them of this form:

$$\exists a \in \mathfrak{F}\Gamma, b \in \mathfrak{F}\Delta : a \vdash_X b$$

That is, the $X$-consequence relation is preserved in all pairs of covering families, in the sense that some pair of members from each family bear the $X$-consequence relation to each other.

## 8.8   The Representation of Forcing

We shall consider two theorems which characterize, or represent the relation $[\vdash_X$.

**Theorem 2.** First Representation Theorem *For every pair* $\Gamma$, $\Delta$ *of sets of formulas,* $\Gamma[\vdash_X \Delta \iff \Gamma[\Vdash_X \Delta$.

**Theorem 3.** Second Representation Theorem *For every pair* $\Gamma$, $\Delta$ *of sets of formulas,* $\Gamma[\vdash_X \Delta \iff$ *for some formula* $\alpha$, $\Gamma[\vdash_X \alpha \& \alpha[\vdash_X \Delta$.

**Lemma 3.** Equivalence of the two representations *For every pair* $\Gamma$, $\Delta$ *of sets of formulas,* $\Gamma[\Vdash_X \Delta \iff$ *for some formula* $\alpha, \Gamma[\vdash_X \alpha \& \alpha[\vdash_X \Delta$.

*Proof.* The right to left direction of this equivalence is a simple (in effect) soundness proof which we can omit with a clear conscience. The hard direction, from left to right, we prove by double induction on the cardinalities of $\Gamma$ and $\Delta$.

In the basis case, the cardinalities of the two sets are less than or equal, respectively to the X-level of $\Gamma$ and $\Delta$. In such a case the only way that $\Gamma[\Vdash_X \Delta$ can hold is if there is an $X$ proof $\gamma \vdash_X \delta$ between some pair of formulas, say $\gamma \in \Gamma$ and $\delta \in \Delta$. By singularity, it must follow that $\Gamma[\Vdash_X \alpha$ and that $\alpha[\Vdash_X \Delta$, for some formula $\alpha$.

As the hypothesis of induction, assume that the result holds for cardinalities of $\Gamma$, $\Delta$ up to n.

In the first part of the induction step, we assume that $|\Gamma|$ is greater than $\ell^X(\Gamma)$ (else the result would hold trivially by singularity), and that $\Gamma[\Vdash_X \Delta$. Now it follows that there must be pairs $\gamma_i, \gamma_j$ of distinct members of $\Gamma$ such that the $X$-level of the set $\Gamma^{ij} = \Gamma_{ij} \cup \Pi\{\gamma_i, \gamma_j\}$ is equal to the $X$-level of $\Gamma$, and that $\Gamma^{ij}[\Vdash_X \Delta$. As before we indicate by $\Gamma_{ij}$ the set $\Gamma$ with the pair $\gamma_i, \gamma_j$ removed. Moreover the set $|\Gamma^{ij}| = n - 1$, so that the hypothesis of induction gives us the existence of some formula, let us call it $\alpha^{ij}$, such that $\Gamma^{ij}[\vdash_X \alpha^{ij}$ and $\alpha^{ij}[\vdash_X \Delta$.

If, for each one of these pairs $\gamma_i, \gamma_j$, we gather together the corresponding results gained from the hypothesis of induction, we shall have, after using a [PIG] rule and the fact that $X$ has coproducts:

$$\Gamma, \coprod\{\text{PPAIRS}(\Gamma)\}[\vdash_X \coprod\{\alpha^{ij}\}\ (i, j) \in \text{PAIRS}(\Gamma)$$

The use of the other [PIG] together with [Cut] results in the following:

$$\Gamma[\vdash_X \coprod\{\alpha^{ij}\}\ (i, j) \in \text{PAIRS}(\Gamma).$$

But since each element of the coproduct $X$-proves $\Delta$, so does the coproduct which serves as the formula $X$-forced by $\Gamma$, which $X$-forces $\Delta$. This ends the first induction step.

The second induction step is, once again, the dual of the first in which we replace pairs $\delta_i, \delta_j$ from delta with their coproducts, which we must be able to do for at least some pairs without increasing the level of $\Delta$. Then we simply use the same kinds of moves (except dualized) to get the existence of some formula $X$-forced by $\Gamma$ which $X$-forces $\Delta$. $\square$

But this serves as a guideline for the proof of the first representation theorem, which goes as follows:

Suppose $\Gamma[\Vdash_X \Delta$. Then, as we showed in the equivalence lemma,

$\Gamma[\vdash_X \alpha$ and $\alpha[\vdash_X \Delta$.

But then by the allowable uses of monotonicity, $\Gamma[\vdash_X \alpha, \Delta$ and $\Gamma, \alpha[\vdash_X \Delta$.

But then, by [Cut], $\Gamma[\vdash_X \Delta$.

# Nine

# Forcing and Practical Inference

PETER SCHOTCH

### Abstract

In this essay we consider two variations on the theme of forcing. In one of these we restrict the number of possible logical covers of a given premise set by specifying certain
subsets, which we call *clumps*, and requiring that any cell which contains a member of
a clump must also contain the other members. The other variation allows for redefining
the notion of logical cover in order to require that the cells not only be *logically* consistent but also *practically* consistent. In other words, in this mode we require of any
logical cover that it recognize our theoretical (and perhaps also practical) commitments,
by defining the cells to be those subsets (if any) which do not prove (in the underlying
logic) any denial of those commitments.

## 9.1   Introduction

What we might call the *pure* or perhaps *general* theory of the forcing
relation is all very well in a theoretical setting. That shouldn't come as
much of a surprise since our treatment of forcing tends to be abstract
and general. On the other hand, sometimes we want to study inference
in something more closely resembling ordinary life, more ordinary than
mathematical life at least. In these cases the general theory is too spare.
In fact we shall distinguish two ways in which one might wish to come

down from the Olympian heights of generality to no greater altitude than a foothill might boast.

First a sketch of the general theory:[1]

We consider logics $X$ which satisfy the usual structural rules:

[R] $\alpha \in \Gamma \implies \Gamma \vdash_X \alpha$

[Cut] $\Gamma, \alpha \vdash_X \beta \ \& \ \Gamma \vdash_X \alpha \implies \Gamma \vdash_X \beta$

[Mon] $\Gamma \vdash_X \alpha \implies \Gamma \cup \Delta \vdash_X \alpha$

For these logics, we understand the notion of consistency in the manner of Post:

> **Definition 1.** $\Gamma$ *is consistent,* in *or* relative to *a logic* $X$ *(alternatively,* $\Gamma$ *is* $X$-*consistent), if and only if there is at least one formula* $\alpha$ *such that* $\Gamma \not\vdash_X \alpha$.

Where $X$ is a logic, the associated consistency predicate (of sets of formulas) for $X$ is indicated by $\text{CON}_X$.

> **Definition 2.** *Any formula, the unit set of which is not consistent, is said to be an* absurd *formula.*

Having a notion of consistency, we go on to define a certain relation between pairs of formulas of the underlying language of the logic $X$ (mention of which is often suppressed when it is unlikely to lead to confusion) which we term *non-trivial denial.*

> **Definition 3.** $X$ *has* non-trivial *denial if and only if for every non-absurd formula* $\alpha$ *there is at least one non-absurd formula* $\beta$ *which is not* $X$-*consistent with* $\alpha$.

---

[1] The definitive account is presented in the essay 'Preserving What?' in this volume.

Two formulas which are related in this way are said to deny each other. We also say each is a *denial* of the other.

---

**Definition 4.** *Given a set of formulas $\Gamma$, we say that an indexed family of sets (starting with $\varnothing$) is a* logical cover *of $\Gamma$ provided: For every element $a$ of the indexed family, $\mathrm{CON}_X(a)$ and*

$$\Sigma \subseteq \bigcup_{i \in I} \mathbb{C}_X(a_i)$$

---

where $\mathbb{C}_X(a_i)$ is the $(X)$ logical closure of $a_i$, which is to say

$$\{\beta \,|\, a_i \vdash_X \beta\}.$$

When $\mathfrak{F}$ is an $(X)$ logical cover for $\Gamma$ we write $\mathrm{COV}_X(\mathfrak{F}, \Gamma)$. We shall refer to the size of the index set of the indexed family in this definition as the *width* of the logical cover, indicated by $w(\mathfrak{F})$.

And now for the central idea.

---

**Definition 5.** *The* level *(relative to the logic $X$) of the set $\Gamma$ of formulas, indicated by $\ell^X(\Gamma)$, is defined as*

$$\ell^X(\Gamma) = \begin{cases} \min_{w(\mathfrak{F})} [\mathrm{COV}_X(\mathfrak{F}, \Gamma)] & \textit{if this limit exists} \\ \infty & \textit{otherwise.} \end{cases}$$

---

In other words, the $X$-level (of incoherence or inconsistency) of a set $\Sigma$ in a logic $X$ is the width of the narrowest $X$-logical cover of $\Sigma$, if there is such a thing, and if there isn't, the level is set to the symbol $\infty$.

---

**Definition 6.** *Finally, we define the relation of $X$-level forcing which, as its name suggests, is derived from some underlying logic $X$.*

$\Gamma \lceil \Vdash_X \alpha$ *if and only if, for every division of $\Gamma$ into $\ell^X(\Gamma)$ cells*

---

> *for at least one of the cells* $\Delta$, $\Delta \vdash_X \alpha$.

## 9.2  Dirty Hands

Now this is all very well in general, for that most abstract plane of logical existence on which epistemology intrudes not at all upon how we reason. However this is seldom a good representation of real inferential life. When we face the world of applications, there may well be non-logical considerations to weigh in the balance.

In real life, we have commitments. Some we clasp to our bosoms after striving to acquire them, while others fall upon us unbidden. At this point, some of our opponents may become existentialist enough to declare that they themselves renounce all commitments and refuse to be bound by anything but their own mighty wills. Such as these have put themselves not only beyond polite society, but also beyond science.

If the mission statement of science includes the aim of framing bold hypotheses and then suffering these to be tested, science involves commitments. We see this as soon as we begin to think about how hypothesis testing works. It is clear that, whether we construct a new experiment, or merely use data previously gathered, we have to assume that the laws of science hold, except of course for the one that we may be testing. It simply makes no sense to talk about testing all the laws of science at once. Testing them against what? We are committed, in this endeavour, to the correctness of whatever bits of science are not being tested.

This is merely one example, though it is a particularly compelling one. But what does it mean to say that we are committed to this or that principle? This much at least: For the duration of our commitment, we shall brook no denial of the principle in question. In other words, we shall treat any such denial as a sort of practical contradiction.[2]

---

[2] Such was a popular device in Buddhist logic, where a paradigm of absurdity was the sentence 'Lotus in the air,' which we might take as an Eastern version of 'Pie in the sky.'

Apart from worrying about commitments we are clearly confronted with cases when merely having consistent cells is not enough, even if we expand our horizons to include *practical consistency*. Cases, that is, in which we want to insist on the integrity of certain of our data. We may be prepared to carve up our premise set into subsets, but we wish to place limits upon how much carving can be done.

## 9.3   Σ-Forcing

Whatever else we may mean by commitment, intolerance of any denial of the commitment must be high on the list. There may come a day in which an argument is so convincing that it releases us from one or more of our commitments, but when that happens, it goes without saying we are no longer committed to whatever it was that previously claimed our allegiance. So we aren't saying that commitment is forever, even commitment worthy of the name. Commitments come and go – an ever shifting pattern as we fail to renew our subscription to one theory and subscribe instead to another.

While our commitment is in force, however, while we are still bound by it, we shall not suffer any denial to be concluded except in the special circumstances noted below. This is the grand picture at any rate, and as is the case with all such, the devil is in the details. One thing to give us pause here is the recognition that our logical commitments are in no way inferior to our other commitments,[3] which places definite limits upon how much refusing we can do.

Think of it this way: We want to treat the denials of commitments, we refer to the set of these by Σ, as absurd – in some wider sense than logically absurd perhaps, but absurd nonetheless. Since we shall be dealing with these commitments in the manner of forcing, there will be some underlying logic $X$ in terms of which initial inferences take place. Given what we have said so far, no member of Σ can be a(n $X$) consequence of a singular set and still be blocked. Earlier we defined as singular the sets that suffer no diminution in any logical cover. In other words, our ability to block these bad conclusions has the same

---

[3]Though we wouldn't follow Quine in giving them a more central place in our 'web of belief.'

limit as our ability in ordinary forcing to block the inference to logical absurdities.

But might we not change this? It all depends upon how we choose to regard the notion of singularity for sets. For the most part, we have been thinking of the singular sets as *defined*, as we did above. If we stick with that line, then the analogy between practical absurdity and logical absurdity continues to hold. On the other hand, we have the option of regarding singularity as a primitive predicate of sets (of formulas) which might be the victim of whatever we want to stipulate in the way of *exceptions* to the way we have understood the idea previously.[4]

We might, that is, choose to excommunicate all those sets which were previously singular but consist of unit sets of members of $\Sigma$. To carry out this program we would also have to limit ourselves to those commitments the denials of which are not $X$-consequences of the empty set. We shall examine the upshot of this alternative stern approach below, but we should note here the existence of opposition to it. Some of our friends have suggested that striking off some sets previously regarded as singular is contrary to the spirit of preservationism.

The most strongly held intuition behind the notion of forcing is this. In the face of problematic inferences in the underlying logic, we fall back to looking at inference from subsets which are problem free. Under any such regime, those inferences in the underlying logic, from sets which cannot be partitioned, *must* be reckoned correct in the derived inference. To deny this is to break the connection between the derived logic and the underlying logic, a connection which forms a large part of the the justification for preservationism as a revision rather than a replacement theory.[5] *That* is one of the things that separates preservationism from alternative approaches to paraconsistency.

We reply that any *general* scheme for setting aside those $X$-licensed inferences, even though they must survive partition, would indeed be anathema. But we are not suggesting anything so general as all that. What we must do is balance our distaste for jettisoning inferences which

---

[4]In effect, this was the approach taken when the topic was introduced in Schotch and Jennings (1989).

[5]For a discussion of these terms, consult the first chapter of this volume.

seem otherwise unassailable with our distaste for practical absurdities. In the sequel we shall present both approaches side by side.

Imagine a case in which there is a physical theory which provides us with plenty of well-confirmed predictions and also, unfortunately, other predictions which are simply absurd, in practical terms at least. Lets say, for instance, that the theory predicts that some physical constant $e$ has an infinite value. What shall we do? A philosopher will immediately say that we have disconfirmed the theory and that we must get rid of it at once. A natural scientist might well have an entirely different slant on things.

A scientist is apt to regard a theory as rather like a salami. Late at night while working in the lab, a scientist overtaken by hunger might go to the fridge and take out a salami to make herself a snack. Alas, there is some mould on one end of the salami. Does she throw it out? Probably not. After all, when faced with a salami which has mould on one end, no law compels us to eat the mouldy part. Cut a few slices from the good end! And the same goes for our theory. Don't use the mouldy part of that either.

In fact, why not cut away the mouldy part of the theory entirely? In order to make it sound better, we could refer to this operation as 'renormalization.' Of course it would be better if we didn't have to resort to this sort of thing, but the world being the kind of place it is, we often do. Show her a physical theory which does all that her renormalized theory does, without invoking that somewhat disreputable operation, and our scientist will embrace it with open arms. Later, at some learned conference or other, she and her colleagues might have a good laugh at the bad old days of renormalization, and proclaim that the younger folk in the profession have it much easier than they did.

But right now there is no such theory and the lab is waiting for our experiments and the journals our articles. There are promotions to get and prestigious fellowships. There are even prizes to win and often respectable amounts of cash are involved. Little wonder then that nobody is prepared to twiddle their scientific thumbs while awaiting a more worthy theory.

This makes philosophers sound a lot purer in spirit than scientists, but it really isn't so. Consider the ever-fascinating realm of moral philosophy. Here we have a rather similar problem. We have two grand approaches to moral theorizing which we might term axiological and deontological. Each of them 'sounds right' in the sense of agreeing with many of our central moral intuitions. But not only are they not compatible, each is refutable by appeal to a central intuition highlighted in the other.[6] In other words, we cannot abandon axiology for deontology or vice versa in order to gain a more secure foundation for morals.

So it seems that in moral philosophy as in physics, we make do. We use the non-mouldy part of the theory and pretend as well as we can that the mouldy part doesn't really exist. If we generalize our notion of $X$-consistency, we can make our logic conform to this behaviour. We can agree that it is a stop-gap measure, one to be used as a last resort, but evidently a last resort is needed.

The central idea is that we get all the mould into one set called $\Sigma$. Less colourfully, $\Sigma$ contains the $(X)$ denials of each of our commitments so that every member of $\Sigma$ is a sentence which we would like to exclude from the output of our theory.

---

**Definition 7.** *A set $\Gamma$ is $(X)$ $\Sigma$-consistent indicated by $\mathrm{CON}_X^\Sigma$, provided that $\Gamma \vdash_X \alpha \implies \alpha \notin \Sigma$.*

---

Evidently, $\Sigma$-consistency implies the usual sort.[7]

From this, the definition of $\Sigma$-logical cover and $\Sigma$-level is obvious. In those definitions we merely replace $\mathrm{CON}_X$ with $\mathrm{CON}_X^\Sigma$. The revised notions will be denoted by $\mathrm{COV}_X^\Sigma$ and $\ell_\Sigma^X$ respectively, while the account of forcing which uses $\Sigma$ will be represented by $[\Vdash_X^\Sigma$. It should be clear that there will be, in general, far fewer $\Sigma$-logical covers for a given set $\Gamma$ than there are logical covers.

Not all of the old rules will hold if we modify singularity by removing members of $\Sigma$; there is bound to be some cost associated with

---

[6]Thus deontological theories are vulnerable to 'lifeboat' counterexamples while axiological theories are vulnerable to 'scapegoat' counterexamples.

[7]In the more general calculus where sets are allowed on the right, this definition can be stated more simply using $\Gamma \nvdash_X \Sigma$.

banishing certain contingent sentences. The earlier form of [Ref] had it that:

$$\frac{\Gamma \cap \Delta \neq \varnothing}{\Gamma[\Vdash_X \Delta}$$

when sets are allowed on the right, and $\alpha \in \Gamma \implies \Gamma[\Vdash_X \alpha$ when they aren't.

This will no longer hold when either $\Gamma \cap \Sigma \neq \varnothing$ or $\Delta \cap \Sigma \neq \varnothing$. What we require is a more general form of [Ref], namely:

$$[\text{Ref}_\Sigma] \frac{\Gamma \cap \Delta \neq \varnothing \,\&\, (\Gamma \cup \Delta) \cap \Sigma = \varnothing}{\Gamma[\Vdash_X^\Sigma \Delta}$$

or

$$[\text{Ref}_\Sigma](\alpha \in \Gamma \,\&\, \alpha \notin \Sigma) \implies \Gamma[\Vdash_X^\Sigma \alpha$$

We get back the usual form of [Ref] by replacing $\Sigma$ with $\varnothing$. In fact this move collapses $\Sigma$-forcing into vanilla forcing. We also get back [Ref] if we don't tinker with the description of singularity.

Tweaking the notion of singularity also requires other changes. We cannot inherit quite as many inferences from the underlying logic $X$ as we did. It remains true that any $X$-theorem will also be an $X$-$\Sigma$-forcing theorem, since the members of $\Sigma$ are contingent by stipulation, but it will no longer be the case that every $X$-consequence of a unit premise set will be preserved. We must drop all those unit sets the members of which belong to $\Sigma$. Of course this means that such sets cannot figure in the generalization to $X$-forcing of the rule [Mon] of monotonicity.

$\Sigma$-forcing is a true generalization of forcing and not one of those approaches which use something akin to *counter-axioms*. Neither do we simply add the denials of all members of $\Sigma$ to every premise set and proceed from that point by ordinary forcing.

The difference is simply that on the counter-axiom approach, or the modified forcing method, the denials of members of $\Sigma$ are, one and all, consequences of every premise set. This is not true for $\Sigma$-forcing since, for example, each 'bad-guy' in $\Sigma$ is contingent; none will be $\Sigma$-forced by the empty set. Neither will any of the denials, presumably 'good-guys' – although not so good that we want to be able to infer them from an arbitrary premise set.

Having said that, we must acknowledge that while $\Sigma$-forcing might provide the basis for some operation like renormalization in physics, it can't be the whole story. This is because we don't simply block the unpalatable in the latter case, we also replace it with the palatable. So if the raw theory tells us that the value of $e$ is infinite, we not only snip that out, we replace it with what we take the actual value to be. One can imagine different ways this might happen, including adopting extra 'non-logical' axioms, but more work would need to be done before something convincing could be offered.

## 9.4   A-Forcing

This is another of the variations on the notion of forcing which reduces the number of logical covers to be considered in calculating whether or not certain conclusions follow from a given premise set. In many applications, unadorned forcing seems to do a bit too much violence in breaking up premise sets (and conclusion sets too, perhaps). If we think of forcing as a candidate for an inference relation to use when reasoning from sets of beliefs, this quickly becomes evident. Representing the belief set of an individual $i$ by $B_i$, it might be argued that in most cases $B_i$ has a level greater than 1. It might even be argued that $B_x$ must have a level of at least 2 if $i$ is rational.

The conflict between this motivation and ordinary forcing or $\Sigma$-forcing, is that we usually identify within some $B_i$ natural *clumps* of beliefs. Thus, while the whole set of $i$'s beliefs may have level 2 or more, we expect and allow $i$ to draw inferences from certain consistent subsets of $B_i$. In other words, we refuse to allow logical covers to prejudice the integrity of any clump of beliefs. In effect, we rule out all those logical covers which do not respect clumps.

For example, if Simon is unable to start his car one morning, he may come to believe, as the result of inference, that his distributor is at fault. In general, we would be willing to allow such reasoning as correct even though $\ell(B_S) = 2$ and there exist covering families of the appropriate width which would prevent the following inference:

$B_S \big[ \Vdash_X$ Simon's distributor is at fault.

We would say, in this situation, that the set of Simon's beliefs about cars and about his car in particular (or at least a respectable subset of these) is immune. The question of which subsets of $B_i$ are to be counted as immune is not to be conclusively settled on logical grounds. This determination must depend upon many factors, not least the identity and circumstances of $i$.

For ease of exposition and to avoid unnecessary complications, we stipulate that the immune subsets of any premise set have level 1.

Our formalization of the intuitive idea of immunity involves a function $A$, defined on sets of sentences and having as the value for a given set $\Gamma$, a set of subsets of $\Gamma$. In other words,

---

**Definition 8.**

*For all sets* $\Gamma : A(\Gamma) \subseteq \mathcal{P}(\Gamma)$, *where* $\mathcal{P}(\Gamma)$ *is the set of all subsets of* $\Gamma$,

---

with $A(\Gamma)$ being interpreted informally as the set of all immune subsets of $\Gamma$. In distinction to the definition of $\Sigma$-forcing, we need make no change in the definition of consistency, but rather to the definition of logical cover. To this end we introduce the notion of a logical cover relative to both the underlying logic $X$ and the function $A$, indicated by $\mathrm{cov}_X^A(\mathfrak{F}, \Gamma)$:

---

**Definition 9.**

$\mathrm{cov}_X^A(\mathfrak{F}, \Gamma) \iff [\mathrm{cov}_X(\mathfrak{F}, \Gamma) \ \& \ (\forall a \in A(\Gamma) \exists x_i \in \mathfrak{F}) a \subseteq x_i]$

---

Thus we allow only those logical covers which do not break up the immune subsets of $\Gamma$. It seems most natural in this setting to consider some single conclusion presentation of the inference relation since we do not usually think of conclusion sets as forming clumps. In either case, however, the definition of the relation we shall call '$\Vdash_X^A$' will be obvious.

There are, of course, many conditions which might be placed upon $A$-functions, each giving rise to a distinctive sort of $A$-forcing. Some are of great interest in the studies of modality mentioned earlier in this volume, while others recommend themselves mainly to the inferentially minded. To recover ordinary forcing, we simply set $A(\Gamma)$ empty, that is,

$$\Gamma\big[\Vdash \alpha(\Gamma\big[\Vdash \Delta) \Leftrightarrow \Gamma\big[\Vdash^A \alpha(\Gamma\big[\Vdash^A \Delta) \;\&\; A(\Gamma) = \varnothing.$$

The other end of this spectrum is not obtained by setting $A(\Gamma) = \Gamma$ since this might violate our restriction on the level of immune subsets. The right condition is instead

$$\mathrm{cov}_X(A(\Gamma), \Gamma),$$

(which obviously reduces to $A(\Gamma) = \Gamma$ when $\ell(\Gamma) = 1$.) This turns out to be one of the modally interesting relations particularly useful in discussions of deontic logic.

Under A-forcing we cannot break up immune sets. This may be expressed in the form of the following rule, dubbed [A], if the underlying logic $X$ is productival.

$$[A]\frac{\Gamma\big[\Vdash_X^A \alpha_1 \;\&\; \ldots \;\&\; \Gamma\big[\Vdash_X^A \alpha_k \;\&\; \exists a \in A(\Gamma) : \{\alpha_1, \ldots, \alpha_k\} \subseteq a}{\Gamma\big[\Vdash_X^A \Pi(\alpha_1, \ldots, \alpha_k)}$$

where $\Pi(\alpha_1, \ldots, \alpha_k)$ is the product (in $X$) of the $\alpha$'s.

## 9.5   Wrap-up

What seems most interesting about forcing and its near relatives is that they actually have *room* to make some accommodation for the actual world. Think about making changes in classical logic or intuitionism to the same end. It isn't even clear what changes those might be. Perhaps many-valued logic, as many of its champions have averred, is one of these attempts to meet the real world, if not halfway, then at least part of the way.

However, forgetting for a moment the deafening howls of protest at such a statement, it is undeniably difficult to see many-valued logic, unless we are talking about a completely Boolean many-valued logic, as any species of classical logic. That is rather the point of classical logic, isn't it? It is as big as any logic can get over that language, having a Post number of $0$.[8] So we can't add anything to classical logic, but neither can we take anything away without the residue being resolutely non-classical.

On the other hand. both $\Sigma$-forcing and A-forcing are recognizable as kinds of forcing. Both are defined in terms of level and preserve that property. At bottom, that is a near definition of what we might call the general notion of forcing.

---

[8]The Post number of a logic $X$ is the number of non-trivial distinct proper extensions of $X$.

# Ten

## Ambiguity Games and Preserving Ambiguity Measures

BRYSON BROWN

### Abstract

Brown (1999) applied preservationist ideas to generate consequence relations first exploited by relevance and dialetheic logicians. The central lesson of the paper was that a systematic application of ambiguity can produce consistent images of inconsistent premise sets, allowing us to systematically constrain the consequences that can be inferred from them. Here we present several different ways to apply ambiguity and the preservation of ambiguity measures to obtain paraconsistent logics. The first uses ambiguity to project consistent images of inconsistent premise sets. The second shifts the focus from the syntactic to the semantic, allowing some atoms to receive ambiguous assignments, that is, assignments that differ from instance to instance. Finally, the third extends the second with a simple game that captures the consequence relation of first-degree entailment, dealing symmetrically with triviality on the right as well as the left. The chapter ends with the observation that preservation of a consequence relation under a range of images offers a new way of applying the general theme of preservationism to produce new (and sometimes better-behaved) consequence relations.

## 10.1 Ambiguity

Brown (1999) began a line of work that has applied preservationist ideas to generate consequence relations first exploited by relevance and dialetheic logicians. The starting point of this approach was the realization that, by treating certain sets of atomic sentences as ambiguous, we can produce consistent *images* of inconsistent premise sets. In this chapter we present several different approaches to using ambiguity and the preservation of ambiguity measures to arrive at some familiar consequence relations.

The first of these approaches uses ambiguity to project consistent images of inconsistent premise sets. The second shifts the focus from the syntactic to the semantic, allowing some atoms to receive ambiguous assignments, in other words, assignments that differ from instance to instance. The third extends the second with a simple game that captures the consequence relation of first-degree entailment. Along the way, dualization of these tricks is applied to cope with triviality on the right as well as the left.

We begin with the original, syntactic story of premise sets and their consistent images. A set of formulae, $\Gamma'$, is a consistent image of $\Gamma$ based on $A$ (which we write $\mathrm{ConIm}(\Gamma', \Gamma, A)$) iff $A$ is a set of atoms, $\Gamma'$ is consistent, and $\Gamma'$ results from the substitution, for each *occurrence* of each member $\alpha$ of $A$ in $\Gamma$, of one of a pair of new atoms, $\alpha_f$ and $\alpha_t$.

A first crude measure of how far $\Gamma$ departs from consistency is the cardinality of the smallest set of atoms $A$ such that for some $\Gamma'$, $\mathrm{ConIm}(\Gamma', \Gamma, A)$. But this measure seems to assume that treating an atom as ambiguous carries a fixed, equal cost. We can still offer a reasonable measure, assuming only that treating any atom as ambiguous carries a non-zero cost. This makes the set of least sets, each of which is sufficient for projecting a consistent image of a premise set, $\Gamma$, a good measure of $\Gamma$'s inconsistency. So we define the *ambiguity set* of $\Gamma$, $\mathrm{Amb}(\Gamma)$ as

$$\{A | \exists \Gamma' : \mathrm{ConIm}(\Gamma', \Gamma, A) \wedge \forall A', A' \subset A, \neg \exists \Gamma' : \mathrm{ConIm}(\Gamma', \Gamma, A')\}.$$

This is the set of smallest sets, $A_1 \dots A_n$, where for each $A_i$ there is some $\Gamma'$ such that $ConIm\Gamma', \Gamma, A_i$.

Extensions that require adding more elements to some of the minimal projection bases are unacceptable. However, some acceptable extensions of $\Gamma$ will rule out some of these minimal projection bases by, in effect, insisting on one or a few of the bases. For example we might extend $\{\alpha, \alpha \rightarrow \beta, \neg\beta\}$, whose Amb set is $\{\{\alpha\},\{\beta\}\}$, by adding $\beta$ to it; the ambiguity set of $\{\alpha, \alpha \rightarrow \beta, \neg\beta, \beta\}$ is just $\{\{\beta\}\}$, since treating '$\beta$' as ambiguous is both necessary and sufficient to produce a consistent image of the original set. So we will regard $\Delta$ as an acceptable extension of $\Gamma$ so long as some elements of $\text{Amb}(\Gamma)$ are also in $\text{Amb}(\Gamma \cup \Delta)$:

$$\text{Accept}(\Delta,\Gamma) \Leftrightarrow \Gamma \subseteq \Delta \ \& \ \text{Amb}(\Gamma \cup \Delta) \subseteq \text{Amb}(\Gamma).$$

Many consequence relations, including the classical consequence relation, can be defined as preserving the acceptability of all acceptable extensions; in this case, our new consequence relation is:

$$\Gamma \vdash_{\text{Amb}} \alpha \Leftrightarrow \forall\Delta: \text{Accept}(\Delta,\Gamma) \rightarrow \text{Accept}(\{\alpha\}, \Gamma \cup\Delta)$$

It follows that the ambiguity set of the closure of $\Gamma$ under $\vdash_{\text{Amb}}$,

$$\text{Amb}(\mathbb{C}_{\text{Amb}}(\Gamma, \vdash_{\text{Amb}})) = \text{Amb}(\Gamma).$$

By including the necessary literals in $\Delta$ we can acceptably extend $\Gamma$ to eliminate all but an arbitrary member of $\text{Amb}(\Gamma)$. But any $\vdash_{\text{Amb}}$ consequence of $\Gamma$ must be an acceptable extension of the result. It follows that every minimally costly way of resolving $\Gamma$'s inconsistency *remains available* when we close $\Gamma$ under this consequence relation.

## 10.2 The Logic of Paradox

Graham Priest's *logic of paradox* (LP) is intended to be a dialetheic logic; it is often presented as a simple illustration of such a logic. Priest's original semantics for LP used Kleene's strong 3-valued matrices, treating the non-classical value, which is a fixed-point for negation, as *designated*. But in general, the same consequence relation can be given very different interpretations; in particular, the consequence relations determined by the preservation-of-ambiguity and LP are identical.

This was originally shown by an induction on the formulae of a propositional language. The idea was to establish a one-to-one relation between LP valuations and valuations, determined by sets of valuations all of which treat certain atoms ambiguously. To distinguish the new values from the old, we replace T and F in the LP valuations with 1 and 0. The pairs of valuations agree on the formulae assigned true and false, mapping T into 1 and F into 0. But the formulae assigned Both by the LP valuation are treated ambiguously. Each instance of each of them is replaced with one or another of a pair of new atoms, one of which receives the value true, and the other false. We quantify across all the resulting projected images, and assign a formula the value 1 if the formula receives the value 1 in some such image. Every sentence assigned either T or Both by the LP valuation thus receives the value 1, while the rest receive the value 0. The resulting ambiguity-generated true/false valuations are the Scott valuations that determine the LP consequence relation (see Scott 1974).

However, we can give a simpler proof by showing how 'truth tables' for the two logics match up. There are two ways in which an atom can acquire the value 1 in the Scott valuations produced above. It can be assigned the value 1 at the outset, or it can be one of the atoms treated ambiguously (obviously, if it's one of those, some image of $\Gamma$ will substitute the replacement atom assigned 1 for it, and so it receives the value 1 in this second way). Let's distinguish these two values as 1 and 1$\prime$. The difference between them, of course, is just that formulae assigned 1 receive that value in every projected image, while formulae assigned 1$\prime$ receive 1 in some image and 0 in some image. Now consider how these values combine with $\neg$ and $\wedge$. If a sentence is assigned 1, then its negation is assigned 0 in every image, and so gets the value 0 in the Scott valuation. But if a sentence is assigned 1$\prime$, then its negation is also assigned 1 in some image, and so gets the value 1 in the Scott valuation, and the value 1$\prime$ in our new truth tables. Of course 0 works just as the classical 0 in the tables, so we get as our new truth table for '$\neg$' what is shown on page 179 (top).

This, of course, is isomorphic to the strong 3-valued Kleene negation.

Now we turn to conjunction. Consider $\xi$, a formula of the form $\phi \wedge \psi$. Once again, we consider the three values, 1, 1$\prime$ and 0. If both $\phi$

| $\Phi$ | $\neg\phi$ |
|--------|------------|
| 1      | 0          |
| 1/     | 1/         |
| 0      | 1          |

and $\psi$ get the value 1, so does $\xi$; $\xi$ gets the value 1/ if one gets the value 1/ while the other gets the value 1, or both get the value 1/. Finally, if either or both get the value 0, so does $\xi$ of course. So our truth table is

| $\wedge$ | 1  | 1/ | 0 |
|----------|----|----|---|
| 1        | 1  | 1/ | 0 |
| 1/       | 1/ | 1/ | 0 |
| 0        | 0  | 0  | 0 |

Again, the table for $\wedge$ is isomorphic to the table for the strong 3-valued Kleene conjunction. The other connectives can be defined in the usual way. It follows that our ambiguity-based consequence relation is identical to LP's.

Another way to present this preservationist reading of the LP consequence relation focuses on the semantic side rather than on images of the premise set. *Wildcard valuations* allow inconsistent sets of sentences to be 'satisfied,' by treating a set of 'wildcard' atoms in a way that allows ambiguity.

Let L be a propositional language with $\alpha_0$, $\alpha_1$, $\alpha_2$,... the atoms of L, and $\phi_1$,...$\phi_n$,... the formulae of L. A wildcard valuation begins by selecting a set of atoms, $W$, to be the wildcards. We assign values to the sentences of L first by assigning 0 or 1 uniformly (that is, in the usual way) to each atom not in $W$.

Call this assignment $A_{At-W}$. Next, we assign 0 or 1 to each *instance* of an atom in $W$ in each formula of L.[1] We call the resulting assignment $^W A_{At-W}$. From here, we assign 0 or 1 to each complex formula, using the usual truth functional interpretation of the connectives.

---

[1] This allows each instance of a wildcard atom in each sentence of L to receive either value freely.

The result is a wildcard valuation, $^W V_{At-W}$. Let $V_{At-W}$ be the set of all such valuations based on a given $A_{At-W}$.[2] We quantify across $V_{At-W}$ to obtain a more stable valuation based on all the wildcard valuations for each wildcard set W. Let $VAt-W$ be the valuation determined by this quantification over the members of $V_{At-W}$. Then $\mathbf{V}_{At-W} \in L$ $\rightarrow \{1,0\}$, where

$$\mathbf{V}_{At-W}(S) = 1 \text{ if } \exists V \in V_{At-W} : V(S) = 1,$$
$$\mathbf{V}_{At-W}(S) = 0 \text{ else.}$$

Finally, we define our consequence relation in the usual way:

$$\Gamma \vdash_W \alpha \Leftrightarrow \forall V_W[(\forall \gamma \in \Gamma, V_W(\gamma) = 1) \Rightarrow V_W(\alpha) = 1].$$

## 10.3   Restoring Symmetry

LP is inelegant for the same reasons that singleton forcing is inelegant; it copes with inconsistency on the left, but leaves the dual triviality on the right untouched. In LP, classical contradictions on the left don't trivialize, but classical tautologies on the right do – any such tautology follows from every premise set. Further, in its multiple-conclusion form LP eliminates the triviality of inconsistent premise sets, but trivializes all conclusion sets whose closure under disjunction includes a tautology. First degree entailment (FDE) is a closely related logic that treats inconsistency on the left and its dual on the right symmetrically, eliminating the trivialization found in classical logic altogether. Brown (2001) presents an ambiguity-based account capturing the consequence relation of first degree entailment.

This treatment of FDE requires careful development of the symmetries of the consequence relation. The first step towards re-establishing the symmetries of classical logic in our ambiguity semantics for LP is to dualize the property to be preserved. In the first step we used ambiguity to project consistent images of the premise set. Now we will use ambiguity to project *consistently deniable* images of conclusion sets. Let

---

[2] So $V_{At-\emptyset}$ is just the singleton set of one classical valuation on L.

Amb*($\Delta$) be the set of minimal sets of sentence letters whose ambiguity is sufficient to project a consistently deniable image of $\Delta$. We require that any sentence from which $\Delta$ follows be an acceptable extension of every acceptable extension of $\Delta$, where acceptability is now consistent deniability:

$$\Gamma \text{ is an Amb*}(\Delta)\text{-preserving extension of } \Delta \Leftrightarrow \text{Amb*}(\Delta \cup \Gamma) \subseteq \text{Amb*}(\Delta).$$

We write this as Accept*($\Gamma,\Delta$). So a set $\Gamma$ is acceptable as an extension of a commitment to *denying* $\Delta$ if and only if extending $\Delta$ with $\Gamma$ doesn't make things worse, in other words, does not require any more ambiguity to produce a consistently deniable image than merely denying $\Delta$ does.

This leads to a right-to-left consequence relation in which individual sentences are placed on the left and sets of sentences on the right:

$$\gamma \vdash_{\text{Amb*}} \Delta \Leftrightarrow \forall\Delta\text{:Accept*}(\Gamma,\Delta) \implies \text{Accept*}(\Gamma\cup\{\alpha\},\Gamma).$$

In English, a set $\Delta$ follows from a formula $\gamma$ if and only if $\gamma$ is an acceptable extension of every acceptable extension of $\Delta$, a set we are committed to denying.

These two asymmetrical consequence relations can be combined to form a symmetrical one: Simply treat sets on the left as closed under conjunction and sets on the right as closed under disjunction, and demand that both of the following consequence relations apply:

$$\Gamma \vdash_{\text{Sym}} \Delta \Leftrightarrow \exists\delta \in \text{Cl}(\Delta, \vee): \Gamma \vdash_{\text{Amb}} \delta \; \& \\ \exists \gamma \in \text{Cl}(\Gamma, \wedge): \gamma \vdash_{\text{Amb*}} \Delta.$$

Or, by linking the set-set relation to an underlying formula-formula relation, we can put it this way instead:

$$\Gamma \vdash_{\text{Sym}} \Delta \Leftrightarrow \exists\delta \in \mathbb{C}(\Delta, \vee), \exists \; \gamma \; \in \text{Cl}(\Gamma, \wedge): \gamma \vdash_{\text{Sym}} \delta, \text{ where} \\ \gamma \vdash_{\text{Sym}} \delta \Leftrightarrow \{\gamma\} \vdash_{\text{Amb}} \delta \; \& \; \gamma \vdash_{\text{Amb*}} \{\delta\}.$$

The upshot of this manoeuvre is a logic sometimes called K*. The consequence relations of FDE and K* agree except when classically trivial sets appear on both the left and the right. In those cases the triviality of the set on the other side ensures that the property we're preserving on each side is trivially preserved. So K* trivializes when classically trivial sets appear on both the left and the right. FDE demands a little more subtlety.

The trick is to produce consistent images of premise sets and non-trivial images of conclusion sets simultaneously, while requiring that the sets of sentence letters used to project these images be *disjoint*.[3] Then $\Gamma \vdash_{\text{FDE}} \Delta$ if and only if every such consistent image of $\Gamma$ can be consistently extended by some member of each non-trivial image of $\Delta$ based on a disjoint set of sentence letters, or (now equivalently): $\Gamma \vdash_{\text{FDE}} \Delta$ if and only if every such non-trivial image of the conclusion set can be extended by some element of each non-contradictory image of the premise set while preserving its *consistent deniability*.

First degree entailment is, of course, the base of relevance logics, which add to it different accounts of the relevant conditional. The standard semantics for FDE due to Dunn adds two new truth values called 'Both' and 'Neither,' to the two familiar ones. In this section we present a new preservationist reading of the job these two values do. On this reading, they express two different treatments of ambiguity in a way that can be captured in a simple game.

The value 'both' is a designated fixed-point for negation; similarly, the value Neither is a non-designated fixed-point for negation. The consequence relation for FDE preserves Both-or-True from left to right, or (what is the same, in a multiple-conclusion setting) Neither-or-False from right to left.

Consider the following recursive definition of a Dunn valuation, defined on a classical sentential language. We use lower-case Greek letters as variables ranging over the formulae of the language. The definition applies a simple way of identifying Dunn's four values with the subsets

---

[3]In effect, ambiguity allows us to capture the results of using 'both' and 'neither' as (respectively) designated and non-designated fixed points for negation, while insisting that the two sets of ambiguously treated letters be disjoint ensures that we never treat the same sentence letter in both of these ways.

of the set of traditional truth values, {T,F}: Both = {T,F}, True = {T}, False = {F} and Neither = Ø. An assignment to the atoms, $V_{at} \in At \rightarrow$ {Both, True, False, Neither} is extended to the rest of the language according to the following rules:

1. $F \in V(\neg A)$ iff $T \in V(A)$

2. $T \in V(\neg A)$ iff $F \in V(A)$

3. $F \in V(A \wedge B)$ iff $F \in V(A)$ or $F \in V(B)$

4. $T \in V(A \wedge B)$ iff $T \in V(A)$ and $T \in V(B)$

5. $F \in V(A \vee B)$ iff $F \in V(A)$ and $F \in V(B)$

6. $T \in V(A \vee B)$ iff $T \in V(A)$ or $T \in V(B)$

Note that $T \in V(A)$ entails that A receives a designated value (either Both or True), and the consequence relation preserves this from left to right, while preserving (in a symmetrical, set-set consequence presentation) Neither or False from right to left.

We will prove that our new, symmetrical ambiguity logic is FDE by comparing truth tables, as we did for LP. The truth tables we use emerge from the game mentioned at the beginning of this chapter. The result shows that the *work* of a Dunn valuation can be done by a game that has nothing to do with peculiar truth values, because we can arrange the results of the game in tables isomorphic to Dunn's 4-valued tables for FDE. The game has two players named 'Verum' and 'Falsum.' It begins with a formula and a partial classical valuation, which matches the values assigned to the atoms receiving the values T or F in the corresponding Dunn valuation. Atoms that have not received such a classical value are divided between the players. Verum receives all the atoms assigned the value Both in the Dunn valuation, while Falsum receives all those assigned the value Neither.

The game is over a selected formula of the language. For Verum, the object of the game is to assign classical values to the instances of her atoms in such a way that the whole formula receives the value T. For Falsum, the object is to assign classical values to all the instances of his atoms in such a way that the whole formula receives the value F. Each player is free to assign either classical value to each distinct instance of any atom they've been assigned.

This game is either a won game for Verum or a won game for Falsum. If it's a won game for Verum, then the Dunn valuation assigns either True or Both to the formula. If it's a won game for Falsum, the Dunn valuation assigns either False or Neither to the formula. Moreover, the Dunn valuation assigns the value True to the formula if and only if the game is won for Verum even if she and Falsum exchange their assigned letter instances; similarly, it assigns the value False to the formula if and only if the game is won for Falsum even if he and Verum exchange their assigned letters. The preservationist consequence relation based on this game preserves won games for Verum from left to right, or, equivalently, won games for Falsum from right to left. That is, if every game on the left is won for Verum, some game on the right is also won for Verum.

We represent each game as a triple, $< \phi, V_c, D >$, where $\phi$ is the formula, $V_c$ is the partial classical assignment, and D is a function from $(At-At_c)$ to {Verum, Falsum} that assigns the atoms not assigned a value by $V_c$ to either Verum or Falsum. A game can be won in two ways. In the first case, $V_c$ together with the division of the remaining atoms fixes which of Verum and Falsum wins regardless of which set of atoms is given to Verum and which is given to Falsum; in the second, the win depends also on which of the two sets of atoms is assigned to which player.

**Proof:** By induction on the number of connectives in $\phi$.

1. Base: For the atoms the result is trivial. The atomic game is won for Verum (Falsum) in the first way if and only if the partial classical valuation assigns it the value T (F). It's won for Verum (Falsum) in the second way if the atom is assigned to Verum (Falsum).

2. Induction hypothesis: This holds for formulae with up to $n$ connectives.

3. Induction step: Let $\phi$ be a formula with $n + 1$ connectives. We will deal with $\neg$ and $\wedge$ here; the rest of the connectives can be

defined in terms of these in the usual way.

4. $\phi$ has the form $\neg\psi$: We have four cases to consider. First, suppose that the $\psi$ game is won for Verum in the first way. Then the game resulting from an exchange of letters between Verum and Falsum is also won for Verum. This implies that Falsum can force the value T on $\psi$ by some assignment of T and F to his letters. But this is exactly what Falsum must do to ensure $\phi$ receives the value F. So $\phi$ is won in the first way for Falsum. Second, suppose that the $\psi$ game is won for Verum in the second way. Then the game resulting from an exchange of letters between Verum and Falsum is won for Falsum. That is, the letters assigned to Verum would allow Verum to force the value F on $\psi$. But this is exactly what Verum must do to assign the value T to $\phi$. So $\phi$ is also a won game for Verum. The third and fourth cases parallel these two, with Verum and Falsum trading places, so if $\psi$ is won for Falsum in the first way, $\phi$ is won for Verum in the first way, and if $\psi$ is won for Falsum in the second way, $\phi$ is won for Falsum in the second way as well.

5. $\phi$ has the form $\psi \wedge \xi$: Here we have eight cases to consider, since both $\psi$ and $\xi$ can be won in either way for either player. However, the cases go through very straightforwardly. First, suppose both $\psi$ and $\xi$ are won for Verum in the first way. Then Verum can force the value T on $\phi$ whether she plays her own atoms or Falsum's atoms – that is, the A game is won for Verum in the first way as well. But if either or both of $\psi$ and $\xi$ is won for Verum in the second way, then Falsum wins the $\phi$ game on an exchange of letters, and $\phi$ is won for Verum in the second way. If either or both of $\psi$ and $\xi$ is won for Falsum in the first way, then $\phi$ is won for Falsum in the first way, while if both $\psi$ and $\xi$ are won for Falsum in the second way, $\phi$ is won for Falsum in the second way. $\square$

We can summarize the results of this theorem in the following tables.

| $\phi$ | $\neg\phi$ |
|---|---|
| won $_1$ for Verum | won $_1$ for Falsum |
| won $_2$ for Verum | won $_2$ for Verum |
| won $_2$ for Falsum | won $_2$ for Falsum |
| won $_1$ for Falsum | won $_1$ for Verum |

| $\wedge$ | won $_1$ for Verum | won $_2$ for Verum |
|---|---|---|
| won $_1$ for Verum | won $_1$ for Verum | won $_2$ for Verum |
| won $_2$ for Verum | won $_2$ for Verum | won $_2$ for Verum |
| won $_2$ for Falsum | won $_2$ for Falsum | won $_2$ for Falsum |
| won $_1$ for Falsum | won $_1$ for Falsum | won $_1$ for Falsum |

| $\wedge$ | won $_2$ for Falsum | won $_1$ for Falsum |
|---|---|---|
| won $_1$ for Verum | won $_2$ for Falsum | won $_1$ for Falsum |
| won $_2$ for Verum | won $_2$ for Falsum | won $_1$ for Falsum |
| won $_2$ for Falsum | won $_2$ for Falsum | won $_1$ for Falsum |
| won $_1$ for Falsum | won $_1$ for Falsum | won $_1$ for Falsum |

These tables are isomorphic to Dunn's four-valued tables for FDE: $Won_1$, for Verum and Falsum respectively, corresponds to True and to False, while $Won_2$ similarly corresponds to Both and to Neither. So our logical game between Verum and Falsum does the work of a Dunn valuation.

This trick provides yet another way of applying ambiguity to replace strange truth values – the rules of the game allow Verum and Falsum to treat ambiguously the atoms assigned to them, as they attempt to produce an assignment that makes the target formula True or False, but each player uses the leeway that ambiguity grants her in a particular way.

## 10.4  Ambiguity and Quantification

Recall the *wildcard atoms* considered above as a treatment of LP. Our little game shows that we can also replace the values Both and Neither with wildcards. For each Dunn valuation, we consider the corresponding wildcard valuations. These are wildcard valuations such that:

1. Atoms to which the Dunn valuation assigned T and F are assigned the values 1 and 0 respectively.

2. The rest of the atoms are treated as wildcards, divided between the atoms assigned both by the Dunn valuation and those assigned Neither.

3. If some assignment of T, F to instances of the atoms assigned Both by the Dunn valuation forces the value T on the formula, whatever values are assigned to the instances of atoms assigned Neither by the Dunn valuation, we also assign 1 to the formula.

4. Otherwise we assign 0 to the formula.

The resulting 1,0 valuations each correspond to a Dunn valuation, assigning 1 to every formula assigned a designated value by the Dunn valuation and 0 to every formula assigned an undesignated valuation. So the consequence relation determined by our game also results from considering all the possible assignments to instances of the wildcard atoms, and looking for whether a 'win' for Verum, an ambiguous assignment to the atoms assigned Both by the Dunn valuation that forces truth on the formula, exists among them.

## 10.5   Echoes of Supervaluation

Our approach bears a resemblance to Bas van Fraassen's supervaluations. A supervaluation also begins as a partial, classical valuation, extends that valuation by assigning values to the 'gaps' in every way, and then quantifies across all the resulting extended valuations, conservatively assigning T (F) to a formula $\phi$ only if all the extended valuations assign T (or F) to $\phi$.

   Our ambiguity logics retain both the starting point, a partial classical valuation, and the use of quantification across a range of extended valuations to compensate for the arbitrariness of the extensions of that partial valuation. These devices allow us to achieve our results without adding strange truth values to the mix, just as they do for van Fraassen. By adding the further element of ambiguity, we have been able to capture more restrained, paraconsistent consequence relations that resist the trivialization of inconsistent sets on the left and of sets which are not consistently deniable on the right.

## 10.6   Final Remarks on Preservation

There is another way to express what is preserved by these logics, which opens up a broader understanding of preservation. This approach focuses on preserving the *consequence relation* itself. We can say that the classical consequence relation is preserved here, under a range of minimally ambiguous, consistent (or consistently deniable) *images* of our premises and conclusions:

$\Gamma \vdash_{FDE} \Delta$ iff every image of the premise and conclusion sets, $I(\Gamma)$, $I^*(\Delta)$ obtained by treating disjoint sets of sentence letters as ambiguous is such that $I(\Gamma) \vdash I^*(\Delta)$.

This suggests a new preservationist strategy for producing new consequence relations from old. We can say that the new consequence relation holds when and only when the old relation holds in all of a range of cases *anchored to* the original premise and conclusion sets. This strategy eliminates or reduces trivialization by ensuring that the *range* of cases considered includes some non-trivial ones, even when the instance forming our 'anchor' is trivial.

This idea can also be applied to the weakly aggregative forcing relation; the ambiguity-based treatment of forcing allows ambiguity at the level of formulas, but not within formulas, and uses a maximum number of distinct 'colours' corresponding to the levels of the premise and conclusion sets. The familiar forcing consequence relation can then be presented not as preserving levels of incoherence but as preserving the classical consequence relation itself, under quantification across a range of recolourings of the elements of premise and conclusion sets.

# Nomenclature

$1, 0, 1'$  The three values of LP for Scott valuations, page 178

$A$      A set of atoms, page 176

$A \twoheadrightarrow B$  A surjective function from $A$ onto $B$, page 116

$A_{At-W}$  The pre-wildcard assignment, page 179

$H$      The domain of a meaning function, page 109

$I(\Gamma)$   A consistent image of $\Gamma$, page 188

$L_{\Delta}$     The set of sets which preserve level by union, page 136

$M^*$     The class of covers, page 113

$M_X$     The class of models of an algebraic logic, page 108

$Mod(\Sigma)$  The class of models of the set $\Sigma$, page 111

$R_{K3}$    The canonical frame relation for K3, page 8

$Rxyz$   The objects $x$, $y$, and $z$ stand in the relation $R$, page 4

$Th(K)$   The theory of the class of models $K$, page 111

$V_{At-W}$   The set of wildcard valuations based on $A_{At-W}$, page 180

$Won_1$   The game-theoretic truth value for True and False, page 186

$Won_2$   The game-theoretic truth value that corresponds to the truth values *Both* and *Neither*, page 186

$X, Y$     Variables for logics, page 88

$\varnothing$     The empty set, page 89

$\mathfrak{C}$     Variable for covers, page 113

$\mathfrak{C}^m_\Gamma$     The minimal cover of $\Gamma$, page 114

$\mathrm{ConIm}(\Gamma', \Gamma, A)$     The set $\Gamma'$ is the consistent image of $\Gamma$ with respect to the set of atoms $A$, page 176

$\mathcal{L}$     The language of a logic, page 88

$\mathfrak{F}$     A variable for a logical cover of the set kind, page 94

$\Gamma, \Sigma$     Sets of formulas, page 6

$\Gamma - \Delta$     Set difference, page 112

$\Gamma^+$     An MLPE, page 136

$\mathcal{M}, \mathcal{R}$     Models of a logic, page 108

$\mathcal{M}_{K3}$     The canonical model of K3, page 8

$\Omega$-MLPE     An $\Omega$-consistent-like MLPE, page 139

$\Pi(\Sigma)$     The product of all of the members of $\Sigma$, page 147

$\vdash$     The syntactic consequence or 'proves' relation, page 5

$\alpha, \beta, \psi, \varphi$     Formula variables, page 4

$\boxplus$     The $(n-1)$-ary modal operator, page 5

$\mathrm{CON}_X$     The consistency predicate for the logic $X$, page 89

$\mathrm{COV}_X(A(\Gamma), \Gamma)$     The A-covering relation, page 172

$\cup$     Set union, page 89

$[\Vdash$     The syntactic-level forcing relation, page 11

$\ell_X$     The level function of the logic $X$, page 114

$\ell^X$ — The level function relative to a logic $X$ where the covers are sets, page 95

$\subseteq_\omega$ — The finite subset of relation, page 130

$\frac{2}{n+1}(\alpha_i)_{i\in[n+1]}$ See convention, page 58

$\frac{2}{n+1}(t_i)_{i\in[n+1]}$ See convention, page 58

$\supset$ — The material conditional, page 5

$\implies$ — The meta-language conditional, page 11

$\infty$ — The special value of level functions for absurd formulas, page 95

$\mathcal{L}_n$ — The $n$-ary modal language, page 66

$\leq$ — The 'less than or equal to' relation on the integers, or a general relation of partial order, page 134

$\mathbf{N_q}$ — A logic based on a hyperframes, page 54

$\mathfrak{F}$ — A hyperframe, page 50

$\mathfrak{M}$ — A hypermodel based on a hyperframe, page 50

$\models_X$ — The satisfaction relation of an algebraic logic, page 109

$\square$ — The necessity operator from modal logic, page 5

$\neg$ — The negation operator, page 6

$\langle a, b \rangle$ — The ordered pair of $a$ and $b$, page 4

$\{\alpha_1, \ldots, \alpha_n\}$ — The set of $\alpha_1, \ldots, \alpha_n$, page 22

$G_nX_n$ — The various systems of $n$-ary modal logic, page 74

$\rightarrow$ — The classical conditional (alternative), page 177

$\models$ — Semantic consequence, page 109

$\rhd_3$ — The K3 provability relation, page 7

$\vdash_W$     The wildcard consequence relation, page 180

$\vdash_{Amb}$     The ambiguity set consequence relation, page 177

$\vec{b}$     A sequence of elements of a lattice, page 37

$\vee$     The 'or' operator, page 126

$\wedge$     The 'and' operator, page 6

$^W A_{At-W}$   The wildcard assignment, page 179

$^W V_{At-W}$   The wildcard valuation, page 180

$f : A \to B$   In general, $f$ is a map from $A$ to $B$, page 109

$mng_X$   The meaning function of a logic $X$, page 109

$w(\mathfrak{C})$   The width of the cover $\mathfrak{C}$, page 113

[Cut-1]   A version of [Cut], page 112

[Cut]   The structural rule of inference called [Cut], page 89

[Den*]   The relation of symmetric negation denial, page 127

[Den]   The property that denial commutes with provability, page 91

[K3]   The aggregation rule for the modal logic K3, page 6

[K]   The rules of complete modal aggregation, page 5

[M]   The rule of monotonicity (alternative), page 112

[Mon]   The structural rule of inference: monotonicity, page 89

[N]   The rule of necessitation, page 6

[RM]   The rule of distribution of the $\square$ operator over the $\supset$ connective, page 5

[R]   The structural rule of inference called reflexivity, page 89

MLPE   Maximal level-preserving extension, page 136

[M*]   The rule of level preserving monotonicity for forcing, page 129

[Cut*]   The special version of [Cut] for forcing, page 130

Accept($\Delta$,$\Gamma$)   $\Delta$ is an acceptable extension of $\Gamma$, page 177

Amb($\Gamma$)   The ambiguity set of $\Gamma$, page 176

Cn        The set of connectives of a logic, page 110

FDE      First-degree entailment, page 180

iff        if, and only if, page 50

IL        Intuitionistic logic, page 126

LP        Priest's logic of paradox, page 106

ND       Stands for *negation denial*, page 126

# References

Apostoli, P. and B. Brown (1995). A solution to the completeness problem for weakly aggregative modal logic. *Journal of Symbolic Logic 60*, 832–42.

Avron, A. (1994). What is a logical system? In D. Gabbay (Ed.), *What is a logical system?*, Volume 4 of *Stud. Logic Comput.*, pp. 217–38. New York: Oxford Univ. Press.

Blackburn, P., M. de Rijke, and Y. Venema (2001). *Modal logic*. Cambridge: Cambridge University Press.

Brown, B. (1999). Yes, virginia, there really are paraconsistent logics. *Journal of Philosophical Logic 28*(5), 489–500.

Brown, B. (2001). LP, FDE and ambiguity. In H. Arabnia (Ed.), *Proceedings of the 2001 meetings of the International Conference on Artificial Intelligence*, Volume II, pp. 827–33. CSREA publications.

Brown, B. and P. K. Schotch (1999). Logic and aggregation. *Journal of Philosophical Logic 28*(396), 265–87.

Campbell, R. (1980). Can inconsistency be reasonable? *Canadian Journal of Philosophy 11*(2), 245–70.

Chellas, B. F. (1980). *Modal Logic: An Introduction*. Cambridge: Cambridge University Press.

Costa-Leite, A. (2007). *Interactions of metaphysical and epistemic concepts*. Ph. D. thesis, Université de Neuchâtel.

Cowen, R. (1972). A short proof of Rado's lemma. *Journal of Combinatorial Theory B12*(2), 299–300.

Cowen, R., S. H. Hechler, and P. Mihók (2002). Graph coloring compactness theorems equivalent to BPI. *Scientiae Mathematicae Japonicae 56*(2), 213–23.

Davey, B. and D. Duffus (1982). Exponentiation and duality. In I. Rival (Ed.), *Ordered sets*, pp. 43–95. Dordrecht, Boston: Reidel.

Davey, B. and H. Priestley (1990). *Introduction to lattices and order*. Cambridge: Cambridge University Press.

Fitting, M. (1986). Notes on the mathematical aspects of Kripke's theory of truth. *Notre Dame J. Formal Logic 27*(1), 75–88.

Gabbay, D. (1976). Two dimensional propositional tense logics. In A. Kasher (Ed.), *Bar-Hillel Memorial Volume*, pp. 145–83. Dordrecht: Reidel.

Jennings, R. (1981). A note on the axiomatisation of brouwersche modal logic. *Journal of Philosophical Logic 10*, 341–42.

Jennings, R. and P. Schotch (1981). Some remarks on weakly weak modal logics. *Notre Dame Journal of Formal Logic 22*, 309–14.

Jennings, R. and P. Schotch (1984). The preservation of coherence. *Studia Logica 43*(1/2), 89–106.

Johnston, D. (1976). Temporal betweeness. Unpublished paper.

Johnston, D. (1978). A generalized relational semantics for modal logic. M.A. thesis, Simon Fraser University, Burnaby, British Columbia, Canada.

Jónsson, B. and A. Tarski (1951). Boolean algebras with operators. Part I. *Amer. J. Math. 73*, 891–939.

Jónsson, B. and A. Tarski (1952). Boolean algebras with operators. Part II. *Amer. J. Math. 74*, 127–62.

Kripke, S. A. (1963). Semantical considerations on modal logics. *Acta Philosophica Fennica, Modal and Many-Valued Logics 16*, 83–94.

McKinsey, J. and A. Tarski (1948). Some theorems about the sentential calculi of Lewis and Heyting. *Journal of Symbolic Logic 13*, 1–15.

Nicholson, T., R. E. Jennings, and D. Sarenac (2000). Revisiting completeness for the $K_n$ modal logics: A new proof. *Logic Journal of the IGPL 8*, 101–5.

Payette, G. and B. d'Entremont (2006). Level compactness. *Notre Dame Journal of Formal Logic 47*(4), 545–55.

Payette, G. and P. Schotch (2007). On preserving. *Logica Universalis 1*(2), 295–310.

Priestley, H. (1970). Representation of distributive lattices by means of ordered Stone spaces. *Bull. London Math. Soc. 2*, 186–90.

Priestley, H. (1984). Ordered sets and duality for distributive lattices. *Annals of Discrete Mathematics 23*, 39–60.

Quine, W. V. O. and J. S. Ullian (1970). *The Web of belief* (2nd 1978 ed.). New York: McGraw-Hill.

Schotch, P. and R. Jennings (1980a). Inference and necessity. *Journal of Philosophical Logic 9*, 327–40.

Schotch, P. and R. Jennings (1980b). Modal logic and the theory of modal aggregation. *Philosophia 9*, 265–78.

Schotch, P. and R. Jennings (1989). On detonating. In G. Priest, R. Routley, and J. Norman (Eds.), *Paraconsistent Logic*, pp. 306–27. Philosophia Verlag.

Schotch, P. K. (2004). *An Introduction to Logic and its Philosophy*. Unpublished.

Scott, D. (1974). Completeness and axiomatizability in many-valued logic. In *Proceedings of the Tarski Symposium (Proc. Sympos. Pure*

*Math., Vol. XXV, Univ. California, Berkeley, Calif., 1971)*, Providence, R.I., pp. 411–35. Amer. Math. Soc.

Segerberg, K. (1971). *An Essay in Classical Modal Logic*, Volume I. Uppsala: Uppsala University Press.

Stone, M. (1936). The theory of representations for Boolean algebras. *Transactions of the American Mathematical Society 40*, 37–111.

Tarski, A. and B. Jónsson (1951). Boolean algebra with operators I. *American Journal of Mathematics 73*, 891–939.

Urquhart, A. (1995). Completeness for weakly aggregative modal logic. Manuscript.

# Index

# Contributors

Bryson Brown is a Professor of Philosophy at the University of Lethbridge.

Raymond Jennings is a Professor of Philosophy at Simon Fraser University.

Kam Sing Leung is a recent graduate of the doctoral program of the Philosophy Department of Simon Fraser University.

Dorian Nicholson is a recent graduate of the doctoral program of the Philosophy Department of Simon Fraser University.

Gillman Payette is in the doctoral program of the University of Calgary.

Peter Schotch is Research Professor of Philosophy at Dalhousie University.

Alasdair Urquhart is Professor of Philosophy and of Computing Science at the University of Toronto.